Counseling
Adult Children
of Alcoholics

RESOURCES FOR
CHRISTIAN COUNSELING

RESOURCES FOR CHRISTIAN COUNSELING

(Other volumes forthcoming)

VOLUME TWENTY-ONE

Counseling Adult Children of Alcoholics

SANDRA D. WILSON, Ph.D.

RESOURCES FOR
CHRISTIAN COUNSELING

General Editor

Gary R. Collins, Ph.D.

WORD PUBLISHING
Dallas · London · Sydney · Singapore

Permission to quote from the following sources is gratefully acknowledged:
Children of Alcoholism: A Survivor's Manual, by Judith Seixas and Geraldine Youcha. Copyright 1987. Reprinted by permission of Crown Publishers, a division of Random House, Inc.

Forgive and Be Free by Richard P. Walter, copyright © 1983 by the Zondervan Corporation.

Appendix 2, C.A.S.T., copyright © 1983 by John W. Jones, Ph.D. Used by permission of Camelot Unlimited, Chicago, Illinois.

Silent Scream by Martha Janssen, copyright © 1983 by Fortress Press.

"The Twelve Steps of Wholeness" by Gary R. Sweeten. Christian Information Committee, Inc.

Child's art on pp. 19 and 36 is taken from *It Will Never Happen to Me* by Claudia Black.

The chart on page 118 is adapted from *Healing the Child Within: Discovery and Recovery for Adult Children of Dysfunctional Families,* copyright © 1987 by Charles L. Whitfield, published by Health Communications, Inc.

Library of Congress Cataloging-in-Publication Data

Wilson, Sandra D., 1938–
    Counseling adult children of alcoholics / Sandra D. Wilson.
        p.   cm. — (Resources for Christian counseling : v. 21)
    Includes bibliographical references.
    ISBN 0-8499-0581-8
    1. Adult children of alcoholics—Pastoral counseling of.
I. Title. II. Series.
BV4463.6W54 1989
261.8′322923—dc20   89-37116
                                              CIP

Printed in the United States of America
9 8 0 1 2 3 9 AGF 9 8 7 6 5 4 3 2 1

CONTENTS

EDITOR'S PREFACE

IN 1754 A NOVELIST NAMED Horace Walpole wrote a fairy tale titled, "The Three Princes of Serendip." In those days, Serendip was the name of modern Sri Lanka, and in that setting the fictional three princes had exciting lives filled with unexpected and delightful discoveries. Walpole's story brought a new word into the English language—a word based on the name of the country where the princes had their unanticipated adventures. *Serendipity,* according to my dictionary, is the experience of making happy or interesting discoveries unexpectedly or by accident.

In working on the books in this series, I have encountered a number of surprising "serendipities"—sometimes in the form of authors or topics that appeared unexpectedly. Near the beginning of her doctoral studies, Sandy Wilson wrote to ask if I would consider serving as the "outside resource person" on her academic committee. I accepted, in part because I knew and respected her pastor, but also because I was interested in Sandy's desire to integrate psychology and theology. For me, sitting on that doctoral committee was genuine serendipity.

Sandra Wilson's dissertation topic, dealing with evangelical Christian adult children of alcoholics, was especially interesting—in part because it opened my eyes to an issue that I previously had not seen with such clarity. Sandy showed that she was an expert on this topic, not only because of her in-depth knowledge of the contemporary professional literature, but also because of her counseling work and her personal experiences growing up in a family made dysfunctional because of alcohol.

Even before her dissertation research was complete, I began to wonder if, serendipitously, I had unexpectedly encountered both a topic that was crucial for this series, and an author who clearly was qualified to write this book. After graduation, the new Dr. Wilson had a much deserved vacation with her husband, and began almost immediately to work on the manuscript. Perhaps being asked to write this volume was, for her, a serendipity.

For some authors, a first book can be a weak effort to break into print. But this certainly is not true of Dr. Wilson. Like a seasoned professional, she has produced a volume that is well-written, clearly documented, contemporary, practical, and sensitive to the needs of so many hurting adult children of alcoholics (often known as ACOAs). The author has documented the prevalence of this problem, has shown how often ACOAs are present in our churches, and has cited useful psychological and scriptural guidelines to guide counselors in giving help.

Like all other volumes in the Resources for Christian Counseling series, this book is intended to be practical and helpful. Written by counseling experts, each of whom has a strong Christian commitment and extensive counseling experience, the books are meant to be examples of accurate psychology and careful use of Scripture. Each is intended to have a clear evangelical perspective, careful documentation, a strong practical orientation, and freedom from the sweeping statements and undocumented rhetoric that sometimes characterize writing in the counseling field. Our goal is to provide books that are clearly written, useful, up-to-date overviews of the issues faced by contemporary Christian counselors—including pastoral counselors. All of the Resources for Christian Counseling books have similar bindings and together they are intended to comprise a helpful encyclopedia of Christian counseling.

Unlike *serendipity*, which entered our language many years ago, *adult children of alcoholics* is a relatively new term. But the problem is very old. For centuries—long before the time of Horace Walpole—children have grown up cowering in the horrifying shadows of parents who are addicted to alcohol. Often these grown children have never learned to trust others, to express their feelings honestly, to face the persisting anger, to forsake their negative self-concepts, or to understand how their personalities and lifestyles have been molded and wounded by the experiences of growing up in alcoholic-controlled homes. Frequently these ACOA people occupy our church pews, live in our neighborhoods, work alongside us as fellow employees, or bring their wounds when they marry into our families. It is probable that we all know people who have grown up in alcoholic homes, even though these victims of alcohol-induced abuse often hide their past hurts.

This book will be of help to counselors; but it goes further. Dr. Wilson's perceptive writing can help all of us understand a widespread but long-hidden condition that has become a major contemporary issue in our society. Within recent years, a number of books on this subject have appeared; but I know of none that can surpass this volume in teaching us to understand and help adult children of alcoholics.

After you read the following pages, I hope you will agree with me that finding this book has been a real serendipity.

Gary R. Collins, Ph.D.
Kildeer, Illinois

INTRODUCTION

THEY COULD REPLACE ALL THE CITIZENS of both New York City and Los Angeles with several million left over. If they did populate these cities, New York and Los Angeles would be filled with residents who tend to be anxious, depressed, approval-seeking, guilt-prone, unforgiving, and distrustful of God and others.[1] Most of you work, worship, and/or live with some of them. Who are they? They are the estimated thirty million Americans who are adult children of alcoholics.

Why should you care about them? One reason is that many of them will come to you for help. Adult children of alcoholics are more apt to seek mental health services than adults raised in nonalcoholic families.[2] This tendency of adult children of alcoholics to seek counseling is relevant to pastors as well as to professional and lay counselors since one national survey indicated that people sought help from pastors more often than from any other group of counselors.[3] Further, if you are a Christian people helper, e.g., a pastor, church leader or teacher, or professional or lay counselor, you should care because *millions of these adult children of alcoholics are part of the body of Christ.* According to a 1984 study, 19 percent of the population of the United States has had a "born again" experience.[4] Assuming that adult children of alcoholics are distributed equally throughout the population, this means there could be over 5.5 million Christians who grew up in alcoholic homes. These are some of the "wounded sheep" in the evangelical fold, and they need tender shepherding and care.

What can you do to help? To be effective, your desire to help adult children of alcoholics must be undergirded with knowledge about their special issues and needs. This volume provides information about the family backgrounds, personal characteristics, and common problems of adult children of alcoholics; but it offers more. Since my research and much of my clinical experience is with Christian adult children of alcoholics, I am familiar with their special struggles to appropriate and live out their faith in Jesus Christ as Savior and Lord. In addition, I am a Christian adult child of an alcoholic, and I know the problems and struggles "up close and personal." All adult children of alcoholics tend to share common characteristics and relational problems; but those who acknowledge Jesus Christ as their Savior and "Highest Power" have additional challenges. This book is intended to provide needed information to assist you as you seek to counsel adult children of alcoholics whether Christian or non-Christian. What can you expect to learn?

An understanding of adult children of alcoholics must be based upon a knowledge of the alcoholic family system and the roles children often play in that system. Part I will provide this background information. Part II will describe the personal characteristics and relational patterns frequently noted in adult children of alcoholics. It will include my research findings on the relationships of evangelical adult children with God. The remainder of the book will address counseling issues, both general and spiritual. Practical and proven helping strategies will be described, and they will be consistent with biblical principles.

Who can use this information? If your interest in helping people and in adult children of alcoholics was forged from your personal experience with parental alcohol abuse, this information is for you first of all. You need to be in the process of making peace with your painful past before you can guide others down that path.

Obviously, all mental health professionals and lay counselors should be cognizant of the special needs of counselees who are adult children of alcoholics. Adults who grew up in alcoholic homes often exhibit cognitive distortions, emotional problems, and interpersonal struggles that are strikingly similar. Effective counseling with these individuals will be facilitated by understanding this constellation and knowing how to intervene to promote change.

Pastors and church leaders will be more sensitive and effective shepherds if they, too, understand these issues, because these wounded sheep bring their bruised hearts and battered God-concepts into the pews.

You may be saying, "But I didn't have an alcoholic parent, and I'm not a counselor, pastor, or teacher. I just want to learn more about how to be a helpful friend." Great. This book is for you, too, because you will learn about the resources available to assist adult children of alcoholics. Clearly, caring Christians will be more effective people helpers if they increase their understanding of adult children of alcoholics. But, is that all you need to be effective?

No. The most important thing you need to be an effective helper with adult children of alcoholics, or anyone else, is the finest counseling supervision. I have worked under the supervision of the very best, most knowledgeable counselor for years. He is described in Isaiah 9:6 as "Wonderful Counselor;" his name is Jesus Christ. In my Ryrie Study Bible, the footnote on Isaiah 9:6 states that, "'Wonderful' regularly means supernatural . . . so the phrase refers to Messiah as the supernatural Counselor. . . ." Of course, you should hone your counseling skills and augment your knowledge of adult children of alcoholics; but the most important thing you can do to help them, and others, is to counsel—formally or informally—in a spirit of total dependence on the supervision and guidance of our supernatural Counselor, the Lord Jesus Christ.

PART ONE

UNDERSTANDING THE ALCOHOLIC FAMILY

"LOOK NOT MOURNFULLY into the past. It comes not back again. Wisely improve the present. It is thine," advised Longfellow. "Those who do not learn from the past are condemned to repeat it," warned Santayana.

How do we reconcile these extrabiblical proverbs? More important, how do we who love the Word of God and the God of the Word reconcile verses such as Philippians 3:13, which speaks of "forgetting what lies behind," with such passages as Psalms 105 and 106, which extol remembering the past? Perhaps the answer lies in the *purpose* of remembering.

In Philippians 3:13–14 Paul spoke of forgetting the past in the context of running a race as he pressed on toward the goal for the prize. And in Hebrews 12:1, he exhorted his readers to lay aside encumbrances as they run their race. As I write this, the Summer Olympic Games are taking place in Seoul, Korea, and, by television, I have seen many runners pressing toward their goals. However, I have an even more personal knowledge of Olympic competition. Our son, Dave, was the 100-meter backstroke silver medalist in the 1984 Summer Olympic Games in Los Angeles. Dave will tell you that when he was in the final race that sunny August afternoon there were many

1

things he purposely forgot—all those things that would be encumbrances to his performance. But there were also things he purposely remembered: all those things that would help him reach his goal.

We know Paul did not use the phrase "forgetting what lies behind" to mean volitional amnesia about his entire past, because he frequently related his earlier life when doing so helped him reach his goal—glorifying God. Psalms 105 and 106 speak of remembering the past to avoid the sins of our fathers and to motivate us to praise and glorify God. Again, we see that the *purpose* of remembering the past is the important consideration.

If you were raised in an alcoholic family, or if you care about, counsel with, or minister to someone who was, it is vital to know something about the structure and function of those families. Our purpose in looking back at the family is not to play a blame game, but to gain understanding. It is not to excuse or relieve the adult children of their personal responsibility for change, but to give a context for change that will help Christian adults raised in alcoholic homes reach their goal of glorifying God.

Part I is designed to provide an understanding of the nature of alcoholism, the alcoholic family system, and the plight of children within that system.

CHAPTER ONE

UNDERSTANDING ALCOHOLISM

THE NUMBER-ONE DRUG ABUSE problem in the United States is alcoholism. It is estimated that twelve million American adults are addicted to alcohol,[1] and alcoholism is cited as the second leading cause of death in the United States.[2] Alcohol has been called the most dangerous psychoactive (mind altering) drug because it is a toxin that damages nearly all of the body's tissues and major organs.[3] It has been reported that *every day, in this country alone, more than six hundred people die either directly or indirectly from alcohol.*[4] Truly, alcohol abuse "bites like a serpent, And stings like a viper," as the Holy Spirit warned through the writer of Proverbs so long ago.[5]

Understanding basic facts concerning the impact of alcoholism is a prerequisite to an informed discussion of the issues affecting adult children of alcoholic parents. However, once we move beyond basic statistics and a survey of the physical effects of alcoholism, these facts often appear contradictory and confusing. Nowhere is this more evident than in the areas of definition and etiology (causes) of alcoholism.

DEFINITIONS

Definitions of alcoholism are nearly as numerous as are "experts" on alcoholism. These definitions can be subsumed under either the disease model or the behavioral problem model. There are vigorous supporters on both sides. For example, one prominent alcoholism authority stated that, "Alcoholism is a fatal disease, 100 percent fatal. . . . This disease is an entity as distinct as measles."[6] In contrast, another expert in the field subtitled his recent book, *The Myth of Alcoholism as a Disease.*[7]

The disease concept of alcoholism can be traced to the work of Benjamin Rush and physician Thomas Trotter in the early nineteenth century; but its dominance stems from research done during the 1940s by E. M. Jellinek at the Yale Center of Alcohol Studies. Jellinek defined alcoholism as "any use of alcoholic beverages that causes any damage to the individual or to society or both,"[8] and he was determined to influence public opinion with the conclusion that such use was due to a disease.

The disease concept has been refined in recent years to correct the false impression that alcoholism can be treated in such a way that alcoholic individuals do not have to do anything for themselves. This refinement views alcoholism as a chronic illness wherein the alcoholic is not the passive recipient of a cure, but instead is an active participant who assumes major responsibility for managing his or her own illness. Kinney and Leaton draw a helpful analogy to rehabilitative medicine:

> . . . With physical therapy, accident victims learn to walk again. In these cases, patients are required to take active part in their recovery. To be successfully treated, an alcoholic must also take an active part.[9]

4

This perspective of the disease concept makes it more palatable to Christians who may have choked on the idea that labeling alcoholism as a disease allowed the alcoholic person to abdicate all personal responsibility.

As noted above, there is an alternative to the disease model of alcoholism which considers it entirely a behavioral problem without any physiological component. Adherents of this position suggest that alcoholics drink to intoxication because they have learned that is a quick, dependable way to temporarily avoid facing their problems. However, this view does not explain why many people who drink alcohol in moderation and experience severe life problems do not become alcoholics. This view represents a "minority opinion" among professionals in the field.[10]

Clearly, there is little agreement on just what alcoholism is. In its most severe form, many experts tend to agree; but there is less consensus on what lesser symptoms should be labeled "alcoholic." For example, one popular book in the field distinguishes between the "problem drinker," the "heavy drinker," and the "alcoholic." The latter is defined as, "a person with the disease of alcoholism regardless of whether he is initially a heavy drinker, a problem drinker, or a light or moderate drinker."[11] The "problem drinker" is described as someone who is not alcoholic, i.e., doesn't have the disease of alcoholism, but whose alcohol use creates problems for himself and/or others. The "heavy drinker" is defined as a person who drinks frequently or in large amounts whether or not he or she is alcoholic or causing problems.[12]

I confess I tend to be less precise, and frequently use alcoholism and alcohol abuse interchangeably since, in my counseling practice with adults raised in alcoholic and other dysfunctional families, I focus more on the effects of the drinking behavior than its causes. I am less concerned about whether people are technically alcoholic than if they are abusing alcohol in a manner that is causing problems for themselves and others. For the sake of consistency, I will use the terms alcoholism and alcoholic in this book in the spirit of the model Gravitz and Bowden employ to determine if someone is an alcoholic.

A person is alcoholic if he or she: 1) drinks, 2) gets into trouble repeatedly as a result of drinking—be that trouble with family, career, work, health, or the law—and 3) continues to drink. If somebody drinks, gets into trouble, and drinks again, repeating the cycle over and over, we consider that person an alcoholic.[13]

Whether defined as a disease or as a behavioral problem, alcoholism is characterized by preoccupation with alcohol to the detriment of physical, emotional, social, and spiritual well-being, and by denial of these self-destructive consequences. These characteristics often appear to be legacies bequeathed from parents to children "unto the third and fourth generations" and beyond. Is this due to hereditary or environmental factors? That question raises the issue of the etiology, i.e., the causes of alcoholism.

CAUSES OF ALCOHOLISM

It is widely believed that alcoholism runs in families, and research confirms this ancient piece of folk wisdom. Studies indicate that sons of alcoholic fathers are four times more likely than other sons to become alcoholics, and daughters of alcoholic mothers are three times more likely to become alcoholics than other women. In addition, grandsons of alcoholic grandfathers are at three times the risk of future alcoholism compared with other men. And daughters of alcoholics tend to marry alcoholic men, perpetuating the intergenerational dynamic.[14]

Is heredity or environment the mechanism that propels this intergenerational cycle? And how can the interaction of the two be untangled? Just because something runs in families does not prove it is genetically determined. Consider that speaking Italian runs in families in Italy! Separating nature from nurture is obviously an arduous and complex task. Currently, most alcoholism authorities believe there is a genetic predisposition for alcoholism in some individuals, and this means there must be some biochemical differences between those who are and are not prone to alcoholism.[15]

Some recent studies pointing to genetic predisposition support the thesis of a metabolic etiology as a contributing factor to alcoholism. Kern compared the zinc levels of twenty children, age eight to twelve, from alcoholic homes with matched subjects from nonalcoholic families, and found the zinc levels of the children of alcoholics to be significantly depressed. This result is meaningful because of the separate documentation of depressed zinc levels in adult alcoholics.[16]

"Cells of Alcoholics, Non-drinkers Differ," proclaimed the headline of a recent article describing results of a research team that measured cAMP, a chemical found in every human cell. This chemical increases with alcohol consumption and returns to normal levels when alcohol is taken away. When alcohol was withheld, these researchers found cAMP levels dropped to normal in cells from nondrinkers; but in cells from alcoholics, the levels fell about 75 percent below the norm. The enthusiastic researchers suggested that reduction in cAMP levels "could explain alcohol withdrawal." They further proposed measuring cAMP in teens to predict which are most susceptible to alcoholism.[17] At the risk of dampening the research team's enthusiasm, I want to suggest results like these are not as totally convincing as they might first appear, since the possibility exists that the cellular changes wrought by alcoholism caused the difference in cAMP-level responses. Additional, more sophisticated studies are needed.

Traditionally, researchers have used twin studies and adoption studies in an effort to identify and differentiate hereditary and environmental influences on the transmission of alcoholism. Adoption studies examine children of alcoholic biological parents who were adopted and raised by nonalcoholic families. Dr. Donald Goodwin and his colleagues studied Danish adoptees separated from their biological parents in infancy. These researchers concluded that the fifty-five biological sons of alcoholic parents were four times as likely to become alcoholics as the seventy-eight sons of nonalcoholics. Severe alcoholism was significant only among the biological children of alcoholics, and apart from the alcoholism, the two groups of adopted sons were indistinguishable when considering other types of psychiatric illness.

Goodwin reported a further investigation of the possibility that sons of alcoholics, raised by their alcoholic parents, would be more likely to develop alcoholism than their brothers who had been adopted out in infancy. However, comparison of these two groups of children indicated that sons of alcoholics living with alcoholic biological parents were no more likely to become alcoholic than their adopted brothers. Nevertheless, both groups of siblings were more likely to become alcoholics than sons having no known parental alcoholism. Goodwin concluded that there may be a genetic predisposition for severe alcoholism, and that children of alcoholics are particularly vulnerable regardless of their environments.[18]

Cloninger also investigated adult sons and adult daughters of alcoholics who had been adopted and found their risk of alcoholism increased only when their original biological parents were alcoholics, regardless of any alcoholism among their adoptive parents.[19] Adoption studies like these point to an inherited predisposition to alcoholism which is unaffected by living with an alcoholic parent.

The few relevant twin studies tend to suggest a genetic predisposition toward alcoholism since monozygotic (identical) twins are usually found to have a significantly higher concordance rate for alcoholism than dizygotic (fraternal) twins. However, it is important to remember if genes completely determined development of alcoholism, both identical twins would always be alcoholic, and that was not the case. Clearly, alcoholism is not inevitable in spite of pronounced family patterns.[20]

Studies do not unequivocally support genetic transmission of alcoholism, and although evidence in support of environmental theories is tenuous, such evidence cannot be ignored.[21] It has been noted that if we generalize from Goodwin's results, we find about 80 percent of the subjects with an alcoholic parent will not become alcoholics, and 60 to 80 percent of the alcoholic subjects did not have an alcoholic parent or other relative.[22] This suggests that in many individuals, environmental factors influence the expression and severity of alcoholism. Future research into the etiology of alcoholism may be based on an interactive model that includes both genetic and environmental factors.

I began this chapter by observing that once we get beyond statistics and descriptions of the physical effects of alcoholism, the subject is loaded with confusion and controversy. There may never be agreement about the precise definition and definitive cause(s) of alcoholism, but there is general consensus regarding its emotional and psychological effects on the alcoholic individual.

EMOTIONAL AND PSYCHOLOGICAL EFFECTS OF ALCOHOLISM

The following list of some emotional and psychological effects of alcoholism is adapted from Linda and Dr. John Friel's description of the major indicators of addiction.[23]

1. *Sneaking.* Alcoholics may hide bottles and/or have a few drinks before going out for the evening "just to be sure" in case there is no opportunity to have more later.

2. *Denial.* This includes defensiveness about the alcoholic's drinking behavior and its consequences. Denial is exhibited in comments like, "No way am I an alcoholic. I have a good job and work hard. Sure, I drink two six-packs every night and I've got a couple D.U.I.s, but if you'd quit nagging me, I'd be fine."

3. *Mood Swings.* This characteristic of progressing alcoholism creates an emotional roller coaster for the alcoholic and all those who are along for the ride, especially the alcoholic's family. Alcoholics often go from being irritable, temperamental, moody, and sad to being elated and hyperactive, then back to irritable and sad. The parallel rail on this roller coaster track is the swing from anger to syrupy sweetness.

4. *Blaming.* This is a major component of denial, because alcoholics must find something or someone to blame for the increasing problems caused by alcoholism in order to maintain denial. Alcoholics appear to exhibit an overwhelming reluctance to accept responsibility for their own lives and symptoms.

5. *Rigid Attitudes.* Alcoholics usually engage in dichotomous, all-or-nothing thinking. Everything is black or white, i.e., in extremes, and alcoholics tend to be dogmatic, opinionated, and intolerant of others' opinions.

6. *Loss of Values.* As alcoholism progresses, alcoholics increasingly exhibit the breakdown of moral and ethical boundaries. They may socialize with people whom they formerly avoided and perform acts they previously did not—hurtful acts, sexual acts, illegal acts.

7. *Blackouts.* This consequence of progressing alcoholism is actually physical; but it also has emotional, psychological, and interpersonal effects. Alcoholic blackouts are not those episodes when alcoholics "pass out," but when they cannot remember what they did while under the influence of alcohol, e.g., driving home from last night's party. As a result, they usually experience an increasing sense of confusion and being out of control.

In addition to prevailing consensus on the devastating physical, psychological and emotional effects of alcoholism, there is agreement about its incredible cost. It is estimated that the cost of treating alcoholism and related disorders is nearly 15 percent of the national health bill, or about 117 billion dollars a year.[24] But that shocking figure does not reflect alcoholism's highest cost: the shattered lives of the alcoholic persons and those closest to them—their families. And the vast majority of alcoholics live in families.[25] In the next chapter we will look at some of the life-shattering forces inside the fiercely guarded walls of the alcoholic family system.

CHAPTER TWO

THE ALCOHOLIC FAMILY SYSTEM

A NATIONAL GALLUP POLL in 1982 showed that 33 percent of American families surveyed reported drinking-related difficulties in their families. More specifically, one in three Americans said some degree of drinking behavior was a cause of problems in their immediate families.[1] The major focus of this book is upon the family problems caused by drinking behavior. However, to begin with an examination of the alcoholic family system would give only a distorted view of family life, for parental alcoholism profoundly alters family functioning. So we need to look briefly at functional families to have a clearer understanding of dysfunctional families such as those with parental alcoholism. But even before that, we need to define some terms and examine the common characteristics and functions of family systems in general.

CHARACTERISTICS OF FAMILY SYSTEMS

Any system is made up of interdependent parts linked together in a particular way to perform a common function. All systems have organization, a drive toward homeostasis or equilibrium, feedback mechanisms, and a circular drive of causal events. A change in one component of the system alters all components of the system.

As we apply this to the family, we see that the members of the family comprise the interdependent part, and the structure of the family is the way they are linked together to accomplish the family functions. As we continue to apply the definition of general systems to the family systems, we recognize that different families have different organizational patterns (or structures). We also know that families tend to settle down into familiar— even if painful—patterns of functioning, and it is difficult to make changes; this is an example of the powerful drive toward equilibrium. Further, families have communication systems to provide feedback, and we can observe clearly that when one member of the family changes, e.g., begins to drink alcoholically, all members of the family are affected.

The best way to understand the characteristics of family systems is to imagine a lovely mobile hanging from the ceiling above you. The mobile's function is to give you pleasure as you enjoy its beauty. The structural elements of the mobile are suspended in a delicately balanced relationship with each other. They are separate entities, yet they are connected. The thin wires or strings connecting the structural pieces are the means of communicating changes in the mobile. If you reached up and changed the position of one component of the mobile, all the others would be affected, although that effect may be almost imperceptible. If you did not disturb the mobile again, eventually the separate, but interconnected, pieces would return to their original relationship with each other. (The structural components of the mobile seem to have an "innate sense" of where they "should" be to perform their function.) The mobile could then continue to perform its function of pleasing you.[2] Keep in mind our imaginary mobile as we examine functional and dysfunctional family systems.

Three Basics of Family Functioning

I believe all families have three basic functions to perform: maintenance, nurturance, and guidance. These functions serve to meet the diverse needs of various family members.

Maintenance Functions. The family functions to provide for the basic needs of food, shelter, and clothing for its members. The adults in the family assume the responsibility for meeting these needs in functional families, although the offspring may be involved. Throughout Scripture we see this function carried out within families. In 1 Timothy 5:8, Paul tells a young church leader that, "if anyone does not provide for his own, and especially for those of his household, he has denied the faith, and is worse than an unbeliever." Obviously, God takes seriously the performance of maintenance functions in families. Children should be able to expect to receive food when they are hungry and larger clothing when they outgrow what they are wearing.

Nurturance Functions. In my conceptualization of family functions, nurturance goes beyond the basics of food and shelter to the need for love and emotional support. Members of functional families care about and respect each other. In their relationships with each other, they follow the Romans 12:15 exhortation to "Rejoice with those who rejoice, and weep with those who weep." Members of functional families use physical touch appropriately and affectionately. Children are not exasperated and caused to "lose heart" by their parents (see Colossians 3:21). Children are loved by their parents, because parents have *learned* to love them (see Titus 2:4).

Healthy, functional families operate on relationship principles presented in the fourth chapter of Ephesians, especially verses 25–32. This passage describes relationships that build up others with words of truth and tenderness rather than tearing them down with bitterness and malice. These principles could be summarized with one word—grace. Verse 29 speaks of the need to use only words that "give grace to those who hear," and verse 32 specifically calls believers to forgive others because *they* have been forgiven.

13

Even if a family is not genuinely Christian, when it functions properly, its members meet each other's nurturance needs by encouraging each other with graceful words, and by oiling the machinery of their relationship with forgiveness.

Guidance Functions. Children need guidance, and healthy families function to provide that guidance. Children need to be taught to tie their shoes, to look both ways before crossing the street, to play fair, and a thousand other things. The primary responsibility for providing guidance to children falls upon the parents, although older siblings often help. Certainly, the Bible lays the guidance burden directly at the feet of parents (especially fathers).[3]

Young children are not the only members of the family with guidance needs. Parents and older children have guidance needs also, and in functional families these are often met by exchanges of information between the family members. This information is frequently obtained from outside the family system, and in healthy families the family boundary is flexible enough to allow for such infusion of new information.

Additional Family Terms

I have raised the issue of family boundaries, and throughout this book I will be using the term "family dynamics." Some understanding of these terms will be helpful.

Family Boundaries. These are psychological, not geographical boundaries. Functional families have flexible and permeable boundaries; they are neither too rigid nor too diffuse. These families have an appropriate sense of "us"; yet it is not "us against the world." On the other hand, in families with diffuse boundaries, there is no sense of cohesion. People from these dysfunctional families are often heard saying, "I haven't talked to my family in years; we were just never very close." And in families with rigid boundaries, there is a "siege mentality." Like a fortress under siege, no one may enter or leave. Even information is not allowed in or out. The tacit understanding in these unhealthy families is, "We don't air our dirty linen, and we don't need anything from anybody."

There are also boundaries within the family. There are intergenerational boundaries between adults and children. For example, in functional families, sexual intercourse takes place between the adults—husband and wife. Incestuous families have diffuse intergenerational boundaries which allow sexual expression to take place between adults and children. There are also individual boundaries within families, i.e., each member of the family should be able to have a clearly defined boundary around himself or herself. If a young adult child has the opportunity to take a good job in another state, he or she would be encouraged to do so in a functional family. But this adult child would be made to feel guilty about his or her "selfishness" at wanting to "abandon" the family if it is dysfunctional.

Family Dynamics. The word *dynamics* is borrowed from physics. It is used to describe the forces that tend toward generating or changing an action or motion, and it explains how this action or motion occurs under the impact of those forces.[4] Family dynamics are the forces operating within the family system to produce the existing family condition. Obviously, the dynamics in dysfunctional families are going to be very different from those in functional family systems.

FUNCTIONAL FAMILY SYSTEMS

I conceive of all families as falling somewhere on a continuum from "Walton's Mountain" on one end to "Dachau"[5] on the other, as illustrated in figure 2–1.

Do you remember the popular television program "The Waltons"? The family depicted on that program was the epitome of an extremely functional family. The Waltons had their difficult moments and human struggles in their home on Walton's Mountain; but family members knew the importance of living by godly values, communicating openly, and extending forgiveness. They managed to resolve every crisis in fifty-nine minutes. At the end of each episode, they went to bed calling out affectionate phrases of love and encouragement to each other.

At the other end of the Family Functioning Continuum is a situation I describe as "Dachau." By that I mean families so extremely dysfunctional that mere existence in them is actually life-threatening for some members. One overcast afternoon in 1985, my husband and I walked the grounds of Dachau, the Nazi death camp near Munich, Germany. I remember the leaden sky,

The Family Functioning Continuum

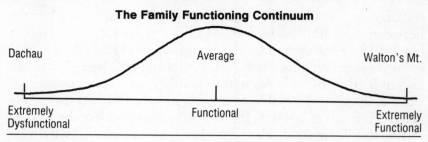

Dachau   Average   Walton's Mt.

Extremely   Functional   Extremely
Dysfunctional   Functional

Figure 2–1

the grotesquely beautiful sculpture symbolizing heaps of twisted corpses disgorged by glutted ovens. I remember these sights as I meet and work with adult offspring from these "Dachau" families. Their leaden looks and twisted, corpse-like existences are hauntingly familiar. But it would be misleading to imply that existence in all alcoholic families is life-threatening. It is not. In fact, the alcoholic family system has a continuum of its own, which is described a little later.

Characteristics of Functional Families

You may be thinking nobody has a family like the Waltons; and I agree (especially about the fifty-nine-minutes part). The bell-shaped, "normal curve" over the continuum depicts the distribution of families in general. As you can see, very few families live near either Walton's Mountain or Dachau. Most families— roughly two-thirds—function in the average range and these millions of functional families have certain characteristics in common.

Safety. There is basic safety in functional families; children do not have to be afraid that Dad will set the house on fire because he was so intoxicated he fell asleep with a cigarette in his hand. In functional families, children do not live in fear of being sexually molested, physically abused, or emotionally abandoned. They do not have to stay awake at night wondering if Dad is going to give Mom a black eye again, because *all* the members of functional families are safe. Functional families provide safety for thoughts and feelings too, so children don't have to live in fear of *emotional* annihilation.

16

Security. If safety provides the assurance that I will be able to *live,* security provides the confidence that I will be able to live my childhood as a *child.* In functional family systems, parents do the parenting, and children are allowed to be children. Seven-year-old children in normal families do not have to plan and cook meals for themselves and younger siblings as often occurs in alcoholic and other dysfunctional families. In normal families, children do not have adult roles thrust on them in a drunken crisis. Instead, healthy parents gradually allow their children to assume age-appropriate responsibilities. Functional family systems are even secure enough to allow conflict between members with the confidence that it can be resolved with respect and honesty.

Stability. Children in functional family systems know the safety and security they experience is going to be there *tomorrow.* They can depend on their parents to be reasonably consistent rather than capricious. Even if the family moves or faces some other major change, children can count on their parents to bring stability to the family by behaving responsibly and predictably. The most important thing parents do to provide stability for the family is to make Jesus Christ Lord of their lives and their home. While I believe a family can function reasonably well without this focus on God, no family can be all it could be—or was intended to be—without the element of personal faith in Christ.

Even with Christ at the center, functional families are not perfect. There may be tension, anxiety, yelling, and crises—but not every day. There may be sadness and even despair—but not usually. When that occurs as a regular way of life, you are not anywhere in the vicinity of Walton's Mountain! You have moved down the slippery slopes of the family continuum to Dachau.

CHARACTERISTICS OF ALCOHOLIC FAMILIES

Alcoholic families have striking similarities, but they also have differences based on the unique dynamics in each home. The alcoholic family system has its own continuum; but, when compared to that of family systems in general, its range of variation is more constricted than that of family systems in general. As illustrated in the alcoholic family continuum shown in figure

2–2, I do not believe the alcoholic family ever reaches what we would refer to as "normal functioning."

In rare cases, alcoholic homes can achieve what I call *mild chaos*. This is a level of pseudo-functioning in which many of the needs of the children are being met with reasonable levels of consistency and an element of security results. Again, the normal curve suggests that most alcoholic families function somewhere between Dachau and mild chaos. In this model, it is not possible for alcoholic families to move into the more functional portion of the continuum depicted by the dotted line.

What happens in alcoholic families to so constrict their range of functioning? To answer that question, we must examine the common dynamics in alcoholic family systems and explore the prevalent patterns of neglect and abuse.

Family Dynamics

The alcoholic family is like other families in many ways: Its members usually work hard, strive to be happy, and hope to love and be loved. However, the alcoholic family is often a "breeding ground of despair hidden beneath the deceptive face of denial."[6] Why? Because alcoholic families clasp a viper to their bosom—the viper of alcohol abuse, which inflicts pain on all it stings, just as the writer of Proverbs warned.[7] To understand this phenomenon and to help those adult children who have been "stung," we must grasp the central role played by alcohol in these families.

Centrality of Alcohol. The major distinguishing characteristic of the alcoholic family is that it is organized around alcohol and the alcoholic. Alcohol use becomes the center and circumference of the family system. Alcoholic behavior becomes the

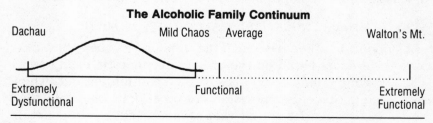

The Alcoholic Family Continuum

Dachau   Mild Chaos   Average   Walton's Mt.

Extremely   Functional   Extremely
Dysfunctional   Functional

Figure 2–2

pervasive family obsession, even when the alcoholic is sober. Always, the family's primary consideration is preventing the alcoholic's need to drink.

Most functional families are less centralized and not so exclusively organized around the needs of one member. In alcoholic families, all other needs, including those of the children, are subordinated to the needs of the alcoholic parent. In figure 2–3 the drawing by a thirteen-year-old child of an alcoholic illustrates her perception of the centrality of alcohol and the alcoholic parent in her home.[8]

The alcoholic's primary need is to be able to drink alcoholically, and he or she does that drinking regardless of the family circumstances or consequences. Please take a moment to reread the last sentence, because it is crucial that we understand the

Figure 2–3

importance of separating "the chicken" from "the egg." Unlike the proverbial chicken-and-egg dilemma, in the case of alcoholism, we *know* which came first! No one is "driven to drink" by external forces such as nagging spouses or noisy children. It may *seem* that way; but the drive to drink is internal, whether biochemical or learned.[9]

In applying this to the family we can say that no parent drinks alcoholically because of the chaotic condition of the home; the home is in a chaotic condition because the parent drinks alcoholically. And that alcoholic drinking shapes every element of the family system. Specifically, the family's central focus becomes distortion of reality to permit ongoing denial of alcoholism.[10]

Denial and Distortion of Reality. When you stop to think about it, alcoholic families face quite a remarkable challenge: sufficient distortion of reality to allow both the continuation of alcoholic drinking by one or both parents, and the denial of parental alcoholism. This challenge is met in many creative ways; but they all involve distortion of reality by denial of facts and feelings.

Denial of facts. Of course the major fact that must be denied is that the alcoholic parent's behavior is negatively affecting the family. This necessitates an illogical and/or faulty explanation of what has been denied. There must be a way to account for increasing drinking, erratic or violent behavior, mood swings, and memory lapses that both explains the reality and denies it simultaneously. This explanation frequently involves the creation of another problem. This "problem" can be outside the family, such as a stressful job, or inside the family. Either way, the solution is always the same—drinking.[11]

The distorted logic in alcoholic families reverses cause and effect. So instead of confessing, "My problems are the result of my drinking," the alcoholic testifies (and the family corroborates), "I drink because I have problems."[12] For example, the father comes home drunk and yells at the mother and the children, causing the baby to become frightened and cry. Father pours himself a drink and says, "I need a drink to relax; this house is a zoo!" Magically, the problem has become the solution. There are many variations on this theme: "Dad doesn't have a drinking problem; he's just under a lot of pressure at work." And the old familiar standby, "If you were quieter/better/

20

smarter/prettier/slimmer/more affectionate, etc., I wouldn't drink so much." This familiar refrain can be sung by the alcoholic to either spouse or children; but the effect is always the same—the problem has become the solution.

Denial and distortion of reality require that the real problem is never identified and addressed. This can produce some bizarre situations and rules. Consider the family where Mom is too drunk to let the family's well-trained old dog outside, so it messes in the house. The rule becomes: The dog cannot go in the house. Does that address Mom's alcoholism? No. Winter comes, the old dog freezes to death, and Mom still drinks alcoholically. And no one may even remember why that rule was made. Rules are an important part of any family system, and this is particularly true in the alcoholic family.

Rules for denial. The rules in alcoholic families are not the kind that are written out and posted on the refrigerator door with magnets. These are *unspoken* rules that silently and forcefully shout their commands to family members. The following is a list of informal but binding rules I have identified. They all have the same purpose—to facilitate denial of reality.

1. *The alcoholic parent's use of alcohol is the most important thing in the family's life.* Over and over this is demonstrated as all other family priorities and needs, including the children's needs, fade into an alcoholic fog.

In an emotionless voice, Gary recalls,"I didn't figure it out for a year or so. Eventually I caught on that the only reason my dad went to see me pitch was to buy beer and drink it during the game, because my mom wouldn't let him bring it in the house. When she found out about him driving home with me from my games when he was loaded, she got mad and they had a big fight. He never went to any more of my games. It was obvious to me even then that the only important thing to him was being able to drink, and when I no longer served that purpose—too bad for me."

2. *Alcohol is not the cause of the family's problems.* We have already looked at how this rule enables the problem to become the solution. Many adults raised in alcoholic families report that when they would plead with their sober parent to do something about the alcoholic parent's drinking, they were told the "real

problem around here is that you're selfish and don't appreciate all the things he (or she) does for you."

3. *The alcoholic is not responsible for his or her dependency.* This rule fosters a feeling of helplessness and hopelessness in the family. Sometimes this rule can be a distorted extension of the disease concept of alcoholism. Remember, even if there is a strong genetic predisposition to alcoholism, the alcoholic is responsible for participating actively in the management of his or her chronic health problem.

4. *The status quo must be maintained at all costs.* When we discussed characteristics of all family systems, we noted that there is a strong drive toward equilibrium, i.e., maintaining the status quo. This is seen dramatically in alcoholic families. Children adopt various roles in the family to allow the alcoholic equilibrium to remain undisturbed. The next three rules are extensions of this one.

5. *Everyone in the family must be an enabler.* An enabler is anyone who prevents the alcoholic person from experiencing the consequences of his or her drug-induced behavior. Enabling spouses are usually referred to as co-alcoholics or codependents because they are dependent on their alcoholic spouses in much the same way those individuals are dependent on alcohol. An enabling wife phones the boss to say that her alcoholic husband has "the flu" when he is actually hungover. An enabling husband excuses his wife's drunken behavior at a party by explaining that his wife's doctor gave her some new medication for "nerves." Children are not born enablers; but codependency is the core curriculum in alcoholic families and children learn what they are taught.

6. *No one may discuss what is really going on in the family, either with one another or with outsiders.* Alcoholic families tend to be closed systems, i.e., they have very rigid and impermeable boundaries which prevent the transfer of useful information in or out. As one spouse of an alcoholic said to her child, *"There's nothing wrong with this family, and don't tell anyone!"*

Even *within* the family, the "no-talk" rule prevails. Eileen told me that she and her older sister never discussed their fathe 's alcoholic and abusive behavior until both were in their thirties. She was shocked to learn that her sister had shared her own feelings of terror, guilt, and anger. As adults, each finally sought help for personal and family problems without the knowledge of the other. When finally they shared this, they wept together over the years of isolated misery that could have been moderated if they had been able to comfort one another as children. But as children, they could not reach out and comfort one another without breaking the no-talk rule.

And children understand at a very early age that their basis of attachment to the family unit is their willingness to corroborate the family story ("Alcohol is not a problem here") and comply with the family rules no matter how dysfunctional those rules may be. Again, please stop and reread that last sentence, because it is essential that you fully grasp its significance if you are to understand the issues discussed in the remainder of this book.

7. *No one may say what he or she is really feeling.* This is an incredibly powerful rule and deserves to be discussed in more detail, for just as perceptions are denied and distorted in alcoholic families, this rule requires the denial and distortion of congruent feelings.

Denial of feelings. It has been noted frequently that adults from alcoholic families have difficulty identifying, feeling, and expressing emotions. They often exhibit a kind of emotional numbness. Children in alcoholic homes are not born with this emotional numbness; they have to be taught the rule that produces this disorder, and most of them learn well and early.

"Feelings were a luxury I couldn't afford in my family," said Angela with a wan smile. "It hurt too much. So I learned to hold my breath, or concentrate on the junk on television—anything just so I wouldn't think about what was happening. Because when you're little and you let yourself think about it, you start to feel scared, real scared." Angela's comments address one of the major functions served by denial of feelings—protection from emotional pain.

Children in alcoholic homes usually are not given the opportunity to talk about their disturbing feelings in order to receive comfort and encouragement, even when they have experienced acute trauma. One daughter of an abusive, alcoholic father and an emotionally disturbed mother remembers one night as she sobbed in pain after being raped by her father. Her mother came in and told her to stop crying because she would, "wake the baby." The adults closest to these children teach and model denial of feelings as the method of choice in coping with emotional distress, so that is what the children learn.

Actually, some feelings are allowed in most alcoholic family systems, as long as they are on the *pleasant* end of the emotional continuum. You have to be middle-aged or older to remember a Saturday morning radio program for children called "Let's Pretend." I remember it well, and if you do too, you will recall that every program ended with the sentence, "And they lived happily ever after!" Alcoholic families are engaged in a daily dramatization of "Let's Pretend"; however, everyone in the family does not live happily ever after. This threatening reality requires that displays of pleasant emotions be *demanded* of children in alcoholic families to validate the family myth that there is no problem in this family.

Jeff grew up in a family in which he was told constantly, "Nobody likes a frowny face. Smile, Jeff, smile." At thirty-two, Jeff is angry not only that he was not allowed to express the overwhelming sadness he experienced as a child, but that he was given the clear message that by having such feelings he risked emotional abandonment by the family ("nobody likes . . ."). As an adult, Jeff continues to smile even as he describes his anger. Jeff's experience is not uncommon in alcoholic families. These are what I call "moon families," for just as we always see only one side of the moon, these families are allowed to exhibit only one side of the emotional spectrum.

Functional family systems allow the appropriate expression of a broad range of feelings, in contrast to the narrow range permitted in alcoholic families. Figures 2–4 and 2–5 may be helpful in

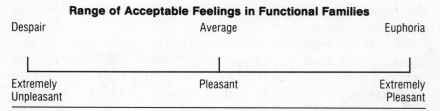

Range of Acceptable Feelings in Functional Families

Despair	Average	Euphoria
Extremely Unpleasant	Pleasant	Extremely Pleasant

Figure 2–4

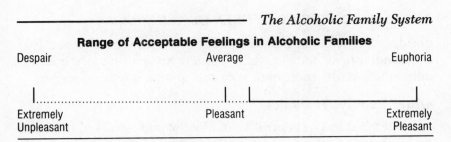

Figure 2–5

depicting the differences between acceptable emotions in functional and in alcoholic families. The range of acceptable feelings that can be expressed appropriately is represented by solid lines, and unacceptable emotions by dotted lines.

It is reasonable to assume that members of alcoholic families are rarely, if ever, genuinely euphoric, although they may experience refreshing respites of very pleasant emotions occasionally. The continuum in figure 2–6 illustrates the range of feelings probably experienced in most alcoholic family systems.

If you compare the continua illustrating acceptable and probable feelings in alcoholic families, you will notice there is little overlapping of the solid lines. What do the children in these families do with their fear, anger, sadness—the emotions which fall outside the overlapping area? They distort and deny them in an effort to corroborate the family's "no-problems-here" story. Typically, these children gradually develop an "affective anesthesia," which leads to the emotional numbness that we see in most adult children of alcoholics. Why do these children do this? Because accepting and validating the family myth is part of their basis of attachment to the family. Their only alternative is complete emotional abandonment. When you consider that

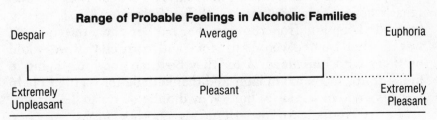

Figure 2–6

children in alcoholic homes usually live with a heightened fear of abandonment because their parents are chronically unavailable emotionally, their course of action makes a lot of sense.

Other Family Dynamics

In addition to the centrality of alcohol and denial of facts and feelings, there are other dynamics operating in alcoholic family systems. Several of these are confusing communication, control strategies, and increasing chaos manifested in patterns of neglect and abuse.

Confusing Communication. Communication in alcoholic families is characterized by secrecy, unclear messages, and repetition. These confusing communication patterns all serve the primary purpose of the alcoholic family by facilitating distortion of reality and denial of alcoholism.

Secrecy. There are few straight answers in alcoholic homes. Of course, *the big secret* is the presence of parental alcoholism, and all the secrecy and evasion are designed to protect the big secret. Gordon remembers well the secrecy surrounding his alcoholic father's drug-induced behavior. "When I asked why my dad was lying on the front porch when I left for school, I was told he was too sleepy to go up to bed. Actually, he was so bombed out the night before he tripped and fell and was too out of it to pick himself up. It was pretty embarrassing to have my friends see my father asleep on the front porch."

Unclear messages. Messages in alcoholic families are usually unclear because they are mixed and/or misdirected. Mixed messages are very confusing to children in these families. Rebecca remembers her mother announcing in the presence of her alcoholic father, "Obey your father," then conspiring with Rebecca and her brother to circumvent their father's orders. Rebecca also recalls her mother joining in with her father to punish her for trying to keep him from throwing her mother down the stairs. "I was terrified that he would kill Mom, and terrified that we would be there with him alone. After they beat me good for trying to break it up, she came in later and thanked me for trying to help her. I wanted to scream at her, 'Why didn't you try to help me?'"

"I love you—leave me alone" is another mixed message frequently received by children in alcoholic families. Unclear messages in these homes can be mixed, but they also can be misdirected.

If misdirected messages were charted on paper, they would form triangles. For example, Person One complains to Person Two about Person Three, who is not present. The complaint may be valid, i.e., it is a message worth delivering; but this communication pattern is confusing and triangular because the message is not directed at the appropriate person. In functional families, Person One could go to Person Three and speak the truth in love concerning his or her complaint. Sometimes there is an unspoken expectation that Person Two will tell Person Three how upset Person One is, so Person Three will change without Person One risking direct exposure to Three's anger.

Because there is so much anger in alcoholic families, this triangular mode of communication is very common. Sober parents often use one or more of their children as confidants upon whom they unload their cares, because they have to talk to someone. Children's shoulders are not strong enough to share this burden, and these children report feeling overwhelmed and confused about whether or not they are supposed to convey this information to the drinking parent. Frequently, the request to relay messages is explicitly stated.

Beth still shudders as she talks about the fear she felt when she repeatedly had to deliver her mother's misdirected messages to her angry, intoxicated father: "My mom used to ask me to go talk to my father—especially when he was crazy-mad drunk—when she wanted something from him. I guess she figured he was less likely to kill me than her! All I remember is that I was scared to death to do it and scared to death not to do what she asked. After all, she wasn't quite as crazy as he was so I didn't want her mad at me." Beth experienced this trauma repeatedly, and often she delivered the same messages time after time. This repetitive element is common to the communication patterns in alcoholic family systems.

Repetition. Conversations in alcoholic families often sound like the needle got stuck; the same groove goes around and around playing the same tired tunes. Many adults from alcoholic families report enormous anger at the sober parent for "doing nothing but complaining for years."

Karen says that she has heard the same things from her mother as long as she can remember. "And now when the phone rings at night I hate it, because I'm afraid it will be her with her tired, old litany of complaints about Dad. When I suggest something, she just says, 'Oh, you don't understand,' and nothing changes. I know she'll be calling back again with the same stuff in a few days." Karen has a good understanding of alcoholic family systems now; but as a child, she reports being very confused and angry about why her mother complained repeatedly about her father's drinking but never did anything about it.

Confusing communication patterns of secrecy, unclear messages, and repetition all serve to facilitate the progression of alcoholism. Eventually, families may employ control strategies to moderate the effects of the advancing alcoholism.

Control Strategies. Many researchers who have examined family dynamics and patterns of interactions in alcoholic families have suggested that the family first denies the developing alcoholism problem, but when the problem becomes greater the family may attempt to minimize it by exerting controls to maintain family structure. Strategies are employed to defend against the increasing invasion of alcoholism in the family.

It has been reported widely that children and/or sober spouses often will attempt to hide and/or dilute the alcoholic's liquor. Sometimes the nonalcoholic parent will use one or more of the children as bodyguards for the drinking parent in an effort to control alcohol use. In effect, this is asking a child to control his or her alcoholic parent, and this is an overwhelmingly frightening assignment for any child.

Wendy's face betrays no emotion as she describes being thrust into the role of parenting her alcoholic parent. "Everyone thought it was so cute that my daddy brought me to the bar. I would perch up on that high stool and drink my 'kiddy cocktail' with its cherry and its orange slice. I hated the way that place and my dad smelled, but my mother always told him to take me, and I knew why. Oh, she never said anything, but I knew I was supposed to keep him from drinking so much he couldn't drive home. One night on the way home, he actually hit a kid on a bike. He never stopped, and we never talked about it. I felt terribly guilty, because I thought it was my fault he was so drunk he hit the kid. At least, I know he didn't kill the kid, because I looked back and saw him get up, but I was so scared my dad and I would both go to jail." Long ago Wendy numbed the fear and anger that accompanied having her childhood stolen and, in its place being assigned an impossible task.

Expecting children to parent their alcoholic parent is not a successful control strategy. However some recent research indicates that protecting the observance of holiday rituals may be an effective way to moderate the effects of parental alcoholism. If the family can maintain holiday celebrations without having them dominated by the alcoholic parent's drinking behavior, children seem to have lower rates of alcoholism themselves compared with children from families in which the celebrations had been disrupted or discontinued.[13]

However, as the alcoholism progresses, it is more and more difficult to prevent celebration of the holidays from degenerating into the chaos of a hellish daze. Sadly, this seems to be especially true concerning the celebration of our Savior's birth. Many Christian adults from alcoholic homes still experience panic and sadness as the Christmas holidays approach, then feel guilty and confused about their reaction.

"I sobbed; I just sobbed and sobbed. My family thought I was nuts!" Gloria, a Christian adult child of an alcoholic parent, was describing her response to a television commercial showing three generations of a loving family smiling and singing carols while gathered around a glorious Christmas tree. "I have longed my whole life to share a Christmas like that with my folks; but Dad always ruined it when I was a kid. The time I remember clearest was when I was seven. For some reason, I was especially excited on Christmas Eve that year. When my dad finally came home he was more drunk than I had ever seen him, and as he and my mother argued in the living room, he lost his balance and fell into the tree. He broke branches, smashed lights, and crushed gifts. That was the last Christmas I ever hoped we'd be like other families. Now, I so want to know the joy of Jesus' birth; but it's such a hard time for me, and I worry about ruining it for my family."

The following poem, written by Joan, whose father was an alcoholic clergyman, poignantly captures the atmosphere of an alcoholic family's Christmas hellish daze.

Nativity

Red hood drapes
his black robe's back
candles subdue the sanctuary,
Noel Noel we sing.

At midnight he stands before us
rolling down the words
"There was no room at the inn."
Raising his arms,
they fold down then close.

Fruitcake, poinsettias,
fudge fill our parsonage,
cookies, cards, and packages
for the minister and his family.

His daughter's presents are not wrapped.
Red tissue paper rustles, their shadows
argue against the wall
his voice commanding, "Hurry up."
He's naked swilling clear vodka.
Sobbing she cries, "You'll wake her."

Silent night
Holy night
All is calm
All is bright.

I will stay here
in this closet
until morning when
they call me
to open my presents
all the tags
in her handwriting.[14]

Continued drinking episodes eventually result in the family abandoning control strategies, followed by increasing disorganization and chaos.

Increasing Chaos. Just as alcoholism is progressive, so are its effects on the family system. The alcoholic family becomes increasingly disorganized and chaotic as the alcoholic parent becomes more absorbed with alcohol and the sober parent becomes more absorbed with the alcoholic.

To describe a family as increasingly chaotic does not mean more plates and pans are flying through the air. It means there is an increasing sense that life is out of control, a heightened perception that no one is in charge. This is the polar opposite of the stability which characterizes functional family systems. Stability is the first casualty in the list of characteristics of functional families.

As the alcoholic family further deteriorates, security is the next to go as parental inconsistency, unpredictability, and unavailability escalate. Parental inconsistency teaches children to be hypervigilant because they never know if they are going to receive hugs—or slugs. Like good scouts, they need to be prepared. Parental unavailability may be due to increasing focus on alcohol or to divorce.

My research with evangelical Christian adult children of alcoholics revealed a higher divorce rate among alcoholic families (20.9 percent) compared with nonalcoholic families (9.7 percent).[15] These data support earlier findings, and suggest that many children from alcoholic families are raised by a single parent. Even if the alcoholic parent remains in the home, children in these families often have their childhoods plundered by the necessity to parent each other and, not infrequently, their parents.

Tragically, if help is not sought and received, the characteristic of safety is sacrificed in many alcoholic families. This important and painful subject demands examination; therefore the last major section of this chapter addresses the patterns of neglect and abuse within alcoholic family systems.

PATTERNS OF NEGLECT AND ABUSE

Neglect and abuse in alcoholic homes create environments where the chronic trauma of parental unavailability and neglect is punctuated occasionally by the acute trauma of violence and abuse.

It has been noted by those who study family dynamics that there are many similarities between alcoholic and abusive families. Some of these similarities are limited coping skills, isolation, suspicion of outside intervention, emphasis on family secrets, and unawareness of the extent to which this family differs from the norm.[16]

Based on my clinical experience, research, and review of literature in the field, I believe children in all alcoholic families are targets of abusive attitudes and/or abusive acts. Abuse in these families could be viewed as occurring on a continuum with neglect—actually passive abuse—on one end, and death—the ultimate abuse—on the other. In my view, the dichotomy between neglect and abuse is erroneous and misleading; however, this division facilitates organization and presentation of material on this calamitous subject.

Neglect

Neglect has been defined as "the absence of caring."[17] When applied to children in alcoholic families, it is exhibited as a chronic, pervasive inattention to the legitimate needs of those children. Linda and John Friel list numerous forms of neglect, categorizing them as emotional, physical, and sexual.[18]

Emotional Neglect. The Friels include in this category the failure to nurture, love, set limits, and/or encourage educational or intellectual development. Not listening to or believing the children, and expecting them to provide emotional nurturing to parents also are listed. Last, Friel and Friel note that when a parent is not emotionally present due to mental illness, chemical dependency, depression, or compulsivity, the children are being emotionally neglected.

Physical Neglect. These authors list the following situations as examples of physical neglect: lack of food, clothing, and/or shelter, leaving child alone or in charge of others in age-inappropriate ways, and failure to provide medical care. In addition, Friel and Friel include as physical neglect allowing or encouraging the child's use of drugs or alcohol and failure to protect the child from the abuse of others, including the spouse.

Sexual Neglect. Children have a genuine need to be taught appropriately about their sexuality, and neglecting to do this is a form of passive abuse. Friel and Friel cite failure to teach children about sex (allowing sexual naïveté) and puberty, e.g., menstruation, nocturnal emissions, etc., as examples of sexual neglect.

In addition to emotional, physical, and sexual neglect of children in alcoholic homes, emotional, physical, and/or sexual abuse have been reported widely.[19]

Abuse

While there are obvious differences between physical and sexual abuse, some things are common to both. First, there is the well-documented correlation between these two forms of abuse and their higher incidence in alcoholic homes. The disinhibiting effects of alcohol, which weaken or remove the usual restraints on acting out violent and/or sexual impulses, are generally believed to explain this correlation. This is not the whole story though, since sober parents also inflict emotional and, less frequently, physical and sexual abuse on children in alcoholic families. It is probable that a combination of the disinhibiting effects of alcohol and the dysfunctional dynamics of alcoholic families interact to increase the abuse potential of each.

The other glaring commonality shared by these two forms of abuse is the emotional devastation of the children thus victimized. As adults, they share similar characteristics of self-hatred, distrust of others, and shame (i.e., the sense that I am a mistake rather than that I make mistakes) coupled with symptoms of Post-traumatic Stress Disorder. These symptoms include reliving the abuse trauma through nightmares and/or intrusive memories, emotional numbing, hypervigilance and/or exaggerated startle response, impaired memory, and avoidance of activities that could symbolize the trauma.[20]

It is probable that a five-year-old who is repeatedly beaten, burned, or raped experiences trauma at least as intense as that suffered by soldiers in battle.[21] Further, the child has neither the cognitive development nor the coping skills the adult soldier can employ to moderate the emotional damage of the original trauma. A closer look reveals five types of abuse in alcoholic family systems: emotional, verbal, physical, sexual, and vicarious abuse.

33

Emotional Abuse. This includes mixed messages, double binds (all the choices given the child are negative ones), projection and transfer of blame onto the child, and alterations of the child's reality, e.g., "Dad's not drunk, he's just tired." The latter is actually a form of intellectual abuse according to the Friels. They continue this category with emotional abuses such as not talking at all about the alcoholism, fostering low self-esteem, and overprotecting, excusing, and blaming others for the child's problems.[22]

Verbal Abuse. This category overlaps somewhat with the previous one. In this group are excessive blaming, shaming, name-calling, comparisons, teasing, belittling, ridiculing, nagging, and screaming. In other words, verbal assault.

Physical Abuse. With this form of abuse, we take a quantum leap in trauma induction. Nothing contributes to a child's insecurity and fear more than recurring violence in the home. This is true whether the violence is directed at the child, the sober parent, or the furniture.[23]

Statistics correlating alcohol and physical abuse vary widely. Kempe and Helfer, who first described the "battered-child syndrome," stated alcohol is involved in one out of every three child-abuse cases, and a 1971 report by the Massachusetts Society of Prevention of Cruelty to Children determined in 34.4 percent of abuse cases, alcohol was involved.[24] However, Dr. Claudia Black believes the incidence of physical abuse in alcoholic families is much higher. Her own research indicated 66 percent of children in these families have been physically abused or have witnessed abuse of another family member. Additionally, she has noted that the National Council on Alcoholism estimates as many as 60 percent of alcoholic families currently in treatment have experienced domestic violence.[25]

Research on neglected and abused children of alcoholics has suggested the greater the parental alcohol abuse, the more severe the physical abuse or neglect.[26] And another recent study comparing parenting practices in alcoholic homes found families with two alcoholic parents displayed the highest percentage of abuse and neglect.[27] It is important to understand, however, that the alcoholic parent is not always the violent one.

This is how Bill, a Christian in his late thirties, describes his childhood with an alcoholic father and a battering mother: "I guess you'd call my dad a quiet drunk. He worked long hours and then came home, sat in front of the television and drank himself into a coma every night. My mom was the screamer and hitter. When I was little, she would grab me and bang my head against the wall until I thought she would kill me. I mean I really thought she would smash my brain out. And she always had a good reason to do it. I mean she did it for punishment if I messed up the house. As a kid, I thought this was how all parents disciplined their children." Now, as an adult, Bill's greater anger is directed at his physically abusive mother.

Physical abuse can take many forms, including these noted by the Friels: slapping, shaking, scratching, squeezing, hitting and beating with boards, sticks, belts, kitchen utensils, yardsticks, electric cords, shovels, and hoses. Such abuse also can include throwing, pushing, shoving, slamming against walls or objects, burning, scalding, freezing, overworking, and forcing or withholding food and/or water.[28] In addition, Black believes physical abuse can be more subtle, as when an alcoholic father takes the family for a sixty-miles-per-hour ride down a mountain road at night with the headlights off.[29] This form of physical abuse leaves no visible scars. Neither does another subtle, but damaging form—vicarious physical abuse.

Vicarious Physical Abuse. Vicarious physical abuse is defined as having to watch others be physically abused, i.e., the victim is part of a family system in which another member is being physically abused. Stated plainly: "If you are witness to the abuse of anyone else, then you are also a victim of abuse."[30] Black reports that research relating to domestic violence suggests witnessing violent acts may be just as detrimental to the child's emotional and psychological development as actually being abused. The figure 2–7 drawing by Tom, age twelve, dramatically portrays the state of constant fear in which a child lives when witnessing recurrent violence between his parents.[31] Tom is a victim of vicarious physical abuse.

Since research reports that two-thirds of spouse abusers also abuse alcohol,[32] and since marital violence does not necessarily

Figure 2–7

occur during intoxication only, but is often part of sober behavior, we can assume that there are millions of Toms.

Sexual Abuse. Recently, in a study of more than four hundred adult children of alcoholics, 18.5 percent reported having been sexually abused as children, as compared with 9.6 percent of the adult children of nonalcoholics.[33] In my own recent research, I found that 22.4 percent of evangelical Christians raised in alcoholic homes reported having been sexually abused by a family member as a child or adolescent, as compared with 3.2 percent of evangelicals from nonalcoholic families.[34] While both of these studies report statistically significant differences in rates of sexual abuse, both probably vastly underestimate the incidence of actual sexual abuse in alcoholic family systems.

One article on alcoholism and child abuse reported a study suggesting at least 63 percent of incest perpetrators were "under the influence of alcohol during the incident."[35] Another article stated as many as 80 percent of fathers had been drinking the first time they committed incest with their daughters.[36] Although the statistics may vary, authorities in the area agree, ". . . it has been documented that there is an extremely high incidence of children from alcoholic families who suffer sexual abuse."[37]

In my counseling practice with Christian adults raised by alcoholic and other impaired parents, I have observed that the effects of alcoholism coupled with incest are doubly traumatic. Many of these adults do not realize they were victims of incest because they define it as only sexual intercourse between family members. Voices in Action, a self-help organization for incest survivors, defines incest as "a betrayal of trust involving overt or covert sexual actions—direct or indirect, verbal or physical (which may include—but is not limited to—intercourse)—between a child and a trusted adult and/or authority figure."[38] With this wider definition of incest, all sexual abuse of young children may be considered incest, since they naturally look to adults as authority figures.

In keeping with this broader definition of incest, the Friels cite the following as examples of child sexual abuse: fondling, sexual touching, exposing oneself to, or masturbating in front of a child, mutual masturbation, oral sex, anal sex, and intercourse. In addition, they include sexual jokes, innuendoes, leering, "games," torture (burning, etc.), and "punishment," e.g., enemas. They also list penetration with fingers or objects, forcing children to have sex with each other, enforced sexual activity with animals, and taking pornographic pictures of children.[39]

Vicarious sexual abuse. Just as children can experience vicarious physical abuse, as noted above, they can be victims of vicarious sexual abuse. Forcing children to watch pornography or others being sexually abused illustrates vicarious sexual abuse. Even when the child is not forced to watch, he or she can experience vicarious sexual abuse by just knowing another child in the family is being sexually abused.

The 129 subjects in my research completed a personal data questionnaire which included the question, "As a child or adolescent were you ever sexually abused by a family member?" Since I did not define incest as more than sexual intercourse, it is highly probable the incidents of incest—more broadly defined—were vastly underreported. Nevertheless, as I coded the questionnaire responses for computer analysis, I saw a note in the margin near this question which dramatically captured the essence of vicarious sexual abuse. This female subject had checked the "no" response; but she had written, "I wasn't, but my older sister was, and I lived in constant fear of being next." Clearly, this adult child of an alcoholic father was a victim of vicarious sexual abuse.

Pathological Equilibrium

Why would a family tolerate this suffering for years? While some theorists have suggested that denial of the problem or financial dependence prevented action, others have speculated that the alcoholic's drinking serves a homeostatic function in the family. For example, if the alcoholic uses alcohol to relieve anxiety while expressing emotions, the family deals with an anxious, emotionally isolated person whenever he or she abstains from alcohol. Until the next drinking incident the family receives no feedback, and the alcoholic accumulates unexpressed emotions which may be explosively released during the next alcoholic episode.

This form of pathological equilibrium demonstrates how alcoholic behavior stabilizes the family system around the core pathology of parental alcoholism, despite high costs to individual members of the system. "The system and the individuals within it accommodate to find a point of balance that both denies the presence of alcoholism and insures its maintenance at the same time."[40] This systemic conceptualization also serves to explain why members of alcoholic family systems seem to act in ways which enable drinking to continue.[41]

As the drinking continues, greater distortion of reality is required to permit ongoing denial. This results in an escalation of chaos in the home. All of this chaos contributes to the neglect and abuse of the children, placing these children at high risk for developing emotional and social problems at all ages.[42]

With the family dynamics and patterns of neglect and abuse described above, it is not surprising that alcoholic families are experienced as confusing, chaotic, and unpredictable by the children in them.[43] Chapter 3 will examine more closely the effects of parental alcoholism on children.

CHAPTER THREE

CHILDREN IN THE ALCOHOLIC FAMILY

DURING A SEMINAR FOR THERAPISTS who work with adult children of alcoholics, the leader asked for a volunteer to help demonstrate a screening interview for potential therapy group participants. Chad came to the front and in a soft voice began to describe his childhood with two alcoholic parents. He related an incident that often had been described to him by laughing family members. He had come to regard it as symbolic of his entire childhood.

"My parents—both alcoholics—would vacation each summer with us kids at the Jersey Shore. As my family tells the story, I loved to be put in a tiny, infant lifejacket tethered to the pier where I would splash and play for hours. One afternoon, when

39

my folks were involved in an extended version of their daily cocktail party, they forgot about me. When they remembered, it was real late, the tide had gone out, and there I was, hungry and crying, dangling from the pier."

Hundreds of therapists, most of whom were raised in alcoholic families, listened in silence broken only by muffled sobs of shared pain remembered. They understood, both professionally and personally, that—in one way or another—children in alcoholic families have been left "high and dry" by their parents. As caring Christians we are called to tell the Chads of the world that the Psalmist understood his abandonment and found comfort. In Psalm 27:10 he declared, "For my father and my mother have forsaken me, But the Lord will take me up."

But why would alcoholic parents "forsake" their children, either physically or emotionally? Alcoholic and co-alcoholic parents love their children as much as other parents, I am certain. Perhaps one additional definition of alcoholism will answer the question. In 1977 the American Medical Association defined alcoholism as, "an illness characterized by significant impairment that is directly associated with persistent and excessive use of alcohol. Impairment may involve physiological, psychological or social dysfunction."[1] The concept of *impairment* of the alcoholic individual's capacity to parent is the link between the characteristics of alcoholic families and the experiences of children within those families. The painful truth is that alcoholism turns even the most loving parents into people who are unpredictable, unreliable, and emotionally unavailable; and this causes family problems, especially for the children.

Theorists and clinicians agree in order to develop the security and trust that their dependency needs will be met, children need stability and consistency in their home life. Children's needs for attention, love, and self-esteem must be met for them to develop into well-adjusted adults. From his research on learned helplessness, Seligman has called childhood, "the dance of development," and he notes that when parents are focused elsewhere (e.g., on alcohol or the alcoholic), there is no partner for the dance.[2] As the children are forsaken to dance alone, they learn that no one is there to meet their needs. These unmet needs affect children at all stages of their development.

DEVELOPMENTAL ISSUES

Erikson proposed that healthy child development requires children to master age-specific psychosocial crises.[3] This section briefly outlines the potential and probable impact of alcoholic families on the major developmental tasks of children and adolescents.

Infants

Infants achieve trust through experiencing consistent, nurturing relations with their primary caregiver, usually the mother. Severely neglected children fail to thrive and often die; moderately neglected children may mistrust adults to meet their needs. Parental alcoholism renders the parents either absorbed by the alcohol or by the alcoholic, hence parents may respond inconsistently and insensitively to the needs of the infant. "The inconsistent parenting characteristics of the alcoholic home may engender insecurity and mistrust in the newborn."[4]

Perhaps it seems farfetched to say that infants are disturbed by the quality of their care. Yet, some developmental psychologists hypothesize that infants may be more "thoughtful" than most people have imagined. Research analyzing heart rates has suggested infants begin thinking about unusual events toward the end of the first year of life, and, "by one year of age . . . differences in rearing experiences seriously affect cognitive functioning."[5]

Toddlers

One- to three-year-olds must attain a sense of autonomy within the secure parameters of parental controls. Alcoholic parents tend to undercontrol or overcontrol their toddlers, or vacillate between both extremes. Parental intoxication and/or absence from the home may leave the toddler without the safety of appropriate control. In contrast, overcontrol may occur if alcoholic families perceive toddlers' age-appropriate efforts to do things "their way" as being out-of-control and too reminiscent of intoxication to be tolerated. Confused toddlers may come to feel inadequate and ashamed for attempting normal developmental tasks and may develop an operating belief that life is arbitrarily controlled by external forces. As a result, little attempt will be made to exercise self-control.

Preschoolers

Preschool children need to develop the initiative necessary to satisfy their natural curiosity, to distinguish reality from fantasy, and to try to understand connections between events. Children of this age need predictable, understanding parents who reward honesty, responsibility, and goal-directed behavior. Again, because the alcoholic parent is distracted by alcohol, and the nonalcoholic parent is distracted by the alcoholic parent, preschoolers are not apt to receive consistent, sensitive parenting.

At this stage, children may begin to learn to mistrust their own perceptions of reality because they have such a critical need for attachment to their parents. Children will alter and deny their own perceptions to identify with the beliefs and values modeled by their parents rather than risk abandonment by questioning the family myth. Additionally, behavior occurring during an alcoholic blackout will be denied by the alcoholic parent, and this contributes to the child's distrust of his or her own perceptions. For example, Charlie's father did not remember the brutal beating with a broom handle that produced bruises on his young son's legs and could not understand Charlie's sullen silence the next day. "You hurt me," Charlie explained in response to his father's inquiry regarding his "rotten mood." Charlie's father told him he was lying, that he must have fallen down the front porch steps. Charlie remembers beginning to believe that he must be crazy.

Steve thought he was going crazy, too; and he also thought he was the only one in the house who knew his father was an alcoholic, because no one ever talked about it. Claudia Black reported Steve's memory of an incident which occurred when he and his father were home alone.

His father, in a semi-conscious state from drunkeness [sic], was on the floor, had thrown-up, hit his head on the coffee table and was bleeding. Steve's mother and sister had returned home within moments after his dad had hit his head. They just picked dad up and carried him off to the bedroom. No one spoke to anyone else.

Steve said again he thought, "maybe this is all in my head."[6]

Black asked Steve's mother and sister why they had not talked about this incident with Steve. "They responded, 'because he hadn't said anything, and we hoped he hadn't noticed.'"[7]

Preadolescents

Five- to eleven-year-old children need their parents to reward goal-directed behavior. As previously noted however, children from alcoholic families typically experience their parents as unavailable and uninvolved. The lack of parental investment during these years may produce feelings of inferiority in the child. Also, many children of alcoholics rarely have friends visit for fear of being embarrassed by the alcoholic's unpredictable, poorly controlled behavior. Poor self-concept and poor social skills may jeopardize healthy peer relationships.

"I can't tell you all how much this group means to me," Yvonne whispered, her eyes glistening with tears. "I never had friends when I was growing up. I could never have slumber parties at *my* house like the other girls. In fifth grade I really got brave and invited a classmate over to my house after school one day. She was new and I hoped maybe she would be desperate enough to want me for a friend. As we walked up on the front porch, I thought I was going to die. I could hear my mom and dad screaming and calling each other filthy names. My dad had lost his job that morning and had been drinking all day. The girl—I can't even remember her name—looked at me wide-eyed for a second, then dropped her head and mumbled something about forgetting she needed to get right home after school. I don't think I ever had the nerve to invite anyone over again."

In addition to being embarrassed by parental drunkenness, by this age some children may be aware that the alcoholic parent's behavior presents physical danger from fires, violence, neglect of younger siblings, etc. Jay recounted proudly how he and his sisters came up with the idea of filling several cooking pans with water and leaving them on the kitchen counter each night so they could get to them quickly to put out fires their alcoholic father frequently started when he fell asleep with a cigarette in his hand. This awareness of physical danger also may result in school avoidance or inattention. Joan cried when she was forced to go to first grade and leave her younger sister home alone with their alcoholic mother. Joan had been providing most of her sister's care for nearly a year.

Adolescents

Adolescent children from alcoholic families face their own developmental challenges, especially that of identity formation. Uncompleted developmental tasks from earlier stages leave them unprepared. Children are not born with a sense of personal identity; it is gradually formed from interactions primarily in the family. Children look to their parents as mirrors to reflect their identity. But *alcoholic and co-alcoholic parents are extremely marred mirrors.* Their perceptions of their children are formed in an alcoholic fog; then this cloudy, distorted image is reflected to the children. This lack of clarity hinders adolescents from emerging as separate, fully defined individuals.

Struggles with identity formation experienced by adolescents in alcoholic families are often expressed by confusion about their sexuality. There are equivocal and contradictory findings regarding the role of the same-sex or opposite-sex parent's influence on children's gender identifications. However, one experienced clinician reported he had never seen a male client who rejected his alcoholic father as a gender model, although he had seen several women who did not want to be women because their alcoholic mother seemed so downtrodden.[8] Perhaps this difference is explained by the prevailing cultural bias against female alcoholics as being beneath contempt.

If the challenge of identity formation is successfully met, late adolescents age seventeen to twenty realize their choices can be self-determined, whether or not they synchronize with parental values. However, this rarely occurs in alcoholic families, a fact reflected in the struggles of adult offspring to separate from their parents and establish their own individual lives.

It has been proposed that the harm experienced by children of alcoholics is related to the child's age at the onset of parental alcoholism, i.e., the younger the child the greater the damage. Perhaps parental alcoholism interferes with mother-infant bonding, leading to deep emotional scars which hinder subsequent development. Further, when parents deny the alcoholism and its behavioral consequences, younger children sometimes develop a faulty sense of reality. This creates increasing confusion, distrust, powerlessness and anxiety that could interfere with future emotional growth.[9]

All these developmental deficits add up to a large number of common problems experienced by children in alcoholic family systems.

COMMON PROBLEMS

The dynamics of the alcoholic system discussed in chapter 2 create stress for children in the family, stress from which they cannot escape. In effect, these children—especially young children—are captives in their homes because they lack the mobility and options available to older adolescents and adults within the family.

In fact, children in alcoholic families have been compared to concentration camp captives. It has been said, "Outside of residence in a concentration camp, there are few sustained human experiences that make one the recipient of as much sadism as does being a close family member of an alcoholic."[10] The word "sadism" may be appropriate only for children from the small portion of alcoholic families near the Dachau end of the Family Functioning Continuum discussed in chapter 2. However, if we change "sadism" to "stress" we may have the typical scenario for children growing up in alcoholic homes.

The stress experienced by children in alcoholic families often is shown by physical, emotional, behavioral, and academic problems. Expression of problems appears to vary in male and female children of alcoholics, with females tending toward depressive syndromes and males more inclined to show delinquent or criminal behavior.[11]

Physical Problems

When compared with children of nonalcoholic families, children of untreated alcoholics have been reported to have had more distinct and more frequent diagnoses of trauma and stress-related diseases.[12] Nylander studied 229 Swedish children of alcoholic fathers and found a significant number of psychosomatic symptoms. Compared with same-age children of nonalcoholic fathers, these four- to twelve-year-olds were often neglected and more likely to visit hospitals for headaches, stomachaches, and tiredness, which appeared unrelated to any diagnosable organic illness. Emotional distress and anxiety were exhibited as abdominal pains and sleep problems in girls, and as hyperactivity and attention deficits in boys.[13] Other research results have supported these data. For example, one study compared one hundred children (ages two to nineteen) who had one or two alcoholic parents with one hundred matched controls, and found that serious illnesses and accidents were more common in infancy and childhood in the alcoholic group.[14]

Emotional and Psychological Problems

In her seminal study of 115 children of alcoholics living with their parents, Margaret Cork described them as shamed by parental alcoholism, as feeling unwanted by one or both parents, as being unable to form meaningful friendships because of their disturbed homelife, and as lacking self-confidence.[15] Other clinical observations and research support the conclusion that children of alcoholics appear to be lacking self-confidence and have poorer self-concepts than children of nonalcoholics.[16]

Dr. Stephanie Brown, founder of the Stanford University Alcohol Clinic, has suggested that children need to maintain an image of their parents as good. As a result, children accept responsibility for the alcoholism that has been denied and begin to see themselves as bad. Furthermore, the children's view of others and the developing sense of their own personal identities are constructed on this faulty foundation, i.e., "I am profoundly bad." These children grow up seeing themselves and others in ways that repeatedly reconfirm this view of themselves as bad.[17]

Fear. Cork's study revealing that children of alcoholic parents often feel unwanted is verified by all the literature on this subject. God's Word says that "children are an heritage of the Lord; and the fruit of the womb is his reward,"[18] but in many alcoholic homes the standard *devised* version of this is translated, "children are a burden of this life and the fruit of the womb is a nuisance." This fosters in the child a sense that, "I am in the way," and contributes to one of the most common fears noted in these children: fear of abandonment. This strong emotion of fear, including the fear of abandonment, warrants closer examination, as do the emotions of anger and sadness.

In an alcoholic home, fear is the child's constant companion— sometimes minuscule and inaudible, sometimes monumental and deafening. Usually, children in alcoholic families do not realize that alcoholism is not their fault; they may feel guilty and responsible for their parent's drinking and the resulting family chaos. Children learn that all family life revolves around the alcoholic, and they are left feeling invisible, unloved, and abandoned. Children commonly become confused and fearful during the alcoholic parent's irresponsible, bizarre, and/or violent behavior, and they often become hypervigilant and "parentified," i.e., parent-like, as they seek to survive and insure the survival of the family. I have suggested previously that children in these homes live in a traumatic environment filled with the *chronic trauma* of insecurity and neglect punctuated occasionally by the *acute trauma* of violence and abuse. Fear is trauma's Siamese twin.

There are as many different fears as there are threatening situations in alcoholic homes. For children in these homes, even an experience like riding in the car may be an occasion for fear.

> I was terrified of driving with my parents. Both of them drove around drunk all the time. Once I refused to get into the car, telling my Dad he was drunk and I wasn't going anywhere with him. He hit me and shoved me in the car. My mother cried and told me never to criticize my father's drinking again. Look what I had done! I'd really upset him now. How could I spoil such a nice family outing?[19]

Fear of abandonment. This is an especially dreadful type of fear experienced by children raised in these traumatic homes. It has been widely reported that children in alcoholic families worry about arguments and fights between their parents.[20, 21, 22]

47

"Children from alcoholic homes, having experienced parental discord, often fear *abandonment*. 'If mom and dad break up, what will happen to me?' they ask."[23]

To fully appreciate this emotional problem common to children in alcoholic families, we must try to see the world from a child's perspective. If we do this, we recognize that fear of abandonment is rooted not in theory, but in the reality of a child's helplessness and utter dependence upon his or her parents (or surrogate parents) for survival. Children are not capable of caring for themselves and they know this intuitively. They may not be able to articulate the fear that their parents may leave and not return, but—as they experience the insecurity and instability of the alcoholic environment—that fear is there. Even when both parents remain in the home *physically*, children know when parents are not there for them *emotionally*. This *emotional abandonment* has far-reaching effects and contributes to the deep sense of worthlessness seen in both young and adult children from these families.[24]

"I felt like the invisible boy," recalls Marvin. "I'm not kidding, my folks had this amazing ability to totally tune me out. Dad was brain-dead from booze and my mother was either working, screaming or crying. It was like being an orphan, except my parents weren't dead." Marvin knows what it is to be emotionally abandoned or "forsaken" by his parents. As an adult, he struggles with feelings of abandonment whenever he experiences conflict in a relationship or a friend is late for an appointment. Fortunately, Marvin has a personal relationship with Jesus Christ and can testify to the comfort that comes when "the Lord will take me up."[25]

Anger. Anger is a natural response to being treated unfairly. As creatures bearing the *Imago Dei,* we innately sense that we—as well as all human beings—deserve to be treated with respect. Even children of alcoholic parents know on some deep level that they deserve better treatment than neglect and abuse. The anger experienced by these children is repressed and transformed into resentment because alcoholic families are not usually safe places to exhibit anger.

It is important to emphasize that anger is not automatically an emotional problem for children any more than it is automatically a sin. Ephesians 4:26 tells us to "Be angry, and yet do not sin; do not let the sun go down on your anger." This verse presupposes that there is a way to deal with anger quickly and appropriately that prevents it from becoming a sin. Children in alcoholic homes do not have appropriate models of responding to anger, and they usually do not have the opportunity to deal with it quickly and in healthy ways.

It has been suggested that anger is a reaction to blocked goals.[26] This conceptualization also serves to explain the ubiquitous anger in children of alcoholics. Children have a need to feel safe and secure in their environment, i.e., that is their goal. The acts and attitudes of alcoholic and co-alcoholic parents block this goal. This results in anger in the child which is shoved safely out of sight, erupting occasionally as resentment. In effect, the anger congeals into resentment which is cemented into bitterness. As adults, children of alcoholics find these "roots of bitterness"[27] reach back to their childhood although the fruit is borne in painful personal and relational problems in their present lives.

Sadness. I often ask adults raised in alcoholic families if their childhoods were filled with laughing, crying, sighing, yelling, or hitting. None of these adults has ever identified laughter as a characteristic of their early lives at home. Deep feelings of hurt, loneliness, and guilt, which are so frequently noted in children from alcoholic homes, are included under the topic of sadness. It would not be inappropriate to describe many of these children as depressed.

Childhood depression has been divided into three types, and alcoholic family systems are fertile soil in which any or all may flourish:

1. The *affectual* depression group. These children are characterized by expressions of sadness, helplessness, and hopelessness. They tend to be between six and eight years of age.

2. The *negative self-esteem* group. These are characterized by "thought-feelings" based on worthlessness, being unloved, and being used by people. They tend to be eight-year-olds or older.

3. The *guilt* group. These children feel "wicked," guilty, and wish that they were dead. They tend to be older than eleven.[28]

Even a cursory evaluation of these types suggests the dynamics of alcoholic families promote the feelings of sadness, helplessness and hopelessness, worthlessness, and guilt described. Existence in an alcoholic family is no laughing matter, and for many children in these families sadness and/or depression is worn like a heavy overcoat that weighs them down and constricts their movement through life.

While most children of alcoholics survive their emotional pain, coping by acting out their confusion, fear, sadness, and anger, some do not. Suicide attempts and completions are thought to be more numerous among children of alcoholics than children of nonalcoholics. In a recent study of self-destruction and suicidal tendencies in preadolescent children of alcoholics, the fathers of suicide attempters were found to be "significantly more alcoholic" than fathers of non-attempters. The mothers of children attempting to commit suicide also were significantly greater consumers of alcohol.[29] Another survey showed that two-thirds of adolescents who committed suicide had an alcoholic parent.[30] Caine suggested that one-fifth of teenage suicides are alcohol related, and he noted that alcohol is the adolescent's drug of choice for abuse.[31]

Behavioral and Academic Problems

Behavioral problems in children of alcoholics have been the focus of many investigators in the field. Bosma reported that more than 50 percent of children referred to an inner-city pediatric clinic for behavioral disorders had an alcoholic parent.[32] Most studies of behavioral problems experienced by children of alcoholics focus on adolescents. However, in one study of behavior disorders, eight- to twelve-year-old children of alcoholics were compared to groups of control children including a group of children of normal (non-psychiatric, nonalcoholic) parents. Children with parental alcoholism were significantly more disturbed than children of normal parents on twelve of seventeen behavioral variables, including ability to maintain attention, responsiveness to environmental stimulation, ability to restrain aggressive behavior, and social isolation.[33]

In a survey of adolescent children on probation, 82 out of 128 males were children of alcoholics.[34] Several studies of adolescent children of alcoholics suggested drug and alcohol abuse was common. Results from a national survey of more than thirteen thousand adolescents indicate a direct relationship between parental and adolescent drinking behavior: adolescents who reported greater parental use of alcohol and a parental tendency to sanction their children's use of alcohol were more likely to report heavy drinking. Most important, those students who drank to intoxication were more likely to have parents who drank to intoxication.[35] One child from an alcoholic family mirrors the study's findings in this comment:

> I knew that my father's drinking was affecting my life and making the whole family nervous and unhappy. But when I started drinking at about age 14, I never thought that my drinking had anything to do with my father's. I drank because I wanted to.
>
> I got drunk every time, just like him, but I never said to myself, "Hey, you're drinking just like him."[36]

As noted in the earlier discussion of the etiology of alcoholism, there appears to be a genetic predisposition to alcoholic drinking among many offspring of alcoholics. These data must be combined with the role of intrafamilial socialization to reach sound conclusions regarding these drinking patterns among adolescent children of alcoholics.

Academic problems of children of alcoholics again raise the issue of interaction of heredity and environment. One study noted a high rate of "mental deficiency" represented by low scores on intelligence tests administered to six- to eleven-year-old children of alcoholics.[37] Problems in academic performance among children of alcoholics considered normal learners may be due to mild, undiagnosed mental retardation; but they also may be explained by the chaotic—even dangerous—environment in which these children live. One child of an alcoholic summarizes parental alcoholism's impact on children's school performances this way:

> Lots of times I wanted to say, "Hey, if you knew what it was like for me! I get it at home, and then I get it worse in

school." I wanted to say, "How smart would you be if you had to lie awake in bed at night in case your mother got it into her head to beat up on you? How much homework would you get done? Could you concentrate in school if you were wondering what you were going to find when you got home?"[38]

The dismal portrait of young and adolescent children of alcoholics sketched above is incomplete, however, without this significant detail: Children of alcoholics do not necessarily demonstrate problems in their youth. Black and Booz-Allen and Hamilton reported some children of alcoholics are "overachievers," while Brown and Cermak[39] have identified what they called a "good kid" syndrome common to the children of alcoholics. This raises the issue of individual differences among offspring in alcoholic families; and these individual differences spotlight the function of roles played by children in these families.

INDIVIDUAL DIFFERENCES

"In a broken nest, there are few whole eggs," says an ancient Chinese proverb. Some alcoholic "nests" seem to be more broken than others, and some "eggs" from those nests appear to be less whole than others. It has been estimated that approximately 10 percent of children in alcoholic homes are what have been called "invulnerables." These are children who not only have survived, but who also have grown into healthy adults.[40] Several moderating factors have been identified which suggest explanations for the wide range of adaptation and adjustment success seen among children from alcoholic families.

Moderating Factors

Recent studies have examined these resilient "invulnerables" and have identified several factors which moderate the impact of parental alcoholism. A longitudinal study of "resilient offspring of alcoholics" reported that subjects who received predominantly positive responses from their caregiving environment, e.g., emotional support and educational stimulation, were found to be "stress-resistant" despite parental alcoholism.[41] Another study of children of alcoholics found that years of separation from the alcoholic parent had favorable effects on adjustment, as did a larger number of siblings.[42] In addition, the nonalcoholic parent's ability to fulfill the parental role successfully has been shown to significantly offset the alcoholic parent's impact on children in the home.[43]

In a controlled twenty-year longitudinal study comparing children from poor, multiproblem, urban families who had one or two alcoholic parents with children from poor, multiproblem families with nonalcoholic parents, Miller and Jang found children of alcoholic parents had greater socialization difficulties. Also, the greater the degree of parental alcoholism, the greater the negative impact on the children during both childhood and adulthood.

> If both parents were alcoholics, the adult subject fared the worst. The negative impact of an alcoholic mother was greater than that of an alcoholic father, and, of course, nonalcoholic parents had the lowest relationship with the subjects' adult failures.[44]

Recently, Dr. Carol Williams compared the child-care practices of three groups of parents from a neighborhood detoxification program. She found families with two alcoholic parents had the least positive attitude toward their children compared with families in which only one parent was alcoholic. In addition, the two-alcoholic-parent families displayed the highest percentage of abuse and neglect.[45] These findings may help to explain the differences in the negative impact of alcoholism cited by Miller and Jang.

It has been reported extensively that the child's age at the onset of parental alcoholism is also a differentiating factor in the consideration of damage to the child. The younger the child, it is believed, the more severe the impact of parental alcoholism. "He just never had a chance—not a chance. I was the lucky one because I was old enough to figure out how crazy everything was at home. I was in high school when my father's drinking and my mother's violence and verbal abuse got really out of control. I just stayed away from home, working or at football practice when I wasn't in school. But Jerry was five years younger and he got hit with all of it." That's Roger's explanation for the difference in his life as a responsible husband, father, and church leader and that of his brother, Jerry, who now is addicted to alcohol and cocaine, has lost his family, and is currently in prison for forgery.

Roger's and Jerry's lives support the data suggesting that although the risks of maladjustment are higher for children raised in alcoholic families, a range of adjustment exists within these children nevertheless.

In addition to moderating factors such as age of child at onset of parental alcoholism, number and gender of alcoholic parent(s), and availability of nurturing parental substitutes, several authorities have proposed that the role played by each child in the alcoholic family determines the individual child's unique adjustment profile.

Defensive Roles

The role-acquisition process in families is a dynamic interaction between the person acquiring the role and those who project role expectations. Children's roles in alcoholic families may be both a means of defending themselves against the onslaught of an apparently capricious and cruel environment, and a means of increasing the pathological equilibrium of the alcoholic family system. Claudia Black[46] and Sharon Wegscheider-Cruse[47] are the major theorists in the area of children's roles within alcoholic families. Black described three typical role profiles of children in alcoholic families: the "Responsible One," the "Adjuster," and the "Placater." Wegscheider-Cruse has suggested four personality groupings for children of alcoholics: the "Family Hero," the "Scapegoat," the "Lost Child," and the "Mascot."

Before examining children's roles in alcoholic families, a warning is in order. Neither I nor any other writer on issues of adult children of alcoholics intends to imply that children are rigidly cast into their roles. Sometimes children play more than one role simultaneously, or they move from one to another with changes in the family dynamics.

The Responsible One/Family Hero. Black's Responsible One is indistinguishable from Wegscheider-Cruse's Family Hero.

The child in this role, usually the first-born, provides structure and stability, and—through role reversal—takes responsibility for the welfare of the entire family, including parents. Responsible Ones are high achieving, pseudomature, parent-like children who learn to derive self-esteem from performing well at home and school. However, they often take on impossible tasks, thereby setting themselves up for failure. Miller and Ripper list over forty traits in the progression of the Responsible One/Family Hero's increasingly dysfunctional approach to self and others. Here are some of the traits they include.

1. Believes he or she is okay only when doing something for someone or being "good." Tries to please parents, teachers, and others for acceptance.

2. Takes the name of Mommy's or Daddy's "Little Helper."

3. Helps parents control other children; learns to give orders.

4. Needs perfection in life to gain "strokes;" average is not good enough. High achiever in school.

5. All activities focus on helping the family or the family image.

6. Feels comfortable around adults; behaves older than age.

7. Can only feel for others and doesn't recognize own needs.

8. Becomes very organized and scheduled; acquires ability to take control in crises.

9. Believes that asking for help shows weakness.

10. Feels overwhelmed and resents siblings for not helping out.[48]

Obviously, these children wear the "white hat" in the alcoholic family. However, that coveted chapeau grows heavier with each passing year, and many adult "heroes" find it an onerous burden.

The Scapegoat. The "white hat" is usually taken when the second child arrives in the alcoholic family, but the "black hat" is available for the child willing to play Scapegoat. The child in this role functions to take the focus off parental alcoholism by running away, failing, stealing, drinking, or using other drugs. Remember, every system has a function which all components of the system support. The primary function of the alcoholic family system is to perpetuate parental alcoholism while denying it and the problems it causes. As these families grow increasingly dysfunctional, the family can blame the Scapegoat, thereby relieving the alcoholic parent of responsibility to change. Some of the characteristics of the Scapegoat include:

1. Learns to receive attention by negative means; acts out (expresses anger and anxiety through antisocial behavior) in the home.

2. Takes focus off the alcoholic; gets some sympathy from co-alcoholic parent.

3. Blamed for all family problems; learns that negative behavior brings family together.

4. Receives emotional or physical abuse.

5. Puts up a front of not caring; begins to challenge authority.

6. Stuffs feelings. Acts tough; builds walls.

7. Becomes a troublemaker. Has poor grades; cuts classes at school.

8. Doesn't like routine. Gives up easily, and is addicted to excitement.

9. Avoids doing anything society says is good; becomes involved in promiscuity, delinquency, and/or hazardous lifestyle, e.g., addiction, abortion, accidents.

10. Is attracted to others who act out.[49]

Clearly, the family's "black hat" can be dangerous to its wearer, both emotionally and physically. But what is the Scapegoat's payoff? Family reunification: Children in this role learn very early that if they cause problems in the family, their parents will stop fighting and start working together to take care of the problems.[50]

The Adjuster/Lost Child. If a third child comes along, a child who makes no demands is needed. Claudia Black terms this child the Adjuster; Sharon Wegscheider-Cruse calls him or her the Lost Child. This is the child who contributes to the family by making no demands and by not being a problem. The child in this role becomes a loner, preferring the privacy of playing or fantasizing in his or her room to participating in the family's chaos. This child is often described as "so good I don't even know he's around." These are the lonely, forgotten children who "slip through the cracks" in alcoholic homes. Some of their traits include:

1. Doesn't know how to get attention.
2. Doesn't feel like he or she fits into the family.
3. High rate of allergies, asthma, accidents.
4. May hide under the bed, in the attic, etc. during stressful situations.
5. Has difficulty making friends in school. Feels like an outcast (peers ridicule him or her), and is willing to do anything for friendship.
6. Average student; not involved in any school activities.
7. Stays out of situations that would draw attention to self.
8. Socially immature, sexually naïve, and feels controlled by everyone.
9. Neglects own needs.
10. Cries alone. Feels a lot of hurt, fear of abandonment, very low self-esteem, but "stuffs" feelings.[51]

The Adjusters/Lost Children find by the time they get on stage that everything has already been done by their older siblings, so they just fade into the scenery.

The Placater/Mascot. Black describes the Placater as the child who smooths over conflicts in the tense, angry alcoholic home by trying to calm distraught parents or divert their attention away from momentary crises. She quotes a five-year-old child from an alcoholic home who, in the midst of a family crisis, said to his crying mother, "Don't worry, Mom, I won't remember all of this when I grow up."[52] Wegscheider-Cruse proposes a role similar to that of the Placater, which she calls the Mascot. This child is the family clown and pet who uses silliness and humor to smooth over family conflicts. Mascots are the center of attention and are dependent on others' approval for their own self-worth. Other characteristics of this role are:

1. Usually youngest child; is overprotected by the family.
2. Learns to get attention by being cute; tries to be everyone's friend.
3. Changes personality like a chameleon, depending on who is present.
4. Protected from family secrets.

5. Gets average grades; acts as "class clown."

6. Is never really listened to or taken seriously.

7. Has many acquaintances but few real friends; can get along with almost anyone.

8. Is sensitive but never shows emotions; smiles while crying inside.

9. Acts younger than his or her age.

10. Hyperactive: is always doing something. High incidence of Ritalin (drug prescribed to manage attention deficit disorder) abuse.[53]

Placater/Mascots and Scapegoats serve similar purposes in the alcoholic family: They divert the family's attention from the alcoholic.

Alcoholic families raise their children to accommodate the unhealthy behaviors of the alcoholic and all who enable the persistence of alcoholic drinking. These children learn to survive in the alcoholic family system by acquiring various behavioral roles at great cost to their personal freedom and emotional well-being.

HOLD IT IN

A review of the roles described by Black and Wegscheider-Cruse highlights the fact that most of the roles appear positive— or at least not negative. In a recent study, four out of five adult children of alcoholics described themselves as being overly responsible, caretaking children, or as adjusting, detached children.[54] Many children from alcoholic homes display a pseudomaturity that enables them to appear very stable and well-functioning on the surface. They have learned to swallow their fear, anger, and sadness. They hold it in just like "the best little boy in the world" described here by Peter Nardi.

Michael was doing very well in school. In fact, he was the brightest kid in class, the teacher's favorite, one of the best-behaved. He never created any disciplinary problems and always hung out with the good crowd. The best little boy in the world. "Why can't we all be like Michael and sit quietly?" Sister Gertrude would say in her most melodious voice. Conform, be docile, do well, be quiet. Hold it in. Don't tell a soul.

And now he was waiting at the school corner for his mother to pick him up. This was always the hardest moment. What will she look like, how will she sound? Michael could tell right away if she had been drinking. The muffled voice, the pale, unmade-up face. He really didn't know what it was all about. He just knew that when Dad came home he would fight with her. Argue, yell, scream, run. Michael could hear them through the closed doors and over the humming of the air conditioner. He wondered if the neighbors could hear, too. Hold it in. Don't tell anyone.

He was still waiting at the corner. She was 15 minutes late. It was so good to go to school and get out of the house. But when 3 o'clock came he would feel the tension begin to gather inside him. He never knew what to expect. When she was not drinking, she would be smiling, even pretty. When drunk, she'd be cold, withdrawn, tired, unloving, not caring. Michael would cook dinner and straighten up the house. He would search for the alcohol, like egg-hunting on Easter morning, under the stuffed chair in the bedroom, in the laundry bag, concealed among the towels, behind her hats in the closet. When he found it, he'd pour it down the sink drain. Maybe then no one would know that she'd been drinking. Maybe no one would fight. Don't tell a soul.

She still hadn't come to pick him up yet. She'd never been 30 minutes late. Sometimes she'd sleep late in the morning after Dad had already left for work, and Michael would make breakfast for his little sister and himself. Then a friend's mother would take them to school. The biggest problem was during vacation time, especially around the holidays. He wanted to play with his friends. But he was afraid to bring them home. He was afraid to go out and play, too, because then she would drink. Michael didn't want to be blamed for that. So he stayed in and did his homework and read. He didn't tell his friends. Hold it in.

And still he was waiting alone on the corner. Forty-five minutes late. Michael decided to walk the 10 blocks home.

He felt that he was old enough now. After all, he took care of his little sister a lot. He took care of his mother a lot. He was responsible. He always did what people told him to do. Everyone could count on him for help. Everyone did. And he never complained. Never fought, never argued, never yelled. The best little boy in the world. Hold it in.

When he got nearer to home, Michael's heart felt as if it were going to explode. Her car was there, the house was locked tight. He rang the bell. He rang and rang as he felt his stomach turn inside out. He climbed through a window. No one seemed to be home. He looked around the house, in all the right hiding places. Finally, in the closet in his own bedroom, he saw his mom in her slip, with a belt around her neck, and attached to the wooden rod. She was just sitting there, sobbing. She had been drinking. But maybe no one would find out. Michael wouldn't tell anyone, ever. Hold it in.[55]

Authorities on alcoholic families have suggested that despite an appearance of survival, all children are affected profoundly by growing up in an alcoholic home. These children may "hold it in," but that does not prevent the effects of parental alcoholism from impinging upon their lives. These effects contribute to the development of identifiable personal and interpersonal characteristics in adult children of alcoholics. These characteristics are the topics of Part II.

PART TWO

UNDERSTANDING ADULT CHILDREN OF ALCOHOLICS

PART I PRESENTED one-half of the knowledge base necessary to counsel effectively with adult children of alcoholics as we looked back to examine alcoholic families and their effects on the children living in them.

Part II provides additional understanding needed to work with adults from alcoholic families as we look around at these adults and examine their personal, relational, and spiritual struggles.

CHAPTER FOUR

CHARACTERISTICS OF ADULT CHILDREN OF ALCOHOLICS

"WHAT IS PAST IS PROLOGUE," Shakespeare wrote in *The Tempest.* Shakespeare's insightful observation has received support from an unlikely source: late twentieth-century cognitive psychology. Psychologists who study problem solving in this field have noted a phenomenon called *rigidity,* which describes the ever-present tendency of individuals to go beyond the information given them. "[For] present stimulation is interpreted in light of past experience, even though we are often not aware of it."[1] What does that textbook jargon mean? It means all our todays are shaped by our yesterdays. It means "what is past is prologue."

What is past may also be prison—a prison of recurring painful patterns of thinking, feeling, and relating. This is the prevailing

63

conclusion of professionals who have observed that adults raised in alcoholic families are particularly susceptible to emotional, physical, relational, and spiritual problems. "The National Association for Children of Alcoholics considers adult children of alcoholics as having an adjustment reaction to familial alcoholism which is recognizable, diagnosable, and treatable."[2]

What does this mean to Christian helpers and/or to Christians who come from families where alcohol reigned? It means there is a sense in which all Christians are alike; yet we are all vastly different.

Every person is identically and entirely bankrupt spiritually ("There is none righteous, not even one," Romans 3:10). There is no way any of us can pay our sin debt. If we are Christians, truly Christ-ones, it is because we have declared our spiritual bankruptcy and accepted Jesus Christ's payment for our sin. But this divine transaction is still not concluded, for our inconceivably gracious Heavenly Father deposits in our spiritual account "every spiritual blessing in the heavenly places in Christ" (Ephesians 1:3). So we see we are created equal spiritually in that we are all equally bankrupt, but—through faith in Jesus as Savior—we are all equally rich. Yet while the ground is level at the foot of the cross, it is pretty uneven elsewhere!

Personally, each of us is uniquely and completely different. Much of that difference is attributable to genetic endowment. But, much of the difference is due to that which our earthly parents deposited in our personal accounts. Healthy, wise (but imperfect) parents consistently (some with greater frequency than others) deposit substantial sums of love, affirmation, encouragement, discipline, comfort, and biblical values in their children's personal accounts. When these children mature, they draw upon these deposits to face the challenges of adult life, and they invest these deposits in the lives of others, especially their children. People who enter adulthood near personal bankruptcy have no emotional "nest egg" with which to handle their inevitable "rainy days" and they have little or nothing to invest in the lives of others.

In a healthy family, children's needs for security, warmth, nurturance and guidance are met most of the time. These children enter adulthood with a sense of security and trust that is inside of themselves. In dysfunctional families, these needs are not met enough or at all, and these children enter adulthood with a sense of incompleteness, mistrust and fear inside of themselves, along with a strong need for some kind of security outside themselves.[3]

That is Linda and John Friel's view of adult children of alcoholic and other impaired parents. Many others agree that the personal deficits of these adults are seen in recognizable personality characteristics and self-defeating relational patterns.

The characteristics of alcoholics began to be addressed in the field of counseling in the 1950s. Later, literature in the field cited studies on the alcoholic's family, including the children living in the home. Only recently, beginning in the late 1970s, have the personality characteristics and relational issues of the adult children of alcoholics begun to appear in the literature.

The overview in figure 4–1 displays many of the unhealthy characteristics most frequently noted among adults raised in alcoholic homes. This list is representative, not exhaustive. It is important to note that the literature in this area highlights the problematic and unhealthy characteristics of adults from alcoholic families; but all of these adults have many positive, healthy

Characteristics of Adult Children of Alcoholics: Overview[4]

Personal			Interpersonal
MENTAL	*EMOTIONAL*	*PHYSICAL*	*RELATIONAL*
Confusion	Fear	Migraine headaches	Distrust
Memory gaps	Guilt	Ulcers, colitis, other	Intimacy problems
All-or-nothing	Shame	digestive problems	Crisis orientation
thinking	Depression	Muscle tension	Hard to have fun
Perfectionism	Sadness	Sleep disorders	Over-dependent
Indecision	Anger/Rage	Stress disorders	High tolerance for
Hypervigilance	Resentment	Eating disorders	inappropriateness
Compulsive	Loneliness	Allergies	Manipulative
thinking	Anxiety/Panic	Chemical	Controlling
Self-devaluing	Numbness	dependency	Over-responsible
Self-hatred		Sexual dysfunction	Approval addiction

Figure 4–1

traits as well. In addition to examining these unhealthy characteristics, we also will address the issue of individual differences among adult children of alcoholics. Finally, we will consider several current attempts to explain these characteristics.

GENERALITIES

Dr. Janet Woititz and others have written extensively on the common characteristics of adult children of alcoholics. These characteristics have been identified from clinical practice, from personal experience, and more recently, from research. Woititz concluded that, "There are certain generalizations that recur in one form or another,"[5] and she suggested that adult children of alcoholics, and those helpers working with them, need to examine and discuss these generalizations.

Woititz has noted the following characteristics in adult children of alcoholics:

1. They guess at what normal behavior is.
2. They have difficulty following a project through from beginning to end.
3. They lie when it would be just as easy to tell the truth.
4. They judge themselves without mercy.
5. They have difficulty having fun.
6. They take themselves very seriously.
7. They have difficulty with intimate relationships.
8. They overreact to changes over which they have no control.
9. They constantly seek approval and affirmation.
10. They usually feel that they are different from other people.
11. They are super responsible or super irresponsible.
12. They are extremely loyal even in the face of evidence that the loyalty is undeserved.
13. They are impulsive and tend to lock themselves into a course of action without giving serious consideration to alternative behaviors or possible consequences. This impulsivity leads to confusion, self-loathing, and loss of control over their environment. In addition, they spend an excessive amount of energy "cleaning up the mess."

Perrin added seven characteristics to the Woititz list.

1. They look for immediate, as opposed to deferred gratification.

2. They seek tension and crisis and then complain about the results.

3. They avoid conflict or aggravate it, but rarely deal with it.

4. They fear rejection and abandonment, yet are rejecting of others.

5. They fear failure, but sabotage their success.

6. They fear criticism and judgment, yet criticize and judge others.

7. They manage their time poorly and do not set their priorities in ways that work out well for them.[6]

Woititz and Perrin generated their list of characteristics from clinical observations of adult children of alcoholics. Only recently have these characteristics been investigated more formally. One study investigated perceptions of past and present emotional and interpersonal situations in more than four hundred adult children of alcoholics. The adult children of alcoholics in this study most frequently identified difficulty in expressing their needs to others, followed by difficulty expressing their feelings, putting themselves first, and trusting people. They also expressed difficulty in identifying feelings and had problems with intimacy and dependency. Nearly half described themselves as being confused and depressed most of the time.[7]

Writing from her extensive clinical experience with children of alcoholics, Black has observed that, upon reaching adulthood, these children "continue to experience problems related to trust, dependency, control, identification and expression of feelings."[8]

To examine some of these characteristics in more detail, it might be helpful to divide them broadly into personal characteristics and interpersonal or relational characteristics.

PERSONAL CHARACTERISTICS

Following the divisions suggested by column headings in figure 4–1, we will look briefly at some of the mental, emotional, and physical characteristics of adults raised in alcoholic homes.

Mental Characteristics

Scripture says that our very personalities and lives are determined by what we think. "For as he thinks within himself, so he is" (Proverbs 23:7). Distorted thinking patterns are reflected in a host of cognitive (mental) characteristics. However, it could be argued that dichotomous (all-or-nothing) thinking and a sense of mental confusion are the core cognitive disorders.

Confusion. Memory gaps, lack of information and distrust of one's own perceptions are the major elements contributing to the mental confusion observed in many adult children of alcoholics.

Many adults from alcoholic homes report substantial memory gaps as they recall their childhoods. This phenomenon, commonly seen in abuse survivors, leaves these adults feeling confused. I have had adult children of alcoholics, especially those raised near the Dachau end of the Family Functioning Continuum, tell me, for example, "ages five to eleven are a total blank."

In chapter 3 we saw that children in alcoholic homes often do not have some of their needs met on a consistent basis. This may include the need for basic information about the child's physical, emotional, social, intellectual, and spiritual self. These information gaps also contribute to mental confusion.

In addition, children in alcoholic families are often caused to doubt their perceptions of reality. They grow up in a silent system that denies those children's need to talk about and gain mental mastery of their confusing environment. Without being able to check their perceptions of reality with competent adults, these children are often forced to guess at what is normal and appropriate. This leaves them feeling confused. I have heard it expressed as a sense that "something is missing in me." This often leads adult children of alcoholics to a lifelong quest for the missing "something" that will bring order out of their mental confusion.

Perhaps it is this cognitive characteristic that makes these adults such voracious consumers of self-help books. The story goes that if you are an adult child of an alcoholic wanting to meet other adults from alcoholic homes, you should go to a bookstore and wait by the self-help section. This anecdote reflects the idea commonly held by adults raised in alcoholic homes that there is one right way to do everything, and you either know it or you don't. And, to make matters worse, they believe everybody else knows the right way!

All-or-nothing Thinking. Adult children of alcoholics tend to think in absolutes. Everything is always completely black or white, good or bad, right or wrong. And since we are never completely right, we are usually completely wrong. This mental characteristic is seen in adult children's abhorrence of process. Dan frequently asks when he will "get over this and be normal." His concept is like that of many other adult children of alcoholics: they are either "sick" or they are "well." Since they do not feel "well," and since they think in dichotomous absolutes, they fail to appreciate the small increments of positive change in their personal growth processes.

This thinking pattern may be behind the control orientation identified in most adult children of alcoholics. If you grew up in a chaotic family, you long to experience more order and control in your life. And if everything is either all under control or all out of control, you are going to work very hard to control *everything and everyone* in your life.

All-or-nothing thinking also leads to perfectionism, indecision, and self-hatred. The core of perfectionism is the belief that anything less than perfect is total failure. Perfectionism also fosters an illusion that you can control your world: "If only I can *be* perfect, find the perfect spouse, have perfect children, join the perfect church, and get the perfect job, my life will be under control and I will be happy." Alas, this thinking dooms its adherents to lives of guaranteed misery.

Adult children of alcoholics may experience the paralysis of perfectionism which leads to difficulty making decisions. They tend to be indecisive because they can never have perfect command of every fact needed to make perfect decisions. And these adults increasingly devalue and despise themselves as they are forced to confront the limitations of their humanity, namely imperfection. As children, they failed to perfectly control their alcoholic parent's drinking, and as adults they fail to attain their unrealistic and unreachable goal of personal perfection. In extreme cases, this self-hatred leads to suicide attempts and completions. In all cases, it contributes to depression and other disturbing emotions.

Emotional Characteristics

Many authorities working in this field have identified several core emotions experienced by nearly all adult children of alcoholics. Based on my clinical experience, adult children of alcoholics appear to be more similar emotionally than any other way. Core emotions include fear, guilt and shame, depression, anger, and numbness.

Fear. Writing from a totally secular perspective, Wayne Kritsberg has stated, "Fear is the root issue and core emotion of all ACOAs [adult children of alcoholics]."[9] Kritsberg's statement could be expanded to say *sin is the root issue and fear is the core emotion of all human beings since the Fall.* Genesis 3:10 records the first human emotion identified by Adam after sin entered Eden. He said, "I was afraid." And human beings have been afraid ever since.

Adult children of alcoholics fear many things, including rejection, humiliation, weakness, vulnerability, failure, loss, and fear itself. However, it could be argued that their transcending fear is that of all human beings—*fear of abandonment.* Kritsberg also identifies fear of abandonment as the primary core emotion experienced by adults from alcoholic families, but he bases this claim solely on the impact of dysfunctional parent-child relationships in alcoholic families which we examined in chapters 2 and 3. This psychological explanation is sound, but there may be other factors involved.

Human beings may be physically and spiritually predisposed to fear of abandonment. Infants will die if physically abandoned by their caregivers. To avoid physical abandonment and preserve some measure of care, children are forced to adapt to whatever environmental demands they encounter. As we saw in chapters 2 and 3, children in alcoholic families live with chronic trauma and insecurity which heighten a child's intuitive fear of abandonment. In contrast, healthy parents repeatedly assure their children that they are loved, that Mommy and

Daddy will not leave them, and that they will always be part of the family.

When sin entered this planet, human beings legitimately experienced fear of abandonment, because sin separated them from God and they were truly lost—cut off, totally adrift from the only Source of spiritual life. And, just as infants are utterly dependent upon their caregivers to sustain physical life, we are utterly dependent upon God, our heavenly caregiver, to provide spiritual life. From my perspective, only persons—whether or not they were raised in alcoholic homes—who have received spiritual life from God through personally trusting Jesus Christ as Savior, can overcome fear of abandonment at its deepest level.

Guilt and Shame. Guilt wears two faces—true and false. True moral guilt is an appropriate and ennobling emotion that stirs us to change when we stray from a moral standard. For Christians, Scripture articulates the standard. False guilt condemns us when we have broken not the rules of God or government, but the arbitrary rules of parents and other significant people. False guilt tells us we have done something wrong when we really have not.

My research findings and those of others have shown that subjects raised in alcoholic homes were more guilt-prone and self-blaming than those from nonalcoholic families. Jean remembers always feeling guilty that she could not stop her alcoholic father's drinking and make her depressed mother happy. As an adult, Jean has come to realize that she did not do anything to cause either her father's alcoholism or her mother's depression.

Whereas guilt is a feeling that "I have done something bad," shame is a feeling that "I *am* something bad." Guilt is a matter of behavior. Shame is a matter of identity. Some have suggested that "shame may be the most powerful emotion for adult children of alcoholics."[10] Shame is the soul-deep feeling of being fatally flawed, less than—and apart from—other human beings. Carol Ann expressed this feeling of shame when she said, "I have to try twice as hard to be half as good as other people."

This feeling of shame must not be confused with the biblical concept of shame due to sin. This distorted form of shame includes feelings of being different from and worse than others, whereas Scripture reveals that all stand equally condemned for their sin before a holy God.

I have had Christian adult children of alcoholic parents express this feeling of shame as sensing they are "cursed." One of them, Jason, described feeling he was cursed and doomed to a life of loneliness and loss. After becoming a Christian, Jason investigated his genealogy to determine if there was occult involvement that would explain his sense of being under a family curse. Jason uncovered no family involvement that would produce a curse but he has learned how his family background contributed to his *sense* of being cursed.

Children derive their personal identities from their parents and families. The chronic, painful embarrassment and humiliation experienced by children in alcoholic families become internalized as shame. Children are repeatedly embarrassed by the behavior of their alcoholic parents, as was one young man who described his humiliation when the neighbors saw his father "neglect to open the garage door before inserting the car."[11] In addition, children in alcoholic homes are often subjected to humiliating, dehumanizing abuse which contributes to the feeling of shame.

Some adult children of alcoholics describe a feeling of perpetual stage fright in which they experience their intrinsic worthlessness as eternally displayed for all to view and condemn. In addition, shame is expressed by the feeling of being different from other people. This sense of "being different" has been noted in adults raised by alcoholic parents.

Depression. I am including with depression the feelings of sadness and grief commonly identified in adult children of alcoholics. Jael Greenleaf suggests these adults develop an "addictive relationship to depression, retreating into it rather than trying to resolve problems."[12]

Dr. Susan Deakins, attending psychiatrist at Washington Heights Community Service Center in New York, has identified a "lingering sadness that underlies depression" in adult children of alcoholics. This sadness is accompanied by sudden, unexpected outbursts of tears in reaction to kindness.

It happens when people act in a caring manner toward children of alcoholics, a manner never shown by their parents. This brings the realization that one's parents should have offered more emotionally than they did and leads to mourning a relationship that never was.[13]

This need to grieve the losses of childhood is a major issue with adult children of alcoholics who often go for counseling with depression as the presenting problem.

Again, in my own research, depression was present significantly more often in subjects from alcoholic as compared with nonalcoholic families.

Anger. Curiously, for some adult children of alcoholics anger is the only emotion they ever feel; for others it is the one they never allow themselves to feel. Some of these adults—usually men—use anger as a shield to defend against more painful emotions such as depression and fear. Typically, Christian women appear to be extremely uncomfortable with anger and experience it as threatening. This is especially true when "anger" is too pallid a label for the deep, internal rage described by many women raised in alcoholic homes. For both men and women, anger—whether aggressive and overt or passive and covert—spills over onto those closest to them.

Numbness. Mental health professionals have reported widely that adult children of alcoholics exhibit "flat affect." Affect is a psychological term for emotion. I have counseled with many adults from alcoholic families who keep smiling blandly even while they describe scenes of incredible terror or deep pathos. They have developed a kind of emotional leprosy. Leprosy destroys the body's ability to register pain, and growing up in alcoholic families often damages the mind's ability to experience emotions. This is especially true for all those who fall outside the narrow range of emotions both experienced and accepted in alcoholic family systems (see figures 2–4 and 2–5 in chapter 2). Like physical leprosy, emotional leprosy may also have a physical component.

In a recent study of people who repress their emotions, some evidence was found for a physiological basis to emotional numbness.[14] This finding comes as no news to millions of adult children of alcoholics who regard feelings as unnecessary luxuries and embarrassing evidence of personal weakness. However, numbing and repressing feelings profoundly affects us physically, for—as John Powell has observed—"when I repress my emotions, my stomach keeps score. . . ."[15]

Physical Characteristics

In addition to the emotional and mental characteristics listed above, adult children of alcoholics typically exhibit a wide range of stress-related disorders. These include tension and migraine headaches, gastro-intestinal problems, TMJ (Temporomandibular Joint Disorder), and chronic back pain. Many adults raised in alcoholic homes also have respiratory problems, allergies, and other illnesses linked to the immune system.

The work of Hans Selye and others has demonstrated that current life-events perceived as stressful depress the human immune system. More recent research suggests that "short stressful events in early childhood may have long-lasting health consequences."[16] It is reasonable to assume that most adults from alcoholic families experienced—at the least—"short stressful events" in their early childhoods.

In addition to physical problems related to stress and immune system suppression, adult children of alcoholics struggle with various addictions. In one large eating-disorders clinic, approximately 62 percent of the patients were adult children of alcoholics.[17] And, as noted previously, children of alcoholics are at high risk for developing alcohol addiction. Apparently, even if adult children of alcoholics escape becoming alcoholic, they live in bondage to alcoholism through fear. Stephanie Brown had observed nearly all of the participants in her therapy groups for adult children of alcoholics are concerned about becoming alcoholic, if they are not already recovering alcoholics. Some manage their fear by total abstinence, but most vigilantly monitor their drinking behavior, anticipating their own alcoholism as "inevitable."[18]

The unhealthy characteristics of adult children of alcoholics described above are manifested more clearly in certain situations like unexpected events, visits with family, and life transitions such as middle age. However, these characteristics are most clearly seen in relationships. And relationships have their own set of problematic characteristics.

RELATIONAL CHARACTERISTICS

Among the many characteristics listed in figure 4–1 are three core relational issues: distrust, crisis orientation, and codependency. The latter incorporates many of the characteristics listed.

Distrust

My research results supported the widely reported clinical observation that adults from alcoholic families have difficulty trusting appropriately. My subjects (all evangelical Christians) raised in alcoholic homes were significantly more distrustful than those raised in nonalcoholic families.[19]

It is reasonable to imagine that children of alcoholics, who often perceive their parents as unavailable, unpredictable, and unloving, would find it difficult as adults to trust that others will relate to them in a more consistent and caring manner. In fact, these adults may assume there is something intrinsically unlovable about themselves, since their parents, who are expected to love their offspring as a matter of course, were so often apparently unconcerned about them. This impaired capacity to trust has a profound impact on all interpersonal relationships, especially on intimate relationships like marriage. In my research I found the divorce rate among subjects raised in alcoholic homes (32.8 percent) was higher than among those from nonalcoholic families (9.7 percent).

Crisis Orientation

Many adults raised in the chronically chaotic and traumatic environment of an alcoholic home become "adrenalin addicts." These individuals are familiar with frequent emergencies and crises and they often find themselves feeling bored, anxious, and/or depressed when their lives are relatively stable. In reality, they feel most alive in a state of "excited misery,"[20] and they believe that more misery is always just around the corner. This is the *waiting-for-the-other-shoe-to-drop* syndrome that has been observed in many adult children of alcoholic parents.

"I know it sounds silly, but I can't enjoy what God has done in my life because I keep feeling I don't deserve it and it won't last." Carol Ann, the Christian adult child of an alcoholic father, wept as she expressed frustration with her inability to rejoice over her Heavenly Father's work of grace in her life. Carol Ann left home at fifteen to marry an alcoholic whom she later divorced. Her second husband beat her and abused her sons. After she came to know Christ in a personal way, she met and married a Christian man who expressed the respect and love she had always longed to experience. "I find myself actually starting arguments with Hal for no good reason. I guess I figure he's going to leave me anyway, so I might as well give him a reason and get it over with."

Carol Ann's habit of creating a crisis in her marriage is a manifestation of the *Rambo-on-the-Loveboat* syndrome. Children in alcoholic homes become familiar with, even expert in, defending themselves against their dangerous—even deadly—family environment just as Rambo (I am told) is familiar with, and expert in, defending himself against his dangerous and deadly jungle environment. As adults, they often feel as strange and out of place in stable relationships as Rambo would if he suddenly parachuted onto the Loveboat. He would probably need to kick over a few deck chairs and toss some people in the pool to stir things up just as Carol Ann needs to start arguments with Hal. Carol Ann knows the rules for surviving in the jungle of her alcohol-focused childhood, but a loving marriage is a different game with a different set of rules. They are unfamiliar; therefore she is uncomfortable.

A crisis orientation, with its waiting-for-the-other-shoe-to-drop and Rambo-on-the-Loveboat syndromes, obviously has a profound impact on relationships.

There is another characteristic that accompanies a crisis orientation—difficulty having fun. Adult children of alcoholics usually take life, and themselves, very seriously. They tend to find it difficult to relax and have fun. Reflecting on the dynamics of alcoholic family systems, we can understand the basis for this relational characteristic. Life in an alcoholic home is very serious business as we saw in chapter 2. Furthermore, children in these homes often have their childhoods stolen by their needy and incompetent parents. These children seldom have the opportunity to play, be silly and carefree—in short—to be children.

Yet the needs of the child live on in adults from alcoholic homes. Many child-needs accompany these individuals into their adult lives, including the need to play as well as the need to be dependent. Unfortunately, the child-need for *healthy* dependence usually is twisted into the relational characteristic of *unhealthy* dependence, more commonly termed codependence.

Codependence

One of the characteristics of a well-adjusted individual is the capacity for *interdependence.*

> Interdependence means being one's own person, being able to maintain a clear and separate identity from others, while still recognizing the need for help and support from others. It also means being able to get that support in healthy rather than destructive ways.[21]

Adults from alcoholic homes appear to have an impaired capacity for healthy, interdependent relationships. Instead, their interactions are often marked by codependency. This is a broad topic on which entire books have been written and definitions abound.

Definition. Codependency was applied originally to people "whose lives had become unmanageable as a result of living in a committed relationship with an alcoholic."[22]

> As professionals began to understand codependency better, more groups of people appeared to have it: adult children of alcoholics . . . people in relationships with irresponsible people; professionals—nurses, social workers, and others in "helping" occupations. . . .[23]

Melody Beattie, author of *Codependent No More,* defines a codependent person as "one who has let another person's behavior affect him or her, and who is obsessed with controlling that person's behavior."[24] My definition is a modification of Beattie's:

A codependent is a person who is being disrespected and controlled by a person he or she is disrespecting and attempting to control.

Etiology. What are the causes of this over-dependency? "Unhealthy dependencies grow out of our normal dependent state as infants."[25] As we have noted, infants are totally dependent upon their caregivers for survival, hence our dependency needs are rooted in the most basic issue of absolute survival. By the time they reach adolescence, even children in extremely chaotic alcoholic families can survive on their own quite well when it comes to basic safety needs. However, it is the more subtle but powerful *emotional* needs that most often go unmet in these families, which means children from these homes enter adulthood with a "reservoir of unmet needs."[26] These unmet needs for healthy affirmation and love, coupled with neglect and abuse, form a cord of codependency. And there is a third strand in that cord—parental modeling. Codependent adults learned about relationships from codependent models. This three-strand cord of codependency constricts the lives of codependent adults and binds them to unhealthy relational patterns.

Characteristics. If the codependents of the world organized, their theme song would be *It All Depends On You* and their motto would be, "Your wish is my command." A codependent individual wants to be "fairy godmother" to the world, to fix everything and everybody. Codependents are enablers, rescuers, and caretakers. Note that last description: caretaker. Codependents take over the care of and the responsibility for people who could take care of and be responsible for themselves. Parents are caregivers. They provide care for children who cannot take care of themselves. This is not codependency; it is appropriate parental behavior. *Unless a person is a child or is incapacitated by brain damage or physical impairment, that person can be responsible for himself or herself.*

Clearly the unhealthy characteristic of over-responsibility is a required course in the codependency curriculum offered in alcoholic family systems. Children in these families are taught that their behavior controls and determines whether or not their alcoholic parent drinks. Very early they learn to take responsibility for—to rescue—another human being.

People function as rescuers anytime they take responsibility for another functioning human being, even if that functioning is impaired by alcohol and/or painful personal problems. An examination of rescuing will identify the distinguishing marks of codependent relationships. The following list of rescuing moves is adapted from *Codependent No More.* [27]

1. Saying yes when we mean no.

2. Doing something for someone although that person is capable of, and should be, doing it for himself or herself.

3. Meeting people's needs without being asked and before we've agreed to do so.

4. Consistently doing more than a fair share of work after our help is requested.

5. Consistently giving more than we receive in a particular relationship.

6. Trying to "fix" people's feelings.

7. Doing people's thinking for them.

8. Solving people's problems for them.

9. Protecting people from the consequences of their own choices, and/or suffering people's consequences for them.

10. Not asking for what we want, need, and desire.

Rescuing appears to be the epitome of Christian compassion when in fact it is a profoundly disrespectful act. To rescue, we must see the other person as less capable of living responsibly than we are. We rescue victims. We rescue helpless people we believe are incapable of saving themselves, like Jessica McClure, the little Texas girl who fell down a well. In chapter 11 we will discuss respectful relationships based on attributing to ourselves and others the respect of personal responsibility.

If you re-read the unhealthy relational characteristics listed in figure 4–1, you will see how those characteristics not yet discussed fit into the codependency picture. For example, over-responsible, codependent people are totally invested in controlling others. How else are they going to "fix" them? However, codependent adults control primarily through indirect means like manipulation. The need to control must be balanced with the codependent's approval addiction. Therefore, to avoid the risk of anger and disapproval, subtle forms of control are employed. Adult approval addiction is the legacy of unmet emotional needs in childhood and requires the co-dependent person to develop a high tolerance for inappropriate behavior. But that comes naturally to adults from alcoholic homes who cut their relational teeth on inappropriate behavior and often do not even know what normal, healthy relationships are.

Some alcoholism professionals suggest that everybody in our culture is codependent to one degree or another.[28] It is the interesting question of degrees of codependency and other unhealthy characteristics observed in adult children of alcoholics that raises the issue of individual differences.

INDIVIDUAL DIFFERENCES

Before addressing the topic of individual differences, a comment is needed about the similarities between unhealthy characteristics noted in many adult children of alcoholics and other clinical populations.

Mental health professionals recognize that many of the characteristics and problems just described have been identified as part of various emotional disorders, including borderline and narcissistic personality disorders. Impaired parent-child relationships are considered major contributors to the development of emotional disorders, as well as to the development of the adult-child-of-an-alcoholic syndrome, described above. There is general agreement on the importance of the quality and patterns of relationships between children and parents, particularly in the child's early years.

While common patterns of parent-child relationships in the alcoholic family have been noted, a variety of patterns can also exist. It cannot be assumed that parent-child interactions in alcoholic families will be identical; differences in these relationships contribute to differences among adult children of alcoholics.

Personal Impact Continuum

It is amazing that so many adult children of alcoholics have brothers and sisters who are not adult children of alcoholics! In my growth group for Christians raised in alcoholic families we often laugh—and cry—about this. While much of the explanation for this phenomenon is a matter of who has or has not come out of denial, some of it is attributable to the unique perceptions of each child in an alcoholic family.

In a recent study of more than one thousand adult children of alcoholics, 78.2 percent said they had been "highly affected" by growing up in an alcoholic home; 11.1 percent said they had been "moderately affected," and 10.7 percent said they were "not affected."[29] It appears there is a personal-impact continuum along which adult children of alcoholics place themselves based on their perceptions, and perhaps based also on the quality of their relationships with their parents or parent surrogates. Location on the personal-impact continuum may represent an interaction of those two factors and may reflect adult children's perceptions of the quality of their relationships with parents or parent surrogates. In addition to personal perceptions of the parent-child relationship, differences in adult children of alcoholics are thought to be the result of living out the family roles adopted in childhood.

Living Out Childhood Roles

Obviously, all of the characteristics and problems mentioned here are not found in all adult children of alcoholics. Many alcoholism professionals have suggested that the particular characteristics which express the personality of each adult child of an alcoholic are determined by the role that person played in the family as a child. In chapter 3, we considered the various roles which have been identified for children in the alcoholic family. These same roles have implications for those children when they function as adults.[30]

Responsible One/Hero. If children played the role of the Responsible One/Hero in childhood, they tend to be overly responsible and controlling as adults. These adults find it difficult to cooperate, relax, and let others take charge. They tend to be overly serious and self-reliant. Also, these adult Heroes may become enablers for others with chemical dependencies or irresponsible lifestyles.

As an adult, the Responsible One/Hero often goes into the helping professions. I am an example of this phenomenon. As a first-born Responsible One/Hero, I exhibit many of the traits described here. I tend to be overly responsible and depression-prone, and for years I have referred to myself as a "recovering perfectionist."

No matter what careers these adults choose, success is guaranteed because they will work harder than anyone else. However, even if they achieve leadership roles in their professions, they may rarely achieve personal satisfaction from their jobs because of unrecognized, unrealistic goals. Adult children of alcoholics living out this Responsible One/Hero role are most likely to appear to be functioning successfully as adults. Often eldest siblings, these adults tend to be perfectionistic, critical, and depression-prone.

Christian adults raised in this role gravitate to positions of church leadership. They are the church members every pastor loves, for they are tireless workers. However, they may be involved in power struggles—especially with other members raised as Heroes, and they tend to be legalistic. Clergypersons are apt to be Responsible Ones/Heroes if they were raised in alcoholic families.

Scapegoat. Whereas the Responsible One/Hero tends to be a super-responsible adult, the Scapegoat tends to be super-irresponsible. The Scapegoat is at high risk for continuing into adulthood the adolescent drug use commonly associated with this role. Adults living out this role are apt to have legal problems and difficulties keeping a job and/or a spouse. These adult Scapegoats pay the highest price. They may end their lives in jail or by accident or suicide.

A Christian Scapegoat tends to be the black sheep in the congregation's fold. His or her appearance and behavior are frequently an embarrassment to other church members. They may remain "stuck" in Christian infancy if not patiently reparented and discipled.

Adjuster/Lost Child. The adult living out this role tends to remain a follower, avoiding responsibility and leadership. Adjuster adults pride themselves on being flexible. They can "go with the flow," and few things seem to bother them. These adults may have a pattern of blaming others for their lack of satisfaction with life, in contrast to the Responsible Ones/ Heroes who blame themselves for everything.

If Adjuster adults trust Christ and join a church, they will sit near the back and rarely offer to fill leadership positions. They may prefer working with children or taking responsibilities that allow them to remain behind the scenes.

Placater/Mascot. Adults in this role often appear tense and anxious. Placater/Mascot adults may be afraid of conflict or of expressions of strong emotion in themselves or others. They may fail to meet personal needs because of the strong desire to avoid anger. Also depression-prone, these adults often have patterns of passivity in relationships. Because Placater/Mascot adults tend to be silly, their relationships also tend to be shallow and flighty.

Placater/Mascot Christian adults frequently are very popular. They work hard to avoid strife in the church and always have an amusing aside when a church business meeting gets tense. They rarely hold top leadership positions for long, because, although they may accept a responsible job to avoid conflict, they seldom follow through as effectively as the Responsible One/Hero.

CAUSED TO STUMBLE

Several writers have attempted to explain the development of unhealthy characteristics in adult children of alcoholics. Seabaugh has proposed that these characteristics are defenses against narcissistic injuries experienced by children in alcoholic homes.[31] Breen sees the psychological problems of these adults as part of a "subterranean grieving process."[32] Worden and others believe that the characteristics discussed in this chapter are symptoms of post-traumatic stress disorder.[33]

My conceptualization incorporates all of these, but is closest to that of Stephanie Brown. She suggests children in alcoholic families are forced by their dependency needs to accept the cognitive distortions of the alcoholic and co-alcoholic parents that there is no alcoholism in the family and all the problems are caused by something else. It is the acceptance of this family myth, accompanied by a denial of reality, that is the child's basis of attachment to the family.[34]

Most counselors would agree that *adults* are responsible for all their choices, but *children can be "caused to stumble,"* i.e., taught wrong values that lead to sinful choices. This phrase is from the eighteenth chapter of Matthew where Jesus set a child before his disciples as a model of believing trust without which no one will enter heaven. Still speaking of that child, Jesus said, "whoever causes one of these little ones who believe in Me to stumble, it is better for him that a heavy millstone be hung around his neck, and that he be drowned in the depth of the sea" (verse 6). Although the context indicates Jesus' primary emphasis was spiritual, perhaps we could extend this caused-to-stumble concept to volitional areas of life.

Children do not have the same choices as adults. A child of five cannot say to himself or herself, "I don't want to speak English. I think it is a dumb language. The grammar and syntax are too confusing. I think I'll speak French." A child has no choice but to learn the language spoken in his or her family. Alcoholic families speak the language of lies—lies about facts and lies about feelings. As adults, these children make the choices that shape their lives based on these lies.

All children are caused to stumble to one degree or another because all parents are sinful. Jesus implied as much in Matthew 18:7 when he said that stumbling blocks are inevitable. But there is a vast difference between being caused (by sinful responsible parents) to stumble off a three-inch curb and being caused (by sinful alcoholic parents) to stumble off a thirty-foot cliff. I see the unhealthy characteristics of adult children of alcoholics as a combination of their nature of innate sin, their brokenness from being caused to stumble as young children, and their subsequent wrong and sinful choices. And while they are not responsible, in my view, for being taught to speak, think, and live lies, they are responsible, as adults, to enter a process of recovering from their brokenness by learning to walk in truth. After all, even if English is your primary language, as an adult you can choose to learn French!

The common element in each model, including mine, is the powerful force exerted by the alcoholic family upon its children of all ages. Therefore, it is appropriate to look next at the relationships these adult children have with their alcoholic family systems.

CHAPTER FIVE

ADULT CHILDREN AND THE ALCOHOLIC FAMILY

MOST ADULT CHILDREN OF ALCOHOLICS continue to interact regularly with their families. They attend family celebrations and rituals where they may be exposed to alcoholic drinking, and this is difficult particularly if the adult child is recovering from his or her own alcoholism. Adult children of alcoholics may also become embroiled in family arguments over how to manage ill alcoholic parents, i.e., whether to enable them to continue drinking or to intervene to help them stop.

The interactions between adult children and their alcoholic and co-alcoholic parents depend in large part upon whether or not the children and/or parents have come out of their denial. This chapter will describe the relationships of adult children who have never, or only recently, faced the impact of parental alcoholism. In chapter 13 I will talk about new roles adult children can play in their families based on respecting truth, themselves, and their parents.

In chapter 4 we looked at the codependent relational style. Take a moment to re-read the list of rescuing moves on page 79. These behaviors characterize codependent relationships, and nowhere do adult children of alcoholics manifest more codependence than in relationships with their parents. You may remember that codependent individuals are caretakers and rescuers. But the rescuer role is just one of a triad of roles played by codependents. To understand the typical relationship between adult children and their alcohol-dominated parents, we need to look at all three sides of a model called the "Karpman Drama Triangle."[1]

FROM RESCUER TO VICTIM

Picture a triangle with the following words at each corner: rescuer, persecutor, victim. These are the three roles codependents successively play, according to Stephen Karpman, who developed this model. In chapter 4, we looked at the rescuer role in some detail. We could say *we rescue whenever we take care of people who could take care of themselves*. It is not unusual for adult children to loan money to their alcoholic parents, care for younger children still in the home, and otherwise shield their parents from the consequences of their alcoholic and irresponsible behavior.

Bill is a Christian in his early thirties who grew up in a large, chaotic, alcoholic family. Whenever problems threatened to close in, his alcoholic father's solution was to move and "start fresh." "I can't even tell you how many times Dad promised 'things will be better here.' Now he and my mother are moving to Alaska, if you can believe it. He's putting the squeeze on all us kids to help finance this latest 'fresh start.' I was saving for a down payment on a small house I've found, but I guess that's history."

Bill is participating in the rescue, but he is resentful and bitter. He has moved to the next corner of Karpman Drama Triangle, and to the next role: persecutor. People inevitably become angry with the person they have so "generously" rescued because they felt forced to do something they did not want to do and, which, in reality, was not their responsibility. Not only that, the "poor victim," just rescued at great personal sacrifice to the rescuer, does not appreciate—or even acknowledge—the rescue. In fact, when the adult child rescuer-turned-persecutor directly or indirectly criticizes the alcoholic parent's behavior, he or she is well on the way to the remaining role.

Bill remembers many times before when he helped out financially. His inquiries about the possibility of getting repaid were met with a chorus of "what a selfish son you are, always looking out for number one, and after all we've done for you." Welcome to the victim role, Bill. As surely as day follows night, *rescuers end up as victims*. Feelings of shame, self-pity, hurt, disappointment, and depression abound at the victim corner of the triangle. Bill and many other adults from alcoholic homes have said, "I try *so* hard to help. Why am I *always* trampled on? Why does this always happen to *me?*"

Part of the answer to "Why me?" is that the victim role is very familiar to adults raised in alcoholic families. To one degree or another, all truly were victims as children. Many still see themselves as victims even as adults. This familiar victim role is played most consistently in relationships with alcoholic parents, although this progression from rescuer to persecutor to victim is characteristic of all codependent relationships.

Obviously, this relational pattern is painful to the codependent adult children enmeshed in it. However, there is evidence suggesting that no matter how difficult and painful it is for adult children to interact with their alcoholic parents, they often continue to do so because they continue to feel responsible for stabilizing the family system.

IMPRISONING LOYALTIES

Cermak and Brown reported that members joined their therapy groups for adult children of alcoholics not only because they were concerned that their own alcoholism was inevitable, but because of feeling responsible for the welfare of their families.[2] Wood reported the comments of one twenty-six-year-old daughter of an alcoholic father and co-alcoholic mother, both in their mid-fifties. This woman suffered severe allergies, and she said, "The only place I've ever been able to breathe normally is in Arizona. I'd like to move there, but I feel I can't while my parents are still alive. My father, especially, depends on me to cheer him up."[3]

This woman regards herself as a very loyal daughter. Unfortunately for her, the loyalty demanded of children in alcoholic families is a constricting, stifling, imprisoning loyalty. This is the "darker side of loyalties" Gary Smalley and John Trent describe in *The Gift of Honor*. Smalley and Trent suggest that fear of losing that "special place" they have with their impaired and demanding parents impels adult children toward imprisoning loyalties where "making a decision on their own becomes unthinkable; acting on their own becomes unforgivable."[4] In effect, that "special place" is a place of firm attachment to the family which can only be maintained at the sacrifice of truth and personal choice.

Imprisoning loyalties bind adult children to their parents and their families, requiring them to mold their lives around the needs and wishes of their parents. This "darker side of loyalty" impacts the lives of adult children in countless ways. Three of the major ways are reflected in their marriages, their parenting, and their willingness to seek help.

Imprisoning Loyalties and Marriage

Adult children of alcoholics often feel uneasy and guilty when they try to create families of their own. Sometimes these children, especially daughters, marry at an early age to escape the chaos created by their parents only to discover they have created their own chaos. Other adult children delay their marriages to remain undistracted and available to continue parenting their parents. Either way, adult children of alcoholics enter marriage with neither healthy role models nor psychological permission to leave their parents. And it is necessary to emotionally "leave" your parents before you can "cleave" to your spouse.

Leaving and cleaving are guidelines God presents in Genesis 2:24. "For this cause a man shall leave his father and his mother, and shall cleave to his wife; and they shall become one flesh." Leaving is much more than geographical relocation. It involves a *transfer of primary loyalties from parents to spouse,* and this is extremely difficult for adult children of alcoholics.

Gina and Ross learned this the hard way when he relocated the family because of a new job. "Honestly, I took this job to get Gina away from her mom who's a drunk. I hoped she'd be able to concentrate more on me and the kids. But in some ways it's worse, because now she runs up huge phone bills every month calling her dad to check on her mother." Ross could not disguise the anger in his voice as he spoke. Gina fought back tears and tried to describe her feelings. "It isn't that I don't love my husband and kids. I really do. It's just that I feel so guilty going off and leaving my dad alone to cope with my mom. I just feel I should be there to help."

Gina is struggling with divided loyalties and "double-mindedness." Many adult children of alcoholics like Gina live in a "double-minded" condition that James 1:8 says causes a person to be "unstable in all his ways." Perhaps this double-minded loyalty is one explanation for higher divorce rates among adult children of alcoholics—even those who are Christians. As noted in chapter 4, my research study reported 32.8 percent of subjects raised in alcoholic homes had been divorced at least once compared with 9.7 percent of those from nonalcoholic families.[5]

Imprisoning Loyalties and Parenting

If adult children of alcoholics marry and have children, they and their spouses may find it embarrassing and difficult to deal with the alcoholic parents. These adult children have problems setting appropriate limits on the alcoholic behavior and may even expose their children to dangerous situations rather than refute the family lie that no one in the family has a drinking problem.

Candice was sobbing softly as she told about the holiday visit with her alcoholic father and step-mother. "It was happening before I realized it, and it was so familiar. Dad would pile us all in the car and we'd drive around and look at house lights and decorations on Christmas Eve. He was always so drunk he couldn't walk straight, let alone drive safely. We kids were scared to death each time, but we always went. This year it happened again, and there I was squeezed into the backseat of the car with him weaving all over the road."

Candice's voice broke and she had difficulty continuing. "Only this year it was different because I had my baby with me. Oh, God, I can't believe I actually went with that maniac again and took my baby." Candice went on to describe her husband's anger when he returned from last-minute Christmas shopping and realized she and their infant son were gone. "He's still mad at me, and I don't blame him. I hate myself for what I did. I just couldn't tell my father no. When I go back home I feel like a stupid, helpless, little kid again, and I hate it."

Many adult children of alcoholics describe that same "little kid" feeling that Candice felt. They experience "growing down" when they return to their parents' home. This is ironic considering the fact that many of them were forced into "growing up" so fast they lost their childhoods. When adult children feel "grown down" they find it nearly impossible to emotionally separate from their parents.

Imprisoning Loyalties and Seeking Help

It has been said that alcoholics do not have relationships, they take hostages. Apparently they take many of their children hostage for life. Because of imprisoning loyalties so characteristic of alcoholic homes, many adult children find themselves unable to emotionally separate from the alcoholic family system. This struggle to separate often prevents these adults from seeking help for themselves. Beletis and Brown reported conclusions based on treating four long-term interactional groups over a four-year period.[6] These researchers concluded that adult children of alcoholics seeking help felt they were abandoning their families since they were forced to confront the alcoholic denial that is the basis of attachment to, and organizing principle of, the alcoholic family system.

Perrin found the same feelings among participants in his therapy groups for adult children of alcoholics. He noted recurring themes of loss of parental love and need to reconnect with families. Group members felt that by seeking help for themselves and breaking denial, they had betrayed their parents and families and, at the same time, been abandoned by them.[7]

WINGS AND STRINGS

"Honor your father and mother. . ." instructs the Lord in Exodus 20:12. In the original Hebrew, the word for *honor* literally meant to be heavy or weighty. In time it came to mean considering a *person* heavy or weighty, i.e., to consider him or her honorable or important, as in the case of a city official.[8] In Exodus 20:12, children of all ages are exhorted to consider their parents and their parents' influences as important. While all parents and parental influences are important, some are "heavier" than others.

Alcoholic and co-alcoholic parents use their influence to impose heavy burdens upon their children which crush their hopes for healthy, interdependent lives. Often these children are left believing they must continue their childhood roles of stabilizing the family system regardless of personal cost. Instead of receiving a heritage of freeing "wings" formed of biblical values, healthy self-concepts, and permission to separate, adults from alcoholic families often remain tangled in a legacy of binding "strings" which inextricably entwine them and their needy parents.

Nowhere is an alcoholic parent's "heavy" influence seen more clearly, and nowhere do the burdensome familial "strings" bind more powerfully, than in the area of shaping children's concepts of God. As Christian adults, these children often stagger in their spiritual walk under the burden of their distorted God-concepts.

CHAPTER SIX

ADULT CHILDREN AND THEIR CONCEPTS OF GOD

IN CHAPTER 2, WE EXPLORED the alcoholic family system's dark corner of child abuse. Specifically, I discussed physical, mental, emotional, and sexual abuse. But there is an additional form of abuse experienced by children in alcoholic and other dysfunctional families: spiritual abuse.

SPIRITUAL ABUSE

Writing in a secular publication for adult children of alcoholics, Andrew Meacham described spiritual abuse:

Spiritual abuse occurs every time a child is physically, sexually, emotionally or mentally abused, because the message the child gets from the parent is: "I can do anything I want with you." In effect, the child gets the mistaken idea that the parent is the child's Higher Power. It is crucial to the development of spirituality that children are taught the concept of a Power that is both higher than themselves—and higher than their parents.[1]

Even if a family is devoid of formal religious training, a child in that family is learning about the attributes of God as surely as any seminarian. This is true for *any* child in *any* family. This is true for children in alcoholic families in which those children frequently experience neglect and abuse.

This chapter focuses on the effects of childhood spiritual abuse in the lives of adults raised in alcoholic homes. Some of the information is based on observations by other clinicians, Christian and non-Christian, working with these adults. But much of the material in this chapter comes from thoughts and feelings shared with me in groups for Christian adult children of alcoholics. I have been given permission to share these thoughts and feelings with the hope they will help others. In addition, my research examined religious perceptions of evangelical Christian adult children of alcoholics and compared them to those of evangelical adults from nonalcoholic families. The results support the conclusion that "Christian adult children of alcoholics struggle more to believe, appropriate, and live out their faith than do their peers in the pew who are not from alcoholic homes."[2] I believe that struggle is rooted in distorted concepts of God.

It has been stated facetiously that "man creates God in his own image." Perhaps it would be more accurate to say that man creates God in the image of his parents—especially his father. Sara Hines Martin, a Christian counselor and author of *Healing for Adult Children of Alcoholics,* quotes William De Arteaga's statement that:

When a person is injured by the father, his ability to relate to God is impaired. If his primal image of the father is one that is hurtful, his ability to view God in a healthy way is fractured. No matter how much he wants to read the Bible and follow God, if his image of the Abba Father, which

93

Jesus describes, is a drunk person, the child has a severe impediment to prayer, growth, and holiness.[3]

DAMAGED PERCEPTIONS

Dr. David Seamands, pastor and counselor for many years, has described the "severe impediment" of which De Arteaga spoke as damaged perceiving receptors.

> For although the Holy Spirit is the One who reveals the truth. What the listener hears and pictures and feels still has to be filtered through him. The Holy Spirit Himself does not bypass the personality equipment by which a person perceives things. *And when those perceiving receptors have been severely damaged, the biblical truths get distorted.*[4]

Dr. Seamands believes painful relationships with neglectful and/or abusive parents are among the forces operating to damage a person's perceiving receptors.

Remember the concept of rigidity? In chapter 4 we saw the psychological basis for the idea that our todays are shaped by our yesterdays. (". . . present stimulation is interpreted in light of past experience. . . .") *In effect, our todays—including our concepts of God—are perceived with receptors constructed from past experiences.* As children begin to learn, formally or informally, about God their Heavenly Parent, their thoughts and feelings about God are formed in the shadow of their earthly parents. They have no choice, because "present stimulation is interpreted in light of past experience. . . ." Parents, or parent surrogates, are the earliest and most influential authority figures by which to interpret all present and future authority figures, human or divine.

Alcoholic and co-alcoholic parents cast long, dark shadows in which it is nearly impossible for children to form undistorted concepts of God. As adults, these children may enter wary relationships with a Higher Power who bears little resemblance to the God of Abraham, Isaac, and Jacob. And this distorted deity is either "feared or expected to do it all."[5] Some adult children of alcoholics reject any relationship with God. In my experience, these fiercely unbelieving adults resent even the nebulous

Higher Power concept foundational to the Twelve-Step Program of Alcoholics Anonymous, Al-Anon, and affiliated adult children of alcoholic support groups.

If adult children of alcoholics become Christians, they enter the lifelong task of clarifying their concepts of God. However, this task is part of the sanctification process of all Christians, not just of those raised in alcoholic homes. Seamands has observed:

> This is one of the main reasons why the Incarnation was so necessary. The Word had to become *flesh.* God had gone as far as He could in revealing Himself through *words*. . . . Words are subject to the distortions of sinful and damaged hearers. Only when the Word became a human life was it possible for us to see a true picture of God, "full of grace and truth" (John 1:14). But the problem of distortion is still partially with us, for the content of the words we read in the Bible which describe Jesus and the character of God is greatly influenced by our memories and relationships.[6]

DISTORTED DEITIES

How might childhood memories of neglect and abuse and relationships with alcoholic and co-alcoholic parents influence God-concepts? I have identified five major distortions of the character of God common to Christian adult children of alcoholics. Their damaged perceptions of God typically portray him as one of the following distorted deities:

1. The Cruel and Capricious God
2. The Demanding and Unforgiving God
3. The Selective and Unfair God
4. The Distant and Unavailable God
5. The Kind but Confused God.

From the following descriptions of these unbiblical views of God's character, we will see that one's location on the Family Functioning Continuum, described in chapter 2, affects the severity of one's impediment to perceiving God.

The Cruel and Capricious God

This is the image of God formed in children nearest the Dachau end of the Family Functioning Continuum. Christian

95

adults worshiping this God usually do so with fear closer to terror than to the "reverence for God expressed in submission to His will" with which wisdom begins.[7] Almost without exception, adults with this perception of God were repeatedly abused in brutal and unpredictable ways as children. Most frequently, this abuse was perpetrated by the child's father.

Becky's Story. Becky was six the first time she was sodomized by her alcoholic father. For the next five years she lived in the Dachau of her parents' cruelty. Eventually Becky and her younger sisters and brothers were removed from their parents' home. Becky's mother was hospitalized for psychiatric reasons and her father left the city. The children were placed in a reasonably healthy foster home, and Becky totally repressed the memories of her sexual abuse. At seventeen, Becky married a Christian man who led her to faith in Christ, and she served God diligently, but joylessly, for years. At mid-life, Becky sought counseling to relieve anxiety symptoms and to help her learn to trust God. After eight months of working with, and building trust in, her Christian counselor, Becky's painful memories began to emerge.

Reliving the physical pain of her abuse was not as devastating to Becky as re-experiencing the overwhelming sense of parental betrayal and abandonment. And in addition to the pain of her past, she and her husband were experiencing severe financial struggles. "God is so cruel, but it doesn't matter because he can do anything he wants. Who am I to object?" Becky repeatedly cried. "I would not treat my children this way."

It is important to understand that many Christians who experience God as cruel and capricious possess a basically correct theology that informs them otherwise. Becky was no exception. However, in spite of her sound theology, Becky lived daily as if her distorted, cruel, and capricious God was on the throne of the universe.

God as Father. Becky's story is typical of Christian adults raised by an abusive, alcoholic father and an impaired, co-alcoholic mother. And for these adults, the "fatherhood of God" is not a comforting concept. The following poem, written by an incest survivor, captures the spiritual struggles of these Christians.

God

> I've been glad for God the Spirit
> and for God the Son
> because I don't believe
> my heart can ever understand
> that God
> is like a father.[8]

"God is male, and I don't trust men. Men always hurt me. My father and my two ex-husbands were alcoholics," stated one woman in a support group for adult children of alcoholics. This Christian woman's ability to perceive her Heavenly Father as Scripture portrays him has been severely damaged by her earthly father and by other alcoholic men in her life.

Some Christian men and women have reported difficulties saying the opening phrase of the model prayer, "Our Father which art in heaven," (KJV) and they are uneasy when they hear others begin prayers with "Dear Heavenly Father." To these adults, the concept of father is not inspiring and dear; it is dreaded and despised. In spite of Bible studies and sermons, these are the Christians who perceive God as a brutal father, both cruel and capricious.

The Demanding and Unforgiving God

The children who learned to perceive God as demanding and unforgiving did not live quite as near Dachau as those who view him as cruel and capricious. These children may have experienced more neglect than abuse, with the exceptions of emotional and verbal abuse, which may have abounded. Often, these are the children who performed the Responsible One/Hero role in their alcoholic families. And they are still performing for their demanding, unforgiving God.

As Christian adults, these children may describe God as a "scowling taskmaster," as did one member of a group for Christians raised in alcoholic homes.

Paul's Story. "For as long as I can remember, I have seen God as disappointed and angry with me. He was always up in heaven, standing with his arms crossed over his chest, slowly shaking his head, and scowling. God was looking down at me

97

and saying, 'Paul, Paul, Paul, I am so disappointed in you. I expected so much more of you. Now here is your new list of rules; get out there and do better.' I know that sounds ridiculous. And I even know that that is not the God Jesus told us about, but I always feel that I should be doing more to please God. I never do enough."

Paul was the oldest son of an alcoholic father and a depressed mother who, due to financial needs, worked full time. His mother relied on Paul to be her "Big Helper," and he did his best. He remembers trying so hard to take care of his three younger sisters, cook meals, and keep peace between his parents so his mother would not be upset as well as exhausted. But no matter how hard he tried, he could never do enough to please his parents and prevent the increasing deterioration of the family.

Paul usually fills several major leadership positions in his church and is considered a very dedicated worker. However, he tends to be one of the more legalistic and joyless members of his congregation. Paul frequently quotes a portion of Luke 12:48, "And from everyone who has been given much shall much be required. . . ." Paul's demanding and unforgiving God requires a great deal. And this distorted deity never forgives when Paul falls short.

The Selective and Unfair God

I have talked with many Christian adults from alcoholic families who do not believe God is cruel, capricious, demanding, and unforgiving with all his children—only with them. In fact, this selective and unfair God may be the distorted deity most often worshiped by adult children of alcoholics as they carry their sense of being "different-and-not-as-good-as" into their relationships with God. Many of these Christian adults have described their selective and unfair God; Linda is one.

Linda's Story. "I've heard preachers say that God doesn't have favorites, but I have always felt like a second-class Christian. I've always felt second-class at church because my parents never came when I was a kid. I worked hard to be accepted, but I still felt separate from other Christians. God has a different kind of relationship with other Christians. I pretend that I have that same, special relationship, but I don't think I know how. God blesses other people—shows them the palm of his hand. I only seem to get the back of his hand. It was different at first. His salvation love was different from his attitude toward me now in my daily life. Maybe it stays the same for other Christians, but it is different for me."

Unfortunately Linda has not come to the place of the apostle Peter who declared in Acts 10:34, "I most certainly understand now that God is not one to show partiality." Linda's selective and unfair God discriminates against her and treats her more harshly than his other children. Linda gives mental assent to the God of Acts 10:34; but her feelings bow before a distorted, discriminating God who is selective and unfair.

The Distant and Unavailable God

This distorted deity is neither cruel, capricious, overly demanding, nor unforgiving. He is just inaccessible. This distant and unavailable God may actually care for his worshipers, but he keeps his distance and does not get too involved in their lives. This was Lamar's God.

Lamar's Story. "That sermon about how our relationships with our fathers affects our view of God really got me thinking. It's funny—I've always felt God loved me, but I just never felt he was as close and available to me as to other Christians. My wife has a close relationship with God, so I usually ask her to pray for me, especially about important things. And as I think about it, that's how I felt about my dad. He worked almost all the time, and when he was home, he was sitting in front of the television set drinking. He was never violent or mean. I knew he loved me, and I loved him. He was sort of there—but not there—in my life. And that's how I see God—there, but not there."

Chronic parental unavailability, whatever the cause, may distort a child's perception of God so he is seen as eternally inaccessible.

The Kind but Confused God

This God is perceived as benign and ineffectual. He appears weak and rather confused by all the chaos in the world. This distorted deity usually is experienced as somewhat distant also. Jan worshiped this kind and confused God.

Jan's Story. "My mother was the alcoholic in our family. She and my dad are both basically nice people whose lives were always out of control. As I got older, and my mother's drinking got worse, I used to ask my dad to do something—anything—to get her some help. He had a lot of health problems himself and always seemed totally overwhelmed with life in general. I loved my parents, and I know they loved me too, but that never seemed to be enough to make things better. Now, I have a real hard time with the idea of God as omnipotent and sovereign. I seem to dwell on things in my life and the world that show how crazy and chaotic everything is."

Followers of this kind but confused God do not perceive him as the majestic creator and sustainer of the universe. Not only is their distorted deity impotent to solve the problems in the world, he is ineffectual with their personal struggles.

PROBLEMS EXPERIENCING GOD

When I compared nearly seventy evangelical adult children of alcoholics with about the same number of evangelical adults from nonalcoholic homes, I found statistically significant differences in their religious perceptions. For the purpose of this study, I divided "religious perception" into four elements: 1) experiencing God's love and forgiveness, 2) trusting God's will, 3) believing biblical promises regarding God's care, and 4) extending forgiveness to others. I readily acknowledge these four dimensions do not encompass the concept of religious perception; but they address its major components. The reliability of Scripture and the concept of a loving God who is personally involved in the lives of his children to the extent of providing forgiveness for their sins are the *sine qua non* of evangelical Christianity. In addition, the call to extend forgiveness to others is seen as the outworking of a viable faith.[9]

The table in figure 6-1 displays the percentages of each group of Christians indicating they had problems in the four areas listed. Information about the statistical analysis appears below the table.

Subjects' Reported Religious Problem Areas by Group in Percentages

Religious Problem Areas	Adult Children of Alcoholics[a]	Adult Children of Nonalcoholics[b]
Experience God's Love and Forgiveness[c]	44.8%	4.8%*
Trust God's Will[d]	53.7%	11.3%*
Believe Biblical Promises[e]	43.3%	4.8%*
Forgive Others[f]	40.3%	14.5%*

*statistically significant difference

[a]67 subjects   [b]62 subjects   [c]$df = 1; \underline{X}^2 = 26.979; \underline{p} = <.001$

[d]$df = 1; \underline{X}^2 = 26.101; \underline{p} = <.001$ [e]$df = 1; \underline{X}^2 = 25.516; \underline{p} = <.001$ [f]$df = 1; \underline{X}^2 = 10.639; \underline{p} = <.01$

Figure 6–1

Having examined the five distorted deities most commonly worshiped by Christian adult children of alcoholics, it is logical to assume these Christians would have problems trusting God and feeling loved and forgiven by him. These data support that assumption.

In addition, my findings indicate that Christians raised in alcoholic homes may be unable to believe biblical promises or to appropriate comfort and encouragement from them. For example, Psalm 103:13 states that, "Just as a father has compassion on his children, So the Lord has compassion on those who fear Him." But many Christian adult children of alcoholics have had little experience with a trustworthy and compassionate father. This suggests that the very evangelicals who are dealing with more troublesome personality characteristics are the same evangelicals who are less able to appropriate the comfort offered by their faith.

However, it is touching to note that the personal devotional practices of prayer and/or Bible study of evangelical adult children of alcoholics in this study were almost identical to those of the adult children of nonalcoholics. It appears that although evangelicals raised in alcoholic families often strive in vain to experience God's love and to believe He cares for them, they continue to strive.[11]

The preceding quotation reflects the finding that there were no significant differences between Christians raised in alcoholic and nonalcoholic homes in response to questions about frequency of "personal devotional practices of prayer and/or Bible study." In addition, there were no significant differences in patterns of church attendance. These findings suggest that even if the God they worship is one of the distorted deities we have examined, Christian adult children of alcoholics continue to worship him publicly and privately.

SPIRITUAL WOUNDS

In chapters 4 and 5 we discussed the physical, mental, emotional, and relational effects of parental alcoholism in the lives of adult children. "It is as though the child has been wounded and was never properly treated. Like an injury not allowed to heal properly, it carries over into adulthood as a chronic health problem."[12]

In this chapter, we have examined evidence suggesting that Christian adult children of alcoholics also bear spiritual wounds. Scars from the spiritual wounds of childhood spiritual abuse are visible in results of research with evangelical adult children of alcoholics. Chapters 14 and 15 focus on healing spiritual wounds.

PART THREE

COUNSELING ADULT CHILDREN OF ALCOHOLICS FOR RECOVERY

IN CHAPTERS 2 AND 3 we saw that children of alcoholic parents learned to cope with many difficult, dangerous, and sometimes life-threatening situations. As children, they learned to survive in the face of stress and trauma. As adults, they can draw upon their survival strength as they face the challenges of recovering from the damaging effects of parental alcoholism. And as *Christians*, they can call upon the Holy Spirit of God who indwells them to empower and bless the recovery process.

The remainder of the book focuses on that recovery process, which can be compared with a process of rehabilitation from physical injury. Adult children of alcoholics may have been caused to stumble off a cliff by alcoholic and co-alcoholic parents; but the adult children are responsible for the choice of lying at the bottom of the cliff or seeking help to recover from their wounds.

Parts III, IV, and V offer counseling guidelines to those seeking to help adult children of alcoholics in their personal rehabilitation and recovery process. The counseling approach presented may be more directive than that used by some mental-health professionals. Adult children of alcoholics seem to benefit most from counseling that gives them the opportunity to:

1. Explore the past.
2. Connect the past to the present.
3. Identify childhood messages and beliefs.
4. Replace misbeliefs with truth.
5. Learn the skills they missed in childhood, such as identifying feelings, problem solving, and limit-setting.
6. Experience feelings disallowed in childhood, such as fear, anger, and sadness.
7. Receive supportive encouragement which validates them and the recovery process.

These seven elements will be woven throughout the recovery tapestry described in the following chapters.

In Part III, we will consider the broad area of counseling adult children of alcoholics as they initially come out of denial by learning to share honestly, think correctly, and feel appropriately. For convenient organization of material and discussion of these three aspects of breaking denial, they have been divided into separate chapters. However, it should be remembered that this is an artificially imposed separation; they actually occur simultaneously.

CHAPTER SEVEN

REVEALING THE SECRET: LEARNING TO SHARE

DISCOVERY PRECEDES RECOVERY. Discovery of the truth about parental alcoholism and its effects is the first step on the road to recovery from those effects. This discovery of truth and the subsequent erosion of denial, "begins a process of recovery that will involve a major uncovering, in-depth reconstruction of one's life and core identity and an equally in-depth process of construction of a new identity based on acknowledgement of having grown up with an alcoholic parent."[1]

SURPRISED BY TRUTH

Most adult children of alcoholics are surprised by the truth about parental alcoholism. Often this occurs when they seek professional counseling for anxiety, depression, marital problems, or other personal and/or interpersonal problems. Skillful, thorough counselors will inquire about a counselee's family history including patterns of parental alcohol use. An instrument such as the Children of Alcoholics Screening Test (C.A.S.T.) is helpful in determining the presence of parental alcoholism. A copy of the C.A.S.T. and information on ordering it appear in Appendix 2. Dr. John Jones, the psychologist who developed the C.A.S.T., has presented data indicating that six or more affirmative answers to the thirty C.A.S.T. questions reliably identify children of alcoholic parents. Here are five of those questions:

1. Did you ever feel alone, scared, nervous, angry or frustrated because a parent was not able to stop drinking?

2. Have you ever heard your parents fight when one of them was drunk?

3. Did you ever feel responsible for and guilty about a parent's drinking?

4. Did you ever threaten to run away from home because of a parent's drinking?

5. Has a parent ever yelled at or hit you or other family members when drinking?[2]

Adults with high C.A.S.T. scores do not automatically acknowledge the presence of parental alcoholism. In my clinical practice, I have worked with adults who indicated twenty of the C.A.S.T. questions were true yet were incredulous at my suggestion they were raised in an alcoholic family.[3] Their incredulity is consistent with reports in the literature indicating that, even in the face of consistent and disruptive alcoholic behavior, family members deny the fact. To work effectively with these adults, a counselor must understand the purpose and the power of denial.

THE PURPOSE OF DENIAL

Denial systems are constructed for logical, sensible, self-protecting purposes. We all have denial systems that serve to shield and preserve us psychologically. A denial system, originally established for good reasons, becomes a problem when it interferes with present functioning. The greater the perceived threat to a child's psychological well-being which precipitated the denial, the greater the resistance to relinquishing it even in the face of evidence that it is has ceased to be a help and has become a hindrance. For example, if a child lived in a violent and abusive alcoholic home, he or she survived, in part, by numbing feelings. That denial of feelings served a valid purpose for the child. However, for that adult child, denial of feelings interferes with his or her capacity to be spontaneous and maintain close relationships. Even when adults recognize the impact of emotional numbness, they find it very difficult to relinquish that component of their denial system.

Denial systems are eroded gently and slowly more often than they are "broken" suddenly and permanently.[4] This fact speaks to the intrinsic power of denial systems.

THE POWER OF DENIAL

The following excerpt from a review of research on fourteen adolescent males on death row illustrates the power of denial:

> Eight of the 14 had injuries severe enough to require hospitalization; nine had serious neurological deficiencies. . . . Twelve had been brutally abused and five had been sodomized by relatives. Their parents had a high rate of alcoholism, drug abuse, and psychiatric hospitalization. The boys had tried to conceal all this during their trials. They preferred to be seen as bad rather than admit that they were psychiatrically impaired, intellectually inadequate, or victims of sexual abuse. The parents often cooperated with the prosecution (and even urged the death sentence) because they had an interest in concealing their own actions.[5]

These death-row adolescents chose to maintain their base of attachment to their dysfunctional families, thereby avoiding the pain of emotional abandonment, rather than share family secrets. They chose denial of truth, which is deceit. Because surely the power of denial is rooted in the basic deceitfulness of the human heart ("The heart is more deceitful than all else. . . ."[6]), coupled with the need to protect one's self by protecting one's family.

To counsel effectively with adult children of alcoholics, we must understand the incredible power of denial in alcoholic family systems. If parents are still in denial, they will "urge the death sentence," to their adult child's efforts to seek help and recognize the truth about parental alcoholism. *Counselors function as "healthier parents" who urge adult children to recognize denial and to commit to living in truth.*

COUNSELING FOR TRUTH

As Christian counselors and people helpers, we know we worship the God of truth, who calls us to truthfulness. This is a difficult concept for Christians raised in alcoholic homes. During the early *discovery* stage of counseling with Christian adult children of alcoholics, I have found several verses to be particularly helpful:

1. *The wisdom of the prudent is to understand his way, But the folly of fools is deceit* (Proverbs 14:8). Often, adult children of alcoholics seek counseling because they do not understand their own ways of relating, behaving, thinking, or feeling. Understanding their ways requires abandoning the self-protecting folly of deceit and embracing the truth about their past, their present, and their future.

2. *He who speaks truth tells what is right, But a false witness, deceit* (Proverbs 12:17). Adult children of alcoholics need to receive permission from God, their Heavenly Parent, and their counselors, their "healthier parents," to speak truth. They need to know that it is *right* to share the family secret and come out of denial and deceit.

3. *And you shall know the truth, and the truth shall make you free* (John 8:32). I tell my counselees that although the primary meaning of this verse is that truth about the person and work of Jesus Christ makes us free from the penalty and power of sin, truth makes us free in other ways too. All truth is God's truth, and truth about our families and ourselves sets us free from the lies that bind us to a painful past, a crippled present, and a hopeless future.

4. *Behold, Thou dost desire truth in the innermost being, And in the hidden part Thou wilt make me know wisdom* (Psalm 51:6 KJV). Children in alcoholic families are raised with parents who

desire denial and deceit in their innermost being. As adults, they must learn that God, their Heavenly Parent, is committed to truth in every part of them, including their perceptions of their parents and memories of their childhoods.

ERASING THE SECRET

Memories of childhood may be extremely vague or entirely missing for many adult children of alcoholics. Herbert Gravitz and Julie Bowden, two prominent specialists in working with these adults, have stated that almost three out of four of their clients reported "significant memory losses that extend over years of childhood."[7] Of course, this does not mean the memories were not stored. It means they cannot be retrieved due to repression. Repression, the process of unconsciously "forgetting" painful memories, is a logical outgrowth of the denial and distortion of reality that reign in alcoholic families.

A particularly bright and articulate Christian woman raised with a sexually abusive, alcoholic father and a physically abusive, co-alcoholic mother graphically described to me the process of denial and repression in her life:

It was as if my mind was a blackboard held very, very close to my face so I couldn't see around the edges. My thoughts were being written with one hand, while in the other hand was a huge eraser. And that hand was erasing furiously all that was being written. Eventually, the first hand got tired and stopped writing. I mean you just stop thinking about the situation because you'd go crazy if you did. Besides, I knew—or believed then—that my parents would kill me if I told anyone what they did to me, and I thought they could read my mind.

The most effective way to keep a life-threatening secret is to forget the secret. And that is just what this woman did for many years until God brought her into a loving marriage, into a supportive church family, and into a counseling relationship where she felt safe. I agree with Gravitz and Bowden who have observed, "that in appropriate and safe settings, adult children begin to remember more and more of what happened to them as they become freer and freer from fear and denial."[8]

COUNSELING FOR PATIENCE

For adult children of alcoholics, eagerly seeking to reassemble the fragmented puzzle pieces of their pasts, the often slow process of remembering can be extremely frustrating. Some of them want to "walk in, be zapped, and walk out remembering everything," as one woman described it to me when she inquired about hypnosis. I realize there are differences of opinion among Christian mental health professionals regarding the use of hypnosis to activate repressed memories. I neither use nor recommend it.

Again, Psalm 51:6 provides guidance. After stating that God desires truth in our innermost beings, the second half of the verse promises that he will make us know wisdom "in the hidden part." I have found it helpful to encourage Christian adults raised in alcoholic homes to patiently trust God's timing in revealing memories and giving wisdom "in the hidden part." After painful memories have emerged, without exception, these adults have expressed the belief that they would not have been able to cope with the emotional upheaval if they had remembered everything at once. As the counselor models patient trust in God's timing, adult children of alcoholics will be increasingly able to rest in God's sovereign schedule for their recovery.

But what about the individuals who do not have significant memory gaps, or who have recalled their previously repressed memories? They struggle with painful feelings with which they need help.

TAKING TIME FOR THE PAIN

There is an old proverb which says, "The truth will make you free, but first it will make you miserable." So, yes, it really is necessary, and it really is safe to dethrone the tyranny of your past. No pain is so devastating as the pain a person refuses to face, and no suffering is so lasting as the suffering left unacknowledged.[9]

The theme song of adult children of alcoholics seems to be, *I Haven't Got Time For The Pain.*[10] To be sure, there is legitimate pain in coming out of denial and facing and sharing the truth about growing up in an alcoholic family. Adults from these families need to be encouraged repeatedly to pursue truth and take time for the pain that inevitably accompanies it. They need to be reminded that the alternative is to pursue the "folly of deceit" which prevents understanding and results in illegitimate pain.

Past Pain

As repressed memories begin to emerge, adult children of alcoholics may experience many painful emotions. Some of these adults abandon counseling during the initial discovery stage of their potential recovery because the truth is too painful to tolerate. This fact should not come as a surprise in light of Penfield's experiments using electrical stimulation to activate areas of the brain thought to store memories. Many of Penfield's adult subjects recalled memories of events from their early childhood with amazing clarity. However, as the research continued, an unexpected side effect was observed. As the subjects remembered an event, they experienced many of the emotions associated with the event. Several subjects refused to continue the experiment because some of the feelings were so painful.[11] They didn't have time for the pain.

In addition to the *past pain* of emerging memories and recognized truth about their childhoods, adult children of alcoholics also face the *present pain* triggered by coming out of denial and sharing the secret.

Present Pain

Chapter 4 cited reports of individuals who experienced emotional distress when they joined therapy groups for adult children of alcoholics. These adults were sharing the secret and feeling the pain which accompanies that process.

Feeling Disloyal and Aggressive. Many adult children of alcoholics believe themselves to be disloyal children when they begin to speak the truth about their families and parents. Women especially experience getting help for themselves as an aggressive act. At this stage of discovery, adult children of alcoholics need to be encouraged with the knowledge that they can speak the truth without dishonoring their parents, no matter how neglectful or abusive they were.

Feeling Responsible and Trapped. Some adult children of alcoholics have described a resistance to facing and sharing the truth because they feel trapped by recognizing their families' neediness. Their thinking goes like this: "If I see how bad it is, then I will *really* have to fix it!"

Feeling Orphaned and Abandoned. Chapter 4 examined the powerful fear of abandonment often experienced by adult children of alcoholics. Feelings of abandonment—of being left "high and dry" dangling from a pier—are activated frequently when adult children of alcoholics share the truth by revealing the family secret with a counselor or group. If the adult child is the only one in the family who has come out of denial and entered recovery, he or she has chosen to construct a new reality based on truth, not denial and deceit. Thus, these individuals have lost their bases of attachment to their families. They feel like orphans.

COUNSELING FOR TRUST

Adult children of alcoholics in the initial stage of dealing with past and present pain need to be supported emotionally and encouraged to trust God to meet their needs during the recovery process they are beginning. The following approaches have proven helpful:

1. Give counselees continuous reassurance that it is right for them to recognize and speak the truth.

2. Assign for meditation and memorization the Bible verses on truth discussed on page 108.

3. Have Christians from alcoholic homes do a topical study on truth and/or deceit.

4. Have them write out, sign, and date a contract with God to renounce deceit and to commit to "truth in the hidden parts."

5. Frequently remind counselees that you will help them work toward genuine forgiveness. Some Christian counselors prefer to begin with counselees by securing statements of intent to forgive everyone who has ever hurt them. Either way, raising

the issue of forgiveness at the outset frees Christian adult children of alcoholics to experience possibly guilt-inducing feelings of anger and abandonment, knowing they will move beyond those emotions into forgiveness.

6. Have counselees meditate upon and memorize verses like John 14:18 ("I will not leave you as orphans; I will come to you"), Hebrews 13:5b–6 ("For He Himself has said, 'I will never desert you, nor will I ever forsake you,' so that we confidently say, 'The Lord is my helper, I will not be afraid. What shall man do to me?'"), and others that address a sense of abandonment.

7. Address the codependent and irrational sense of responsibility for family members often seen in adult children of alcoholics. Here, as in all aspects of the recovery process, a psycho-educational approach is helpful.

8. Assign and/or provide materials on codependency and characteristics of adult children of alcoholics to augment information provided by the counselor. The Resources listed in Appendix A can be helpful in identifying appropriate materials.

9. Begin teaching counselees about respecting others made in the image of God by letting others be responsible for the consequences of their own actions.

10. Give permission to grieve childhood losses, and direct counselees to Psalm 27 and similar passages that offer comfort and encourage trust in God.

11. Encourage counselees to join a support group or therapy group for adult children of alcoholics. Ideally, this will be a group where Jesus Christ is acknowledged as the *Highest* Power. Unfortunately, there are very few of these groups in existence. You may want to start one, as has been done in the church I attend.

SHARING IN GROUPS

In leading groups for Christian adult children of alcoholics and groups for Christian incest survivors, I have observed a phenomenon that convinces me that revealing the family secret in a group is a powerful experience. Several of the group members were also in individual counseling with me. Nearly all of these individuals stated something similar to this: "It isn't that I didn't believe you when you said what I was feeling was natural for someone from a family like mine, or that I didn't believe the examples in the book you had me read. But it was such a relief to actually hear other people describe just exactly what I was feeling. It was so good to know I am not the only one."

Knowing you are "not the only one" is one of the major benefits of participation in groups. Hearing others describe feelings and experiences similar to yours *validates* and *normalizes* them. Well-organized and conducted groups may become new, healthier, surrogate families to their members. Of course there are some groups that are more effective and helpful than others, just as there are some counselors who are more effective and helpful than others.

In effective groups, participants can be "frogs." I mean they can be authentic and transparent and know they will be accepted "warts and all," just as they would be in functional families. Adult children of alcoholics often spend their lives pretending to themselves and others that they are princes and princesses, i.e., that they are perfect people raised in perfect castles. Support and therapy groups are gatherings of "frogs"— real, hurting people with real, painful problems. The very act of joining a group for adult children of alcoholics is a statement of truth about our "frogishness" and the "frogishness" of our families.

Christian counselors, people helpers, or pastors can begin a Christ-centered support group for adult children of alcoholics. Appendix 1 of this book includes information on a workbook integrating the Twelve-Step Program with Scripture. This workbook can be used for individual or group study. In addition, Appendix 3 contains a Christian adult children of alcoholics "growth group" format not based on the Twelve Steps of Alcoholics Anonymous. Appendix 3 also includes an adaptation of the list of characteristics of adult children of alcoholics. Regardless of the format used, groups provide support and encouragement as *discovering* adult children of alcoholics become *recovering* adult children of alcoholics.

SANCTIFICATION AND RECOVERY

The chart in figure 7–1 summarizes a conceptualization of the parallels between sanctification and recovery.

114

Parallels between Sanctification and Recovery

SALVATION		DISCOVERY
Freedom from the penalty of sin (spiritual death)		Freedom from the penalty of the past (personal death)
↓		↓
SANCTIFICATION		RECOVERY
Freedom from the power of sin (spiritual defeat)		Freedom from the power of the past (personal defeat)

Figure 7–1

In the spiritual realm, our recovery from the effects of sin begins with our salvation experience when we place our trust in the finished work of Jesus Christ at the cross, where he paid the sin debt we could never pay, and rescued us from the penalty of sin—spiritual death. In effect, our new birth is an experience of spiritual discovery that places us on a path of spiritual recovery from the power of sin with its spiritual defeat. This process of becoming more like Jesus is called sanctification. As we cooperate with the Holy Spirit's work in our sanctification process, we are increasingly free from the power of sin in our lives. However, we do not become totally free from the power of sin and completely like Jesus Christ while still in these bodies of flesh. In other words, we do not become "recovered sinners."

In the same way, on a personal plane, discovery is the initial experience of recognizing the truth about parental alcoholism that frees us from the penalty of the past—personal death. By personal death, I mean death to all that God intended us to be. Death to the person he created me to be. In this model, recovery is the lifelong process of becoming increasingly free of the power of the past with its personal defeats. These defeats include twisted God-concepts, mangled self-concepts, broken relationships, and crushed hopes. These areas of personal defeat are some of the recovery issues facing those of us raised in alcoholic homes.

| | Progression of Recovery Issues | | |
ISSUES	DISCOVERY	RECOVERY	MORE RECOVERY
GRIEVING	Identifying losses	Grieving past losses	Grieving current losses
ABANDONMENT	Recognizing I was abandoned	Talking about and grieving it	Increasingly know I can never be abandoned by God
CONTROL	Identifying	Beginning to let go	More trust in God's loving control
DISTRUST	Identifying	Trusting selectively	Trusting appropriately
RESPONSIBILITY FOR OTHERS	Identifying boundaries	Learning to set limits	Being responsible for self with clear boundaries
NEGLECTING OWN NEEDS	Realizing I have needs	Identifying needs	Getting needs met appropriately
ALL-OR-NONE THINKING	Recognizing both/ and choices	Identifying both/ and choices	Practicing both/ and choices
TOLERANCE FOR INAPPROPRIATE	Questioning what is appropriate	Learning what is appropriate	Usually knowing the appropriate

Figure 7–2

Progression of Recovery Issues

The following chart lists eight of the major recovery issues for adult children of alcoholics. It suggests the progressive transformation of these issues during the recovery process. Other clinicians have proposed similar recovery models and have included a category of "recovered" issues.[12] I believe that particular concept is as erroneous as that of "recovered alcoholic" or "recovered sinner."

THE BATTLE FOR TRUTH

In this chapter, we have explored one aspect of the recovery process of adult children of alcoholics. And we have considered ways counselors can help these adults as they risk revealing "the family secret" and learn to share the truth in the initial discovery stage. To summarize, counselors need to:

1. Focus on God's call for truth in every aspect of counselees' lives.

2. Encourage counselees' efforts to take responsibility for themselves and to relinquish responsibility for others.

3. Support counselees as they begin to experience past and present pain.

It is important to add that some adult children of alcoholics report feeling "stuck" during the discovery stage. That is, they seem able to go neither forward, because of intolerance of their increasing sense of isolation and abandonment, nor backward, because they cannot "unlearn" emerging truth. It is at this point of "stuckness" that adults from alcoholic families must wage mental warfare to hold onto their new realities.

In fact, the pivotal battle of recovery is fought in the mind-renewal arena. And in chapter 8, we turn to this subject of renewing the mind and learning more of the truth.

CHAPTER EIGHT

RENEWING THE MIND: LEARNING THE TRUTH

IN THE FIRST CENTURY, A.D., Epictetus said, "Men are disturbed not by things but by the views which they take of them." In the twentieth century, cognitive therapists like Albert Ellis and others have echoed this emphasis on thinking as the determinant of personal well-being.

However, long before Epictetus or Ellis, God told us our thinking shapes our behavior and emotions: ". . . For as he thinks within himself, so he is," declares Proverbs 23:7. What a sweeping statement! Think of it: Who I am is determined by how I think. Jesus reinforced this concept in Mark 7:20 when he said, ". . . it is the thought life that pollutes . . ." (LB). And in Matthew 15:18–19, Christ tell his disciples that words and behaviors are a product of that part of our inner being where thinking occurs.

The classic New Testament passage on the importance of thinking patterns is Romans 12:2. Here God clearly sketches his plan for our transformation process, and the emphasis is on thinking patterns. The verb tense in the Greek indicates continuous action.[1] A literal translation would be, ". . . but keep on being transformed by the continuous renewing of your mind. . . ." It is as if being sinful people raised by sinful parents in a sinful world produces a thinking disorder. And as an aspect of their sanctification, God calls his children to a lifelong process of mind renewal. The biblical concept of mind renewal corresponds to what psychologists call cognitive restructuring. This process of restructuring thinking patterns produces accompanying changes in emotions, actions, and relationships. If every Christian has a sin-based thinking disorder and needs mind renewal, surely Christians raised in alcoholic families, which are characterized primarily by thinking disorders, have this need.

A THINKING DISORDER

Dr. Stephanie Brown, founder of Stanford University's Alcohol Clinic, conceptualizes the issues of alcoholic family members primarily as a thinking disorder.

As alcoholism progresses, the alcoholic and *the family develop a thinking disorder* that explains increasing drinking and denies it at the same time. This disorder includes rationalization and denial, primitive cognitive defense mechanisms, and distorted logic that reverses cause and effect ("I drink because I have problems" rather than "The problems are the result of my drinking") and consistently distorts reality.[2]

Brown and others see the recovery process of adult children of alcoholics primarily as one of learning to think correctly about themselves, their families, and their world.

Miller and Ripper hold this view, and speak of an "internal deception functioning" which allows adult children of

119

alcoholics to distort reality, thus minimizing and rationalizing parental alcoholism and its effects.[3] "Internal deception functioning" has almost a biblical ring to it, echoing the truth that our deceitful hearts are the source of our polluted thoughts.

Whether from a secular or a scriptural perspective then, cognitive restructuring of distorted, deceptive thinking is central to the transformation process. The pivotal battle of recovery, and perhaps of sanctification, is fought in the mind-renewal arena, as we war to take "every thought captive to the obedience of Christ" who is Truth.[4]

Thought/FEELINGS AND THOUGHT/Feelings

We need a crucial reminder at this point. As noted in the introduction to Part III, thoughts and feelings are not separated neatly into two tidy bundles. They are connected and addressed simultaneously in the recovery processes of adult children of alcoholics. As we divide thoughts and feelings for convenience of discussion, we need to remember that some thoughts are more emotion-laden than others. That is, thoughts about parents are more charged with emotions than thoughts about ancient Mesopotamian monarchies. I call these relatively emotion-free thoughts THOUGHT/*feelings*. In contrast, there is usually a great deal of emotion attached to thoughts about our personal family history. These emotion-laden thoughts are *thought/*FEELINGS. It is far easier to be logical, honest, and open to change in the realm of THOUGHT/feelings than thought/FEELINGS. However, it is important to remember that when we are counseling for mind renewal with adult children of alcoholics, we are working in the realm of thought/FEELINGS.

LEARNING A NEW LANGUAGE

In chapter 4, we considered the fact that children do not have the same choices as adults. For example, children have no alternative to learning the language spoken in the family into which they are born. And the family language is more than mere words; it is the thinking patterns underlying the words. "But the things that proceed out of the mouth come from the heart," (the center of cognition in Hebrew thought, and similar to the New Testament word *mind*). This portion of Matthew 15:18 underscores the fact that words are the vehicle of expression by which thoughts are revealed.

Most parents teach their children a "thought language" which accurately reflects the realities of their environment with reasonable consistency. Their goal is to prepare the children to function successfully in life. Alcoholic and co-alcoholic parents teach their children a thought language which distorts and denies the realities of their environment in an effort to protect the parents from facing the problems in their own alcohol-dominated lives. Children in alcoholic families are taught a denial-based, thinking-disorder language that involves the very act of reasoning by requiring faulty construction of reality.

> Individuals must not only deny what they see, hear, feel, but they must also construct faulty explanations for what is really happening. Attachments in the alcoholic family are built on sharing the family's point of view—denying, to some degree, parental alcoholism and adapting the reasoning that explains it.[5]

Young children in alcoholic families have no language options. However, even when they learn about the thought languages of other families, they continue to "speak" their primary thought language because it is the basis of attachment to their family. Counselors must understand that helping adult children of alcoholics learn new ways of thinking about themselves, their families, and their other relationships is like teaching them a foreign language. But it is even more complicated than that.

When learning Latin in high school and French in college, I was not asked to disavow and replace major portions of my primary language. But when working with adult children of alcoholics, we must ask just that. Obviously, this is a formidable task. Children learn languages with facility. But for adults, it requires persistent and patient practice. Although a slow and painful process, it can be done. Knowledgeable, empathic counselors and/or effective support groups can help.

COUNSELING FOR TRUTH

Before we can replace misbeliefs with truth, we need to identify the childhood messages and beliefs in adults from alcoholic families. As we have noted, this process of replacing misbeliefs with truth is what the Bible calls mind renewal in Romans 12:2, and what psychologists term cognitive restructuring. Counselors can assist adult children of alcoholics in their mind renewal by using some of the following ideas.

1. *Review and use some of the counseling strategies presented in chapter 7.* For example, we must have a continual commitment to truth throughout the counseling work. Also, it is essential that adult children of alcoholics learn about the dynamics of alcoholic family systems. Reading assignments on that topic are an important part of the counseling process. Appendix A contains a list of books that would be especially useful.

2. *Become familiar with the basic principles of cognitive therapy.* Christian psychologist William Backus has written *Telling the Truth to Troubled People* to provide this information for pastors, Christian lay-counselors, and other nonprofessional helpers.[6]

3. *Assign books that teach basic concepts of cognitive reconstruction (mind renewal).* Fortunately, there are several excellent books by Christian psychologists.[7] All of these volumes are packed with Scripture.

4. *Have counselees list rules and messages that governed their families.* Have them include both spoken and unspoken rules and messages on the lists. From your knowledge of alcoholic family systems, you may want to suggest additional childhood messages if the list is very short. Sometimes one or two suggestions trigger a counselee's awareness of additional messages. These lists provide adult children with insight into the foundations of their current misbeliefs.

5. *Help counselees see both the present effects of childhood misbeliefs and the need for mind renewal.* As adult children of alcoholics learn more about the effects of parental alcoholism, they begin to realize their parents taught them much that was not true. These adults are encouraged by the scriptural promise of mind renewal. Have Christian adult children meditate upon

Romans 12:2. It can also be useful to have them do a study of the major words in that verse and write their own commentary on it.

6. *Emphasize the value of the Bible as the only perfectly unmarred mirror into which we can look to see God, ourselves, and others.* James 1:23–25 uses a mirror metaphor and speaks of blessings for those who look intently into "the perfect law, the law of liberty," i.e., the Scriptures.

7. *Teach "thought stopping and substitution."* There are various thought-stopping techniques; but one of the simplest and most effective uses three-by-five cards. On one side of the card, have counselees write the word STOP in large, capital letters. Some people like to write it in red. On the other side, a counselee should write a Bible verse or passage that refutes the misbelief he or she is seeking to eliminate. Adult children should keep the cards with them at all times. Changing thinking patterns is hard work requiring many repetitions of the truth. As adult children identify more misbeliefs, they will make more cards.

8. *Identify other sources of new messages and beliefs.* Counselees can gain accurate information from effective support groups, from good books on the topic, and—of course—from *you* as you become increasingly knowledgeable. All of these sources are valuable, although all are imperfect—in contrast to Scripture.

9. *Introduce the concept of learning a new language.* This imagery has proven helpful to counselees as they struggle with the slow process of changing the thinking patterns of a lifetime. This metaphor also provides another perspective on the value of support groups. After all, a second language is learned more quickly when we are around those who speak it.

10. *Provide supportive encouragement by use of Scripture.* Romans 15:4 says perseverance and "the encouragement of the Scriptures" lead to hope, and adult children of alcoholics need hope. Also, direct counselees to use the Scriptures regularly to discover for themselves the encouragement they offer.

11. *Introduce the "new family history" assignment.* Have adult children of alcoholics begin to reconstruct their family story based on the new truths they are learning. It is helpful to have them write out their revised, factual family history.

Pastors and counselors will need to assist in this process because childhood misbeliefs cloud clear perceptions of alcoholic family systems.

These eleven ideas provide general guidelines for counseling with adult children of alcoholics as they learn to identify and discard misbeliefs. Now we will examine ten common misbeliefs noted in many of these adults and discuss specific counseling strategies for each.

COMMON MISBELIEFS

The misbeliefs described here are symptomatic of the thinking disorders typically characterizing adult children of alcoholics. These ten statements, in effect, articulate the denial-based, thought-disorder language learned by children in alcoholic families. Some of them will be described briefly and elaborated upon in later chapters; others will be discussed in more depth. Each is rooted in childhood experiences in alcoholic families. Each needs to be recognized for the lie it is and replaced with the truth.

1. *"I caused it, therefore I should control and/or cure it."* The "IT," of course, is parental alcoholism. The roots of this misbelief rest in the soil of infantile grandiosity. Psychologists use that term to describe an infant's perception of himself or herself being the omnipotent center of the universe. An infant cries, and a caregiver materializes, as if by magic. In the magical thinking of very young children, they have enormous, frightening powers. This fantasy is corrected by reality in most children as they grow older. However, this fantasy flourishes in alcoholic families because it is nurtured by the need to deny and distort reality to relieve the alcoholic parent(s) of responsibility for drinking. Children in alcoholic families are often overtly or covertly blamed for causing parental alcoholism. In most of these children, this misbelief is in full bloom by adulthood.

Seixas and Youcha identify this cognitive distortion as the myth believed most widely and clung to most tenaciously by adult children of alcoholics.[8] They tell of a young college student who recalled that when he was a young boy he saved all his pennies, "convinced that if he could buy his mother a bottle of her favorite perfume she would be so pleased she would stop drinking."[9] Adults raised in alcoholic homes have learned that purchasing an alcoholic parent's favorite toiletry will not produce a cure. Yet many adult children still believe they are responsible for finding the magical substance that will.

A constant flow of truth is needed to erode this misbelief. Reading about the issues of adult children of alcoholics and participating in good support groups are part of the erosion process. Counselors will need to be alert for the lingering effects of this misbelief.

2. *"I caused my parents to treat me as they did."* This misbelief accompanies the previous one. In more detail, it goes like this: "I not only caused my parent(s) to drink, I caused them to neglect and/or abuse me. If I had been as good as other children, my parents would have treated me as well as other parents treat their children."

Again, this myth is founded on the magical thinking of early childhood. It is enlarged by the dynamics of shame-based alcoholic family systems and alcoholic and co-alcoholic parents' needs to deny responsibility for their behavior.

Why would adults blame themselves for the dishonoring and dehumanizing treatment experienced as children at the hands of their abusive alcoholic parents? Brown suggests one answer is the child's critical need for attachment to parental figures.

. . . Children will alter their perceptions, registering an abusive parent as good, because the child must rely on that same parent for comfort. The need for attachment overrides all else.[10]

Gravitz and Bowden offer a similar explanation. These authors have stated that children need to believe they exercise some influence over their environment because it is too frightening for them to consider that nothing they can do will make a difference. They desperately need to convince themselves that if only they were different than they are, their parents would stop drinking, fighting, neglecting, and/or abusing them, and everything would be all right in their family. "So they began playing the 'if only' game very early in an attempt to adapt the world, their world, to their own safety and security needs."[11]

Brown, Gravitz, and Bowden all speak to the safety and dependency needs of children in alcoholic homes. These authors imply that when these children reach adulthood they continue to deny reality about parental responsibility for abusive behavior, because these adult children still need to remain in control and attached to the family.

Often, it is extremely difficult for adults raised in abusive alcoholic homes to acknowledge their parents' responsibility for the abuse. Many of these adults cling to the lie that, "I was a bad child—worse than other children—and deserved to be abused, therefore my parents were justified when they chose to abuse me. If I had been like other children, my parents would have treated my differently." Believing that appears to be easier than accepting the truth that, "No child deserves to be abused; therefore my parents were wrong when they chose to abuse me. My parents' choice to abuse me was a result of what was wrong with them, not a result of what was wrong with me." The lie preserves the illusion of control: "If I would have changed, I could have caused them to change their treatment of me."

Counselors need to help adult children of alcoholics replace that lie with the truth that their parents' treatment of them was beyond their control. However, this new truth is often resisted. Accepting this truth implies that if they were unable to control their worlds as children, these counselees are unable to completely control them now as adults. In addition, this thought/FEELING carries the emotional pain of grieving the loss of idealized parents. Clearly, with adults who were abused in alcoholic families, counseling needs to explore their pasts and connect them to their present struggles. Both patient support and empathic confrontation may be required as counselors assist in this phase of mind renewal.

3. *"If I trust anyone, I will be hurt."* Trusting others is often experienced as very dangerous by adult children of alcoholics because they perceive it as giving others control over them. Therapists working with these adults report hearing them say, "If I trust you, I will have to let down my guard, and then you can hurt me."[12]

Adult children of alcoholics need to be helped to learn to trust *appropriately.* Sometimes Christian adults from alcoholic homes think the Bible instructs believers to trust everyone immediately and completely. Since they experience themselves as distrusting,[13] they may believe they are failures. These Christians may be helped by showing them from Scripture that Jesus did not trust people immediately and completely.[14] Furthermore, that type of undiscerning trust denies the biblical view of humankind's "deceitful . . . and desperately wicked" hearts.[15] The concept of selective and appropriate trusting will be addressed in more detail in chapter 11's discussion of respectful relationships.

4. *"It is too awful; I am hopelessly ruined."* Adult children of alcoholics may become overwhelmed by all the new things they are learning. As they begin to recognize the effects of parental alcoholism on their lives, many see themselves as irreparably damaged and become discouraged. There can be thoughts of,"It's too much; there is no way I can make my life better."[16]

These thoughts reflect the all-or-nothing thinking pattern seen in most adult children of alcoholics. When overwhelmed with their sense of personal brokenness, these counselees need hope that they can change. They need encouragement from Scripture and from learning about the changes in other adult children of alcoholics. These counselees also are helped by learning that their sense of being hopelessly ruined is a normal part of the recovery process.

5. *"I don't have the right to get better if my family isn't getting better."* This misbelief is rooted in an impaired capacity to see oneself as separate from others in the family. When individual boundaries are weak, as they often are in alcoholic families, children are perceived—and perceive themselves—merely as extensions of their parents. If these children begin recovery as adults, they may battle this misbelief, especially in the early stages. Chapter 13 focuses on new family relationships, including the need to lovingly detach if the family is still in denial.

6. *"I don't need any help from anyone."* Individuals who cling to this misbelief think getting help is a sign of weakness. In alcoholic families, problems were denied. Alcoholic and co-alcoholic parents often worked very hard, repeating the same ineffective

attempts to change their situations, rather than reach out for help. To these individuals, seeking help meant acknowledging problems. One of the core beliefs of alcoholics is that they can handle their drinking by self-control without any help from others.[17] Their adult children frequently believe they can recover from the effects of parental alcoholism without any help from others.

Adult children of alcoholics appear to be willing to seek counseling at least as often, if not more often, than adults from nonalcoholic families.[18] However, they usually present depression, low self-esteem, marital conflicts, or other issues as the primary problem. The "I-don't-need-any-help" misbelief may not surface until their presenting problems are connected to their alcoholic family backgrounds. Issues of family loyalty are involved, and counselors need to be sensitive to the mental warfare experienced by these counselees as they enter the mind-renewal process.

The concept of mental warfare is presented in 2 Corinthians 10:4–5, and that metaphor is an apt one for this mind-renewal process. It may be helpful to direct Christian adults from alcoholic families to that passage, and remind them that the Bible extols the wisdom of using counselors when engaged in warfare.[19] Also, Proverbs 12:15 says ". . . a wise man is he who listens to counsel."

7. *"Now that I see my issues, I must change immediately."* Adult children of alcoholics can often be heard saying something like this. "Okay, I see where some of that stuff applies to me. Tell me what to do to change it as soon as possible. I just got engaged and want to be over all this before I get married in four months." This comment reflects the adult child's much cherished, but unrealistic, expectation for a speedy recovery.

Adult children of alcoholics need to become familiar and comfortable with the word "process." To some, it is almost as though that word is obscene. They sometimes facetiously refer to process as the "P-word." Counselors need to help these adults cultivate a process orientation to recovery, and to life. Recovery, like sanctification, is not an event. Recovery is a process. And, "Recovery moves at your pace; you do not move at recovery's pace."[20]

8. *"I must get cured and be perfect."* This misbelief reveals the pervasive all-or-nothing thinking seen in adult children of alcoholics. This misbelief is the flip side of the I-am-hopelessly-ruined misbelief. On a scale of one to ten, all-or-nothing thinking allows only categories of one and ten. There are no categories in between. In reference to this issue, Claudia Black has said that recovery is learning the numbers two through nine.[21]

The I-must-get-cured-and-be-perfect misbelief may emerge after a few weeks or months of counseling, reading books, and/or attending support groups. Typically, adult children of alcoholics believe they should be cured—problem-free—after that. As Gravitz and Bowden have noted,

> If they have not achieved full recovery by this point, they feel they have not achieved anything. If everything is not all right (which it never is), everything is all wrong! Thinking this way is falling into the trap of all-or-none functioning.[22]

Counselors need to be alert to small changes in adult children of alcoholics and point them out frequently, because these adults have difficulty with the concept of *some*— that is, adult children rarely think in terms of *some* change. They tend to think only in terms of total, complete change versus no change at all. And, of course, only total, complete change is perceived as acceptable. As a result, these adults may fail to give God thanks and to validate themselves for the progress they are making. This failure leads to discouragement and a sense of hopelessness. Consistent emphasis on a process orientation to recovery is necessary to challenge this I-must-get-cured-and-be-perfect misbelief.

9. *"I cannot deny anyone anything."* Again, all-or-nothing thinking is reflected in this misbelief. Many adult children of alcoholics believe they have to give and do anything anyone asks of them or they are totally selfish. In this thinking pattern, there are only two categories: denying nothing (a ten) or being completely selfish (a one). There is nothing in between—no options numbered two through nine. As children, adults from alcoholic families learned that the needs and desires of their parents always superseded their own. They may even have been labeled

"selfish" when they expressed legitimate childhood needs. As adults, they find it difficult to set personal boundaries which allow them to choose to do some things for some people rather than to try to do *everything* for everyone.

This misbelief is particularly powerful in Christian adults from alcoholic families. They often distort the New Testament concept of *agape* love, which seeks the welfare of the other,[23] into a kind of "sloppy agape" which seeks to make everyone happy. In relationships with non-Christians, agape love would seek to guide them to a saving faith in Jesus Christ. That is their greatest need, no matter what other problems are in their lives. Frequently, agape love includes refusing to solve others' problems, because people do not come to Christ without a sense of their neediness. And when interacting with Christians, agape love is expressed in a way that would move them toward being "conformed to the image of [God's] Son."[24]

Codependent approval-seeking is the faulty foundation of "sloppy agape." Counselors need to empathically confront adult children of alcoholics with this truth. Direct counselees to the Gospels where, "there were times when Jesus put His own needs for rest and food ahead of ministering to others."[25] The effects of this "I-cannot-deny-anyone-anything" will be discussed further in chapter 11, which describes respectful relationships.

10. *"I have to be in control."* The unabridged version of this misbelief goes something like this. "I have to be in control of myself and everything else or my world will fall apart."[26] This misbelief is more than an expression of a selfish desire to have things one's own way. Controlling is a compulsion to keep tight reins on the awareness and expression of thoughts, feelings, and behaviors. For adult children of alcoholics, it is not that being in control makes them feel happy, it makes them feel safe. The basic issue is safety; therefore the need to give up control may be the most frightening recovery issue faced by adult children of alcoholics.

The control compulsion is expressed in the need of adult children of alcoholics to direct, supervise, regulate, or legislate their own and others' behavior. This compulsion is also seen in their discomfort with surprises, uncertainty, and strong feelings—their own or those of others.

Having gone through childhood with little or no control, it is as if adult children have silently vowed, "Never again." As they enter adulthood, the need to control what happens becomes paramount.

Black distinguishes "external controllers" from "internal controllers."[27] External controllers need to control people and situations to bring more consistency and sense of order to their lives. For example, one adult child reported that it was crucial to him to get his father's car in the garage as soon as possible after his father had driven it across the front yard. "If the neighbors saw Dad's car in the flower bed, they would think there was something wrong with our family or that my father was a drunk." Internal controllers control by diminishing awareness of personal needs and by withholding feelings. The message to themselves is, "I don't have any needs and I don't have any feelings about not getting them met." A child in an alcoholic home may give up trying to heal the family's pain by controlling Dad's drinking. However, personal pain can be masked and control maintained by believing he or she does not need a father who is sober enough to be interested in his child's activities. "And, what's more, I don't care about Dad never coming to any of my ballgames. It doesn't bother me." Black suggests that internal control is operating even without visible external control.

It is important for counselors to realize that the all-or-nothing thinking pattern of adult children of alcoholics makes the idea of giving up control a terrifying prospect. They tend to think in dichotomous categories of being totally in control or totally out of control. Pastors and counselors need to introduce the word "some" into the vocabularies of these adults. In other words, they need to help adult children of alcoholics learn that there are additional alternatives to giving up *all* control or giving up *no* control. Encourage them to begin giving up *some* control in the least threatening areas of their lives. For example, they could let someone else plan the menu for the next church social. Help them see that giving up *some* control provides more options and choices. A less control-oriented lifestyle also enables adult children to experience more energy, creativity, and relaxation.

This I-must-be-in-control misbelief is founded on the illusion that we have the power to control other people and all our circumstances. In reality, we can only *influence* others (with the exception of young children and impaired adults), and our power to control circumstances is limited. When counselors challenge this misbelief with truth about the illusion of control, most adult children of alcoholics will acknowledge that it is irrational. Most will quickly add, however, "But I feel so strongly that I have to be in control that the thought of not being in control scares me to death." Clearly, this misbelief is a thought/ FEELING that will not be changed easily or rapidly.

Ultimately, the compulsion to control is a spiritual matter. Christians raised in alcoholic families struggle with their controlling tendencies and their desires to trust the control of a sovereign, loving God. They may express this struggle with comments like these: "I know God is loving, but I have a hard time trusting him. After all, if he is sovereign—and I know the Bible teaches he is—he allowed all the chaos and pain in my family. If I stop trying to control everything, what guarantee do I have that I won't experience similar or worse pain?" Counselors must be prepared to discuss the knotty issue of God's sovereignty and the existence of evil.[28]

PRACTICING THE NEW LANGUAGE

Throughout this chapter, cognitive restructuring or mind renewal has been compared to learning a second language. As noted earlier, it is complicated and difficult because it requires purposely forsaking much of one's primary language.

The mind-renewal process begins with recognizing old misbeliefs and learning new ways to think correctly. It continues as adult children of alcoholics are helped to practice new, healthier, Christ-honoring choices. One of these choices, described in chapter 9, is learning to experience feelings that were numbed in childhood.

CHAPTER NINE

RECLAIMING THE EMOTIONS: LEARNING TO FEEL

"ALL OF OUR SYMPTOMS ARE FEELING DISEASES," declare Friel and Friel.

Our symptoms are unhealthy mechanisms that we use to keep from feeling our feelings. They smother, hide, distort and mix up our feelings. They turn fear and sadness into rage. They create depression from anger; fear from loneliness. In many cases, they cause a unique distortion in which the rich, full range of normal human emotions is channeled into one or two overpowering feelings.[1]

What are feelings? And why are they so threatening to most adult children of alcoholics?

FEELINGS

Psychologists generally use three terms for feelings. "Emotion" is a broad term which includes feeling, the accompanying biophysiological state, and even underlying chemical changes. "Affect" is a term introduced by psychoanalysts that is used to describe the dominant emotional tone of a person as others perceive it. And "feeling" is the subjective awareness of our own emotional states.[2]

Ideally, our feelings—the experiencing of our emotions—and our authentic emotional conditions would be congruent. For example, we would match the painful emotion of grief with a subjective awareness of that grief. And we would allow ourselves to mourn. Ideally, we would know the full range of human emotions. We would experience subjective awareness of them, and appropriately express them. Clearly, this ideal has a biblical basis in both the Old and New Testaments.

A BIBLICAL BASIS FOR EXPERIENCING EMOTIONS

Ecclesiastes 3:4 paints an emotional panorama by declaring there is "a time to weep, and a time to laugh; A time to mourn, and a time to dance." Laughing and dancing are expressions of great joy, as weeping and mourning are expressions of deep grief. And David, the man "after God's own heart," displayed authentic awareness of these extreme ends of the emotional continuum. Perhaps the clearest expression of David's capacity to congruently experience and express great joy is found in the sixth chapter of 2 Samuel, which describes David's bringing the ark of God into Jerusalem in fulfillment of his long-cherished desire. Verse 12 speaks of David's "gladness," and verse 14 describes him "dancing before the Lord with all his might." In striking contrast to this joyful scene, we see David "deeply moved" with grief, weeping, and crying out in soul-deep despair as he mourned the death of his rebel son, Absalom.[3]

The New Testament also speaks to the full range of human emotions in Romans 12:15 by admonishing us to, "Rejoice with those who rejoice, and weep with those who weep." And David's son, Jesus Christ, clearly exhibited the capacity to authentically experience and express emotions. We are told that Jesus "rejoiced greatly" at the good report of the seventy men he had sent out to proclaim the kingdom of God.[4] And although the Gospels do not say specifically that Jesus smiled and laughed, it is inconceivable that children would have come to him so eagerly if he had not. A different emotional tone is sounded as Jesus anguished over Jerusalem's rejection of him,[5] wept at Lazarus' tomb,[6] and "deeply grieved" in Gethsemane.[7]

FEAR OF FEELINGS

Scripture portrays the full panorama of emotions as acceptable when appropriately expressed. Functional families also permit the appropriate expression of a broad range of feelings. In chapter 2 we discussed the contrast between that freedom to authentically experience all emotions and the unspoken, rule-bound fear of feelings that prevails in alcoholic families. This difference was depicted in continua comparing the range of acceptable feelings in functional and alcoholic families. In our present examination of feelings, it will be helpful to contrast the continua again in figures 9–1 and 9–2. As you may recall, the range of acceptable feelings that can be expressed appropriately is represented by solid lines, and unacceptable emotions by dotted lines.

In chapter 2, we noted that it was reasonable to assume members of alcoholic families are rarely, if ever, genuinely euphoric, although they might experience occasions of very pleasant emotions. A third continuum is presented again in figure 9–3 to illustrate the range of feelings probably experienced in most alcoholic family systems.

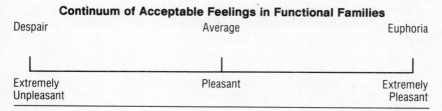

Continuum of Acceptable Feelings in Functional Families

Despair	Average	Euphoria

Extremely Unpleasant	Pleasant	Extremely Pleasant

Figure 9–1

Continuum of Acceptable Feelings in Alcoholic Families

Despair   Average   Euphoria

Extremely   Pleasant   Extremely
Unpleasant   Pleasant

Figure 9–2

As we noted previously when comparing the continua illustrating acceptable and probable feelings in alcoholic families, there is little overlapping of the solid lines. That is, there is a narrow range of emotions that are both acceptable and probable in alcoholic families.

We began this chapter by asking two questions about feelings: What are they, and why are they so threatening to adult children of alcoholics? Thus far we have attempted to answer the first question by examining psychological definitions of feelings and related terms and by exploring biblical patterns of emotional expression. Figures 9–2 and 9–3 help us answer the second question. Adults raised in alcoholic homes frequently experience feelings as threatening because, as children, they learned that most feelings were unacceptable. And expression of those unacceptable feelings often brought loss of parental affection and possible punishment because it failed to validate the "problem-free-family" myth.

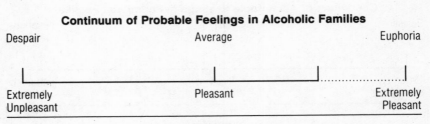

Continuum of Probable Feelings in Alcoholic Families

Despair   Average   Euphoria

Extremely   Pleasant   Extremely
Unpleasant   Pleasant

Figure 9–3

What did these children do with emotions such as fear, anger, and sadness, which fell outside the acceptable range? They learned to "smother, hide, distort, and mix up" their feelings as suggested above by Friel and Friel. The smothering and hiding of emotions is what I referred to as "affective anesthesia." This produces the emotional numbness seen in most adult children of alcoholics. After all, what is the best way for a child to avoid jeopardizing his or her basis of attachment to the family by expressing unacceptable feelings? The answer is: Stop experiencing those feelings. The logic is irrefutable. "I can't express an unacceptable feeling if I don't experience it."

EMOTIONAL LEPROSY

Chapter 4 introduced the concept of emotional leprosy by comparing it with physical leprosy. We noted that just as leprosy (Hansen's disease) destroys the body's ability to register pain, growing up in alcoholic families may damage the mind's ability to experience feelings—especially unacceptable feelings. Adults raised in these families frequently are described as emotional repressers.

Recent research with people who repress their emotions suggests there may be a physiological basis for emotional leprosy just as there is for Hansen's disease.

The ability to tune out feelings like anger and anxiety is reflected in brain function. A recent study of stiff-upper-lip types found they had a lag in the time it took certain information to get from one hemisphere of the brain to the other. The lag was only for disturbing messages, not for neutral ones. . . . *Although experts believe that the represser personality is rooted in psychological experiences of childhood, the findings on brain function provide a tangible marker of the syndrome. In effect, the brain hampers the conscious registering of negative emotions.*[8]

Certainly, one of the "psychological experiences of childhood" deemed foundational to the "emotional leprosy syndrome" could be a child's need to preserve his or her basis of attachment to the alcoholic family by expressing only acceptable emotions—even in times of extreme chaos or violence. The results of the study summarized above suggest that what begins as a parental demand may become an altered pattern of brain functioning. And that pattern of functioning inhibits the registering of negative, painful emotions just as leprosy destroys physical pain sensors.

RECLAIMING LOST EMOTIONS

The effects of emotional leprosy and Hansen's disease, or physical leprosy, are similar in another way. Both result in the loss of parts of the afflicted individual. Philip Yancey tells of a leprous baby who tragically chewed off her own finger because she felt no pain and had no awareness that the finger was part of her body.[9]

Many adult children of alcoholics have lost parts of their emotional selves. Friel and Friel, among others, have noted that these adults exhibit a distortion of emotional expression "in which the rich, full range of normal human emotions is channeled into one or two overpowering feelings."[10] These authors have observed that sadness, fear, loneliness, and shame "all get thrown into the pot together and get expressed as anger."

> In this same way, feelings of tenderness, softness, warmth, safety, closeness and sensuality all get thrown into one pot and get expressed as lust, which is why the spouses of all kinds of addicts say that their sex is great sometimes, but that they feel lonely and empty in the relationship nonetheless.[11]

There is nothing wrong per se with anger. And certainly there is nothing wrong with spouses feeling strong sexual desire for each other. However, if these two feelings are the only ones ever experienced, then something is wrong. Scripture clearly teaches that human beings were created to feel more than just these two emotions.

In part, counseling adult children of alcoholics is a process of helping them reclaim disowned emotions and learn to experience the full range of human feelings. The remainder of this chapter will present some general considerations and guidelines for this reclaiming process.

UNDERSTANDING AND COUNSELING AVOIDANCE OF FEELINGS

Cermak and Brown,[12] Gravitz and Bowden,[13] and others have identified avoidance of feelings as a core issue for adult children of alcoholics. These adult children typically hold a basic belief that feelings are bad and dangerous. Pastors and counselors working with these adults need to understand this.

As we have seen, in alcoholic families children's expressions of feelings often are met with censure and rejection. These children are taught very early that they must hide their feelings to minimize conflicts. They soon learn to disown and deaden feelings. After all, what good are they? Feelings just cause trouble for them and for the family. But avoidance of feelings is more than just a matter of personal comfort; it is often experienced as a life-and-death issue of personal safety.

Feelings as Dangerous

Gravitz and Bowden have noted that in many alcoholic families, the expression of strong emotions like anger often result in immediate, destructive actions.

> The very idea of having a strong feeling is equated with acting out that feeling. Instead of looking at feelings as a *potential* impetus to behavior, children of alcoholics see feelings as a direct immediate *cause* of behavior. In the midst of all this chaos and confusion, they may want to run to their parents, throw their arms around them and weep, but they know that it would not be safe. They cannot even talk about what happened! They know that in order to live in this family—and a five or even ten-year-old cannot say, "To heck with this! I'm going to pack my bags and find another family to live with,"—they *must* ignore their feelings. Shock, anger, terror, or guilt are so scary, so dangerous, so unacceptable, that the best way to deal with them is just not to acknowledge them. Instead, they must be buried deep inside.[14]

At the risk of belaboring the point, people helpers must grasp the fact that adult children of alcoholics experience feelings not so much as an inconvenience but as a threat. Old, childhood fear is involved. This is not the strong emotion or feeling of fear, but the fear of feeling a strong emotion. Counselors need to understand that feelings are perceived as dangerous by many adults raised in alcoholic homes. We need to help these adults recognize the defenses frequently employed to protect against the threat of experiencing authentic emotions. This recognition is a prerequisite to relinquishing emotional anesthetics.

Defenses against "Dangerous" Feelings

Claudia Black recommends asking adult children of alcoholics three questions early in the counseling process. Black suggests counselors ask:

1. What are the two or three feelings that are easiest for you to share?

2. What are the most difficult feelings for you to experience and share?

3. What do you do to defend yourself against experiencing those difficult feelings?[15]

Black believes it is important to address the issue of defenses against feelings because adult children of alcoholics, and others who repress (unconsciously block) feelings, often use addictive behaviors to anesthetize their emotions. These addictions serve as defenses against the threat of consciously feeling unacceptable emotions. At the earliest stirrings of disowned and "dangerous" emotions, repressers experience increased stress. To reduce this stress, they engage in the addictive behavior. It may be addiction to an illegal substance like cocaine, or it may be a legal and socially acceptable addiction to work.

Habitual abuse of substances like alcohol and other drugs has been viewed traditionally as addictive behavior. Recently, other behaviors such as eating disorders, overspending, excessive television viewing, and exercise obsession have been considered addictions. These behaviors have many of the characteristics of drug addictions. For example, these behaviors alter the mood of the "user." Frequently there is increasing preoccupation with the addictive behavior. Tolerance may develop requiring larger and larger "doses" of the behavior to produce the desired mood swing. In addition, despite feelings of guilt and shame and promises to change, adult children continue to use addictive behaviors to cope with the threat of feeling unacceptable emotions.

The triggering event may be external, such as conflict in a valued relationship, or it can be within the individual. In fact, the painful and threatening feelings of shame, guilt, and powerlessness that accompany the addictive behavior may serve to reactivate this cyclical process. From our knowledge of children in alcoholic families, we have learned that feelings of guilt, shame, and powerlessness were their constant companions. However, these internal, emotional companions were too frightening for children to face without adult support and comfort. And since adults in alcoholic homes are usually unavailable to provide support and comfort, those emotions seem "dangerous." These "dangerous" feelings and the resulting "defending addictions" become a cycle, as diagrammed in figure 9–4.

To be effective with adult children of alcoholics, counselors need to be able to identify the addictive behavior(s) these counselees employ to defend against authentic emotions perceived.

In addition to using addictive behaviors to numb unacceptable feelings, adult children of alcoholics also use crises and

Cycle of "Dangerous" Feelings and Defending Addictions

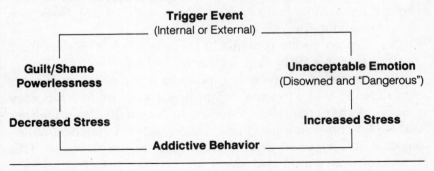

Figure 9–4

relationship addictions such as codependent relationships. Staying absorbed in taking responsibility for someone else's life distracts adult children from experiencing their emotions. And surviving repeated crises in their own or other lives serves the same purpose. Counselors need to understand—and help adult children see—this connection between codependency, crisis orientation, and their functions as emotional anesthetics.

The use of defending addictions, codependent relationships, and crises to anesthetize unacceptable feelings is an exercise in self-protection for adult children of alcoholics. However, they often believe they also are protecting their parents and family from the anger and other "dangerous" feelings they know are shelved in the emotional deepfreeze. A compassionate, knowledgeable people helper can provide the support and encouragement adult children will need as they begin to thaw long-frozen feelings. An important part of that support will come in the form of repeated assurances that, "If you experience intense emotions you do not have to be destructive and you will not go crazy."

"The Feelings Are Thawing and the Dam Is Breaking"

After several weeks of counseling and attending a support group for adult children of alcoholics, Liz was agitated and upset. "I feel like I've had this enormous reservoir of frozen feelings behind a big, thick dam. Now the feelings are thawing and the dam is breaking. I'm feeling all these different, conflicting, confusing feelings I've never had before. Does this mean I'm going crazy?"

"No," her counselor replied, "it means you are experiencing a lot of different, conflicting, confusing feelings."

Liz's counselor went on to explain to her that what she was experiencing was a normal, appropriate part of her recovery process. As her counselor continued to "normalize" her feelings and explain how childhood prohibitions against "unacceptable" emotions affect us as adults, Liz began to visibly relax. This counselor understood that there are several specific strategies that help adult children as they begin to experience a broader range of emotions.

COUNSELING FOR AUTHENTIC EMOTIONS

The following counseling guidelines blend strategies of secular clinicians with interventions developed to meet the special needs of Christian adults raised in alcoholic families.

1. *Explore parental and family expression of emotion.* The purpose of this looking back is not to blame, but to understand. Adult children may be helped by charting intergenerational family patterns of emotional expression. This chart can take the form of a modified genogram similar to those used by family therapists. Figure 9–5 is an example of an abbreviated family-feeling chart.

As noted, figure 9–5 is only an abbreviated version of a family-feeling chart. Counselor and counselee need to work with a very large sheet of paper to fully chart the intergenerational family-feeling patterns. For example, figure 9-5 does not include aunts and uncles and great-grandparents.

The family-feeling chart allows adult children to see patterns of emotional expression. This helps them identify the "imprisoning loyalties" that bind them to similar patterns in their present lives. Identification and insight do not bring change automatically, but they prepare the path for it.

Family-Feeling Chart

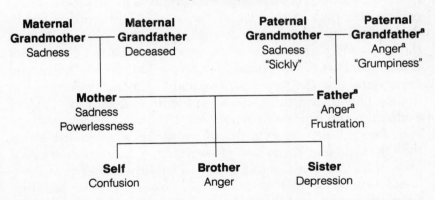

Denotes alcohol abuser, and the emotion(s) typically expressed when this person is intoxicated.

Figure 9–5

2. *Identify childhood messages about feelings.* With information gained from books, seminars, and other sources, counselors will be able to help adult children identify childhood messages about emotional expression. Identifying these childhood messages provides a context for change as these adults struggle to experience authentic emotions.

3. *Identify current misbeliefs about feelings.* "Feelings are dangerous." "Displaying emotion is for sissies." "Showing emotion gives others power over you." These are a few of the misbeliefs that adult children commonly identify. Often it is extremely difficult for these adults to recognize that statements such as these express erroneous beliefs, because, in most cases, *current* misbeliefs and *childhood* messages will line up neatly in matching pairs. Counselors can expect to meet resistance as they assist in this slow process; they will be helped by cultivating patience and by understanding that emotional expression is experienced as weak and dangerous by most adult children.

4. *Give permission to discard misbeliefs.* This hardly seems worth mentioning but is essential in the recovery process. In reality, people helpers are giving permission for adult children to disobey some of their parents' spoken or unspoken rules from childhood. Again, issues of parental and family loyalty emerge.

Adults from alcoholic homes must face the need to choose healthier patterns of emotional expression as part of their recovery process even if this causes them to feel like disloyal children. The entire concept of making choices different from those of one's parents is revolutionary to many adult children of alcoholics. Part of the counselor's role is to help adult children understand that they can still love and honor their parents even if they choose healthier, more authentic and biblical ways of evaluating and expressing emotions.

5. *Present biblical patterns of emotional expression.* Using the Old and New Testament passages cited earlier in the chapter, counselors can assign a study of biblical patterns of emotional expression to Christian adults from alcoholic families. Counselors may want to use their own versions of the continua in figures 9–1, 9–2, and 9–3 to reinforce the fact that Scripture presents appropriate expression of the full range of human emotions as right and good. Discuss with adult children that this

ideal is the pattern followed—imperfectly, to be sure—in well-functioning families. They usually must be reminded of this, because, concerning feelings, as in other areas of life, many adults raised in alcoholic homes do not know what constitutes normal, functional family living.

6. *Help develop a feeling vocabulary.* Many clinicians have noted that before they can help adult children of alcoholics identify their awakening feelings, the adult children need to develop a feeling vocabulary, because, in effect, many of these counselees are emotional illiterates.

Although counselors can give adult children a list of feeling words, it seems to be more helpful to encourage adult children to develop their own lists. If they are unable to expand their lists beyond three or four words—and this is sometimes the case—counselors may want to share their own, more complete lists. Figure 9–6 is an example of a feeling vocabulary chart that is divided into pleasant and unpleasant categories and into levels of intensity.

The sample feeling vocabulary chart shown in figure 9–6 may be expanded to include many other feelings. Adult children of alcoholics often perceive emotions only in extremes such as euphoria and despair. Therefore, a chart showing several levels of intensity helps to reduce their anxieties about experiencing emotions.

7. *Help identify feelings.* To help adult children of alcoholics learn to identify their feelings, Claudia Black suggests

Feeling Vocabulary Chart

Pleasant Feelings			Unpleasant Feelings		
Strong	Moderate	Mild	Mild	Moderate	Strong
loved	liked/cared for	regarded	unpopular	disliked	loathed
love	affection	friendliness	unfriendliness	aversion	hatred
infatuated	fondness	benevolence	disdain	envy	bitterness
vibrancy	excitement	alertness	lethargy	dejection	misery
euphoria	happiness	contentment	discontentment	sadness	despair
delight	gratification	relaxation	disappointment	frustration	rage

Figure 9–6

using a feeling list similar to the one shown in figure 9–7. She recommends that adult children take time daily or weekly to acknowledge to themselves when and where they experienced specific feelings. Black also suggests sharing these feelings with another person.[16]

The alphabetized feeling identification list may be enlarged to include many other emotions. When expanding the list, be sure to include varying levels of emotional intensity.

Making a collage is another method by which adult children of alcoholics may begin to identify their feelings. Using a large piece of poster board, adult children can paste on photographs, magazine illustrations, newspaper pictures, and other materials representing their lives in alcoholic families, their emotions during childhood, or their present lives and/or emotions. Counselors may want to assign this collage-making task as homework. Counselees then can share the completed collage in a support group or with their counselors. This sharing is an important aspect of the recovery process.

8. *Help express emotions appropriately.* As noted earlier, many adult children of alcoholics equate emotions with actions. Many think if they are angry they must scream or hit something or somebody. Or they believe that if they are unhappy they must leave a relationship or situation. Instead of viewing emotions as invariable causes of behavior, counselors need to help adult children learn to see emotions as potential precipitants of behavior.

Feeling Identification List

Feeling	When and Where	Feeling	When and Where
Angry	_____	Fearful	_____
Ashamed	_____	Frustrated	_____
Brave	_____	Guilty	_____
Confused	_____	Happy	_____
Discouraged	_____	Jealous	_____
Embarrassed	_____	Loving	_____
Encouraged	_____	Sad	_____
Excited	_____	Shy	_____

Figure 9–7

In addition, when emotions are expressed, they can be expressed appropriately. Adult children of alcoholics need to have this truth taught and modeled by pastors, counselors, and other helpers. Appropriate expression of emotions involves more than just non-violence. At the least, it also includes being respectful of others, self, and even of unpleasant feelings.

Expressing anger and other potentially destructive emotions can be a frightening challenge to adult children of alcoholics. Expressing them appropriately means more than not punching someone in the nose. Proverbs 18:21 describes another potentially deadly weapon: "Death and life are in the power of the tongue. . . ." Long after adult children have forsaken physical violence as a necessary outworking of frustration and anger, they may continue to struggle with verbal violence. Counselors need to emphasize that appropriate expression of emotions means respectful expression of emotions. And they will need to consistently model this.

When learning to express a broader range of emotions, adult children need assistance to learn respect for themselves as well as for others. Frequently it is difficult for an adult from an alcoholic home to experience and express feelings without a sense of shame and personal weakness. Support groups often prove to be effective resources in correcting this attitude. As adult children of alcoholics begin to openly share their feelings with others, the feelings are experienced as less threatening. And as these adults are accepted and affirmed when appropriately expressing authentic emotions, their sense of shame and weakness slowly dissipates.

Just as adult children may behave disrespectfully toward others when expressing anger, they tend to be disrespectful of themselves when experiencing and expressing sadness or fear. They may describe themselves as "weak and childish" or as "crybabies" in the presence of fear or sadness. Counselors and other people helpers can provide emotional support and comfort, and can remind counselees that Jesus wept. They can also present corrective, biblically-based truth to counter misbeliefs about feelings.

Finally, we can help adult children of alcoholics learn to respect their feelings—even the unpleasant and painful ones.

Claudia Black notes that while positive feelings are the ones people seek, negative feelings can be viewed as cues or signals that give us valuable information.

"When I feel sad, it may possibly mean I need support."
"When I am angry, I probably need to clarify my stance."
"When I am scared I need to let someone else know that."
By viewing the more painful feelings as signals it is easier to accept them and to utilize them constructively. By identifying feelings one is less apt to be overwhelmed by emotion and end up depressed, confused or enraged.[17]

C. S. Lewis once described pain as God's megaphone. Clearly, the shout of physical pain commands our attention. Similarly, painful feelings demand our awareness and direct us to consider needed changes in our mental, emotional, and spiritual lives.

RECLAIMING AUTHENTIC EMOTIONS

Children in alcoholic homes learn that their basis of attachment to the family is rooted in denial and distortion of facts and feelings. Truth and authentic emotions are casualties in such environments when children relinquish valuable parts of themselves—their perceptions, their preferences, and their genuine, congruent, authentic feelings.

Human beings possess an emotional nature. God created us so in his image. When a child is taught to deny and distort emotions, he or she is forced to abandon part of his or her God-designed personhood. Pastors, counselors, and other people helpers can help adult children of alcoholics reclaim their divinely ordained, but frequently disowned, emotions.

PART FOUR

COUNSELING RELATIONAL PROBLEMS

THE FIRST STAGE OF RECOVERY for adult children of alcoholics is a time of discovery when they learn to share the destructive family secret, to think and speak the truth, and to reclaim previously disowned feelings. The nucleus of this discovery process is breaking the denial of parental alcoholism and its effect. This is the necessary boost needed to launch the lifelong recovery process. It is necessary, but not sufficient. The new truths illuminated during the discovery phase must be applied to specific areas of life.

Chapters 10 through 13 will examine four specific problem areas encountered by most adult children of alcoholics. All four areas create difficulties for adult children. All four areas present counseling challenges that can be met with increased knowledge, consistent compassion, and spiritual resources. And all four areas deal with relationships. The first relationship is the one adult children have with themselves.

CHAPTER TEN

COUNSELING FOR AN ACCURATE IDENTITY

SCORES OF BOOKS HAVE BEEN WRITTEN on the related topics of self-esteem and identity (or self-image).[1] Many fine ones are authored by Christians who apply biblical truths to these subjects.[2]

This chapter will focus on the identity struggles that are seen in many adult children of alcoholics, as well as the concerns of some Christians about overemphasis on ourselves, which may result in selfishness and self-centeredness. Most of the chapter will explore misbeliefs about identity and counseling strategies for developing a healthy, biblically based self-image.

ACCURATE IDENTITY OR PRIDE?

An accurate, healthy identity includes self-acceptance founded on realistic self-knowledge. Paul addressed this in

Romans 12:3. The New English Bible renders this verse, in part, ". . . Think your way to a sober estimate [of yourself]. . . ." In this context, "sober" means accurate.

But, some may ask, doesn't all the self-focus necessary to gain realistic self-knowledge promote a selfish, self-centered life? The answer is similar to the response to the question of why we look into the past. As we noted, the danger in looking back is that we might do nothing more than play the "blame game." The value and purpose of looking at the past is to move beyond its bondage and glorify God more fully. The backward family-focus is a temporary phase in the process of moving toward a more complete God-focus in both the present and the future.

The self-focus of this chapter can be viewed as a temporary phase in the progression to comfortable self-forgetfulness. However, what is being called "comfortable self-forgetfulness" eludes many Christian adults raised in alcoholic homes. These adults are like severely sprained ankles swollen many times their normal size. In the pain of their brokenness, adult children loom so large on the horizons of their personal worlds that they obscure the person and purposes of their Savior. They cannot forget themselves, in a healthy and comfortable way, because the sense of shame and neediness throbs in every situation and relationship. They cannot decrease so that Jesus might increase because their self-hatred and self-rejection keep them engrossed in unending quests to "find" themselves and/or "prove" themselves.

Normally we do not live ankle-focused lives. When our ankles are healthy, we forget about them and simply use them to accomplish our goals. However, if you had a badly sprained ankle, no doubt you would become ankle-focused rather quickly. You would be wise to give your ankle special attention to speed the healing process and move beyond your temporarily ankle-focused life.

It could be argued that when we limp through life with twisted self-concepts we are invariably self-centered. In contrast, the Scriptures call Christians to be Christ-centered. This chapter has two major purposes which promote the goal of moving from self-centered to Christ-centered living. The first is to present the biblical basis of the life-transforming, accurate identity which belongs to every Christian, including adult children of alcoholics. The second goal is to present practical counseling suggestions to guide adult children through their temporary, change-oriented self-focus into the self-acceptance and self-forgetfulness which enables them to focus more fully on Jesus Christ.

ORIGINS OF FAULTY IDENTITY

As newborns, we are unable to answer several critical questions. Who am I? Am I lovable? Am I competent? So, at birth, all of us are enrolled in an incredibly effective education system known as the family.

Rosellini and Worden believe that for many adult children of alcoholics, the family is "P.S. Dread."

P.S. Dread can be best described as an informal pedagogical system promoting denial, lies, promises, selfish martyrdom, grandiose fantasies, despair and shame.[3]

Whether the family curriculum teaches predominantly truth (as in well-functioning families) or error, the captive young pupils thoroughly master its contents. Part of the family curriculum is designed to provide answers to questions of personal identity.

Parents as Teachers

Previously, parents were described as mirrors that reflect their child's self-concept to him or her. But parents are also teachers. Under the tutelage of their parents, children form their self-concepts in the informal classroom called home.

Parents teach both verbally and nonverbally, by "lecture," and by "demonstration." Alcoholic and co-alcoholic parents are not prepared for their teaching assignments because they lack healthy, accurate self-images of their own. This weakens their ability to instill that kind of self-image in their children. Archibald Hart has stated that:

There is overwhelming research evidence to show that a high level of self-esteem in the parents produces a more consistent atmosphere of unconditional love and acceptance, and this optimizes the development of high self-esteem in the children.[4]

Many psychological studies confirm the commonly held belief that loving acceptance of children by their parents correlates with positive self-concepts. However, in many alcoholic families, neither parent is emotionally available to provide loving acceptance. As we have seen from earlier chapters, alcoholic families tend to be rigid systems that offer little emotional nourishment to the children in them. Children receive verbal and nonverbal messages that say:

"You're in the way."

"Look at you, you're a mess."

"Why did you spill your milk? Can't you do anything right?"

"Okay, you got three A's, but what's this B for?"

"Can't you ever say anything that makes sense?"

"What's wrong with you?"

"You are so demanding."[5]

Eventually the "you are" becomes "I am," and parental messages are internalized. In effect, parents take up residence within the minds of their children. The old parental messages about the adult child's identity are replayed automatically in every situation that raises the "who-am-I?" question. This gives new definition to the term "instant replay."

Unrealistic Expectations

Thus far we have identified parental self-concepts and related treatment of children as major contributors to the children's self-images. One specific aspect of that treatment in alcoholic families is the pressure of unrealistic expectations.

Georgia described the effects of that pressure as she cried softly. "Somehow, I just always felt that I should have been born an adult. I mean I felt so guilty whenever I needed any help with anything. Mom was so exhausted and angry trying to clean up the messes my dad created with his drinking. My being a kid was a huge burden for her and the whole family."

Georgia and other adult children have described the subtle and not-so-subtle messages they received during childhood which said, "You are a mistake. You are not what we wanted or needed." Often, these messages are delivered in the form of age-inappropriate, unrealistic expectations. Again, the "you are" becomes "I am." For Georgia that meant that the internalized messages of her parents played over and over telling her that she was a mistake and that nothing she did was good enough.

Georgia's experience—so common to adult children of alcoholics—is a striking contrast from the Biblical ideal. In Colossians 3:21, fathers are told, ". . . do not exasperate your children, that they may not lose heart." Paul seems to be saying here that a parent's treatment of a child may have profound and negative effects. As a result, parents should avoid acts and attitudes that lead to those effects. Certainly, unrealistic parental expectations should be avoided for they cause children to "lose heart" and see themselves as never measuring up.

Interactions with Others and the Child's Part

But why, someone may ask, don't the children in alcoholic families see that their parents are treating them inappropriately? As the children get a little older, why don't they learn to disregard the crippling self-concept messages and view themselves more accurately?

Some do, if they have help. Not all adult children have equally faulty and unhealthy self-concepts. As noted in chapter 3, the presence of other, more affirming and appropriate caregivers moderates the negative effects of parental alcoholism on the children in the family. In effect, these other caregivers become surrogate parents who teach the child a more accurate identity curriculum. Apparently, the children transfer their need to maintain their bases of attachment from their biological families to their substitute families. As a result these children are able to learn to see themselves more realistically.

But what of the children who do not have healthier, surrogate parents? Due to their fear of abandonment, rooted in the physical helplessness of childhood and separation from God because of their sin natures, children must maintain their bases of attachment to their families at whatever cost. If they are not offered healthier, substitute families, they remain attached to their birth families. As discussed before, this attachment is maintained by children sacrificing their own perceptions, ideas, and needs, and by "buying the family story." And that story includes not only the denial of parental alcoholism, but the identity-forming parental messages to the children.

It has been suggested that if children did not have sinful natures they would not be affected by their parents' treatment. Jesus, the only perfect child or adult, had no spiritual fear of abandonment because he was not separated from his Father by sin. In Luke 2:40–52 we see the only incident between the child Jesus, at age twelve, and his parents, who wrongly accused and rebuked Jesus in their fear, anger, and concern for him.

> He did not buy their wrong view of the situation, thus troubling Himself within, but corrected it. . . . He did not allow Himself to be embarrassed or "put down" by the rebuke He received. And He certainly didn't develop a bad or lower (even slightly lower) self-image as the result of their verbal wrong. He demonstrated an independence of thought that allowed Him to evaluate what was said and to reject what was wrong without any of that wrong affecting Him detrimentally in any way whatever. In short, He handled their wrongdoing rightly.[6]

There is a great difference in the reasoning ability of a child of twelve and one of five or six. One wonders if the sinless, but fully human Jesus as a child of four or five would have been developmentally capable of such "independence of thought."

At twelve, the sinless Jesus was able to reason independently of his parents. He did not have to "buy the family story." Unfortunately, there are no sinless children in alcoholic (or any other) families. Children in alcoholic families usually grow up believing the misbeliefs they learned about themselves.

MAJOR MISBELIEFS IN FAULTY IDENTITY

All the misbeliefs discussed in chapter 8 have some relationship to the self-images of adult children. However, there are four major misbeliefs directly influencing identity. Pastors, counselors, and other helpers will be more effective as they understand these major misbeliefs.

1. *"I don't deserve to exist."* There are variations of this misbelief that include, "I am a mistake," or perhaps, "I am bad—hopelessly bad."

This misbelief is accompanied by the feeling of existence guilt. Occasionally, the I-don't-deserve-to-exist misbelief and existence guilt are based on overt, verbal messages from parents. For example, one man described being "brainwashed" by his alcoholic father, who often said, "You take up too much room on this earth!"[7] More often this misbelief is rooted in the many subtle verbal and nonverbal messages that convey to the child, "You are too much of a bother."

When adults from alcoholic homes believe they do not have the right to exist, they may develop an attitude that has been called "'subintentional suicide'—a kind of self-destruction by default."[8] This may be exhibited by their involvement in potentially dangerous activities and relationships.

Sometimes the "subintentional" approach to suicide gives way to a fully intentional one. Feelings of worthlessness and hopelessness that accompany this I-don't-deserve-to-exist misbelief may become so painful that suicide is viewed as the only solution. Karen, an adult child who survived a serious suicide attempt, explained it this way: "I really believed I was doing my family and the world a favor."

Christian counselors and other people helpers need to be able to recognize the behavioral signs of this possibly deadly misbelief. They also need to know when psychiatric referral is appropriate to evaluate the counselee's need for antidepressant medication and/or hospitalization. It is safer to err on the side of referring needlessly than to underestimate the possible danger of suicide.

Christian adults from alcoholic homes are helped by having this misbelief challenged from the truth of Scripture. A few verses suitable for that purpose are presented in figure 10–1. These adult children also are helped by reading about and hearing from other adult children who have moved past this misbelief.

2. ". . . *(Because) I'll never be normal.*" This misbelief can be thought of as a continuation of the first. It then reads: "I don't deserve to exist because I'll never be normal." As used in the expression of this misbelief, "normal" means "good enough," which in turn is translated as "perfect."

This thinking reflects the belief that one is "different and less than" others, a belief which has been expressed by most adult children of alcoholics. Jerry—with a shrug of resignation—put it this way, "I've always been a caterpillar in a butterfly world. Somehow other people have some abilities or understand some things I don't have or know that made them butterflies. Worst of all, I won't ever be able to be a butterfly." And Jerry was convinced not only that he was a caterpillar person, but that all the butterfly people in the world recognized and rejected him for his caterpillar qualities.

Jerry is not the first person to see himself as an insect. In Numbers 13:33, ten of the twelve men sent to spy out the land of Canaan reported, ". . . we became like grasshoppers in our own sight, and so we were in their [the Canaanites'] sight." The grasshopper perspective shared by these ten prompted the Israelites to rebel against God's direction to enter Canaan. As a result the nation took a forty-year detour through the wilderness.

Moses was not effective arguing against the grasshopper image of the ten spies. Rosellini and Worden have suggested that telling adult children who feel worthless that they are valuable may only make them think the counselor is a bad judge of character.[9] These authors suggest that adult children need to change their behavior, accept themselves, and make up new rules by which to evaluate themselves. The new rules must be more realistic than the old, internalized alcoholic family rules which taught that, "in order to be 'good' you had to be perfect, so this warped logic led you to believe that perfection was normal."[10]

Biblically based rules would be the most realistic and certainly would refute the warped logic that might lead to the misbelief that perfection is normal. That is precisely the misbelief cherished by many adult children of alcoholics.

3. ". . . *(Since) normal people are perfect.*" This is the final portion of our sentence which reads: "I don't deserve to exist

because I'll never be normal since normal people are perfect."
This three-part sentence is constructed entirely of misbeliefs,
with each phrase building upon the previous one.

Remember Jerry who felt like a caterpillar in a butterfly
world? Jerry believes that "butterfly people," i.e., normal
people, are problem-free and perfect. What's more, only these
perfect, "butterfly people" are valuable and worthy of esteem.
Rosselini and Worden believe this idea is foundational to the
adult child's struggle with an unhealthy self-image and with
perfectionism.

> Underlying these attitudes is the belief that "normal"
> people—the people worthy of esteem—don't have to
> struggle to get what they want, and they don't make mis-
> takes or ask for help or feel fear.
> An adult child mired in self-hate doesn't realize that
> courage doesn't mean the absence of fear. Courage is going
> into the unknown in spite of sometimes overwhelming fear.
> Brave people often quake in their boots.
> Confident people struggle with self-doubt.
> Strong, resolute people sometimes falter, [and] break
> down.
> Successful people make mistakes. (Many would argue
> that you can't be a success without making mistakes—and
> learning from them.)
> . . . This is reality. This is what normal is all about.[11]

Clearly, this normal-people-are-perfect misbelief is unscrip-
tural. From beginning to end, God's Word declares that "all have
sinned"[12] and "There is none righteous."[13] To borrow Jerry's
metaphor, since the entrance of sin into the world, there has
been only one perfect "butterfly person"—Jesus Christ. All the
rest of us are caterpillars.

Accepting their imperfect, sinful "caterpillar nature" is a
prerequisite for adult children to experience the saving grace
of God as well as the liberating freedom of an accurate self-
concept.

4. *"(Therefore) I must pretend to be perfect to live among
normal people."* A more complete rendering of this misbelief is:

"I must concentrate and work very hard pretending to be perfect just to live among, be accepted by, and have any chance in the world of being loved by normal people."

These four major misbeliefs, which shape the inaccurate and unhealthy self-images of many adult children, compose two, related sentences: *"I don't deserve to exist, because I'll never be normal since normal people are perfect. Therefore I must pretend to be perfect to live among normal people."*

The impossible and unrealistic goal of perfection is set during a person's childhood in an alcoholic family. Barbara is an example. Now forty-seven, she recalls with horror her high-school graduation. Barbara finished third in her class of over 250 students. However, her mother refused to attend the graduation ceremonies. Why? Barbara's mother said she was ashamed of her daughter, who "should have been first in the class."[14]

Not many parents are as blatant as Barbara's mother about unrealistic expectations of perfection in their children. This mother's all-or-nothing thinking is apparent: Since her daughter was not number one, she was worthless and a source of embarrassment. In many, usually more subtle, ways alcoholic families train children to believe *Either you are the best or you are nothing.* Or as one man from an alcoholic home expressed it, "Our family motto was: *Second place is no place.*"

How do children survive with the unseen stigma of total badness and worthlessness in a world where everyone else is perceived as perfect and worthy? Some abandon the effort to measure up and live out an "I-am-totally-worthless-and-I'll prove-it" script. But, in Jerry's words, usually the caterpillar dons a butterfly disguise. And adult children become adept at pretending perfection. They act as if they don't make mistakes, feel inadequate, or have hateful thoughts and deep inner fears.[15]

Claudia Black believes that underneath the butterfly disguise, "Little Ms. and Mr. Perfect" know they are imperfect and unworthy and they live in terror that others may find out at any moment.[16] This terror reflects the life-and-death nature of the drive to appear perfect.

Some readers may have noted that this misbelief was worded: "I must pretend to be perfect to live among normal people," not, ". . . to be accepted among normal people." The four major misbeliefs begin and end with the struggle for existence. Counselors will be more effective when they understand that many adult children of alcoholics feel threatened and panicky at the thought of acknowledging weaknesses and problems to others.

The attempt to appear perfect is a rejection of human limitations. It is a rejection, too, of our fallenness. Neither is necessary. Our merciful God resolved the dilemma of our imperfect, fallen natures at Calvary. The application of this truth can free adult children from the wearisome task of dragging an ill-fitting mask of perfection through life.

Skillful, knowledgeable, and caring people helpers can assist in this process. As they counsel for more accurate identities, there are some general considerations and specific strategies that will make pastors, counselors, and others more effective.

COUNSELING FOR AN ACCURATE IDENTITY

Stephanie Brown believes that changing the adult child's identity is the heart of the recovery process. She has stated,

> With the break in denial and acquisition of the label ACA [adult child of an alcoholic], individuals begin a process of recovery that centers on a *transformation in identity*.[17]

Faulty, Role-Based Identity

Adult children usually develop an inaccurate, performance-based identity. Remember, there are only two possibilities in the all-or-nothing thinking pattern prevalent in alcoholic families—only a one or a ten. And children in these families have been taught that they are zeros. Repeatedly they are reminded how they fail; therefore they conclude they are, indeed, worthless. It is as if at some point they say to themselves, "My worthless personhood deserves only rejection and humiliation. Perfect performance is my only hope to earn acceptance and recognition."

The role played by a child in an alcoholic family usually becomes his or her external identity. Fulfilling the role is a way to be validated so the child can feel worthwhile momentarily. The roles, sometimes called defensive adaptations, served valuable purposes in childhood. But for adults, the defensive roles, "often constitute the core of the individual's problems in interpersonal relationships and the only sense of self at the same time."[18]

Why is it important for counselors to understand this? Because when we ask adult children to abandon the defensive childhood roles that are creating problems in their lives, we are asking them—in effect—to relinquish the basis of their identities. And if we take away the basis of identity, we leave only a sense of worthlessness. In the place of a faulty, performance-based identity, counselors and other helpers must present the basis for an accurate, biblically based identity.

Accurate, Biblically Based Identity

To have an accurate self-concept, all of us need to see ourselves as God sees us. We will be unable to do that—or help others do that—without the biblical answer to the "Who-am-I?" question. Scripture is the only unmarred mirror into which individuals can look to see themselves realistically. If pastors and counselors invite an adult child to behold his or her image in the scriptural mirror, what will be seen?[19]

First, the Bible reveals that human beings are made in the image of God. However, that image has been marred, for Scripture reflects God's view that humankind is—as theologians say—utterly depraved, or sinful. This means no one is capable of doing anything of eternal value in and of themselves, and everyone is separated from God now and forever.

But, the Bible also clearly shows God's view of us as objects of his unconditional love. When Christ died to pay for all our sins, God expressed his love by meeting our greatest need, which is to be in right relationship with him.[20] It is an unfathomable paradox. Human beings are totally corrupted by sin, yet of such value to God that he would make provisions for them to become his children and be part of his eternal family.[21]

How might adult children of alcoholics and others respond if they learned to see themselves as God sees them? Ideally, non-Christians would recognize their need to trust Christ as Savior and Lord.[22] Even if they do not, they can have the basis for an accurate identity if they see themselves both as sinners and as objects of God's love. Christian adult children could be released from the bondage of a performance-oriented lifestyle and experience what David Seamands calls "Healing Grace."[23] Certainly, Christian adult children who learn to see themselves accurately would overflow with renewed praise to God for his love and grace.

COUNSELING GUIDELINES

Counselors and other helpers can assist adult children of alcoholics develop an accurate identity and experience the benefits cited above. The remainder of the chapter presents specific strategies to reach that goal.

Some of the counseling strategies or change steps listed below have been mentioned in previous chapters. Others will be expanded in future chapters. This demonstrates how the process of recovering from the effects of parental alcoholism is a multifaceted one. For example, counseling for correct thinking will affect self-concept, and counseling for accurate identity will influence relationship patterns. Chapter topics are not in watertight compartments; and some change steps listed below "leak" from one to another.

1. *Review counseling suggestions from chapter 8.* Many of the ideas to promote mind renewal will be helpful, because developing a new, accurate identity is part of the mind-renewal process.

2. *Teach the concept of parents as "marred mirrors."* This is part of the basic, ongoing process of connecting the past to the present. Help counselees understand that the faulty, performance-based identities of their parents impaired the parents' ability to teach any other basis of identity. Adult children of alcoholics seem to identify easily with the marred-mirror metaphor. It reflects the fact that the parents' self-images were marred by their own parents, who also were marred mirrors. This intergenerational perspective is important for balance. It is also biblical.[24]

3. *Identify childhood "labels" and identity messages.* Have counselees list the verbalized and nonverbalized labels attached to them as children. Discuss the messages the labels conveyed about personal identity.

4. *Identify current identity misbeliefs.* Describe how parental messages from the past repeatedly get replayed as identity misbeliefs today. Have adult children prepare a list of misbeliefs for discussion during counseling.

5. *Present the biblical basis of an accurate identity.* As homework, ask counselees to read one or more books on this topic. Several I recommend are listed under number two in the notes of this chapter. Have counselees take notes or mark the most pertinent passages for discussion. Emphasize that if Christian adult children would appropriate the truth that they are loved by God and fully accepted by him in Christ, it would revolutionize their self-images.

6. *From Scripture, list elements of every Christian's identity.* Ask counselees to begin a notebook of Bible verses that describe various aspects of every Christian's identity. For each verse, have him or her write the reference, a personalized summary, and a past, present, or future application. Figure 10–1 is a sample page from such a notebook.

Each page of this notebook could be headed with a statement such as, "These verses tell me what my Heavenly Father really thinks about me. They tell me who I am. Lord, help me believe you and not what others (or my mental replay) may say."

Accurate Identity Notebook
(Sample Page)

───

Ephesians 1:6
I am accepted in Christ. I can survive my sister's rejection because God accepts me. I feel that acceptance at church. I will start spending more time with my new church family.

Ephesians 1:7
I am forgiven of all my sins and washed in the blood of Christ. I do not need to continue to punish myself for past sins.

Ephesians 2:10
I am God's workmanship, created in Christ Jesus for good works. When I messed up at work today I felt like a worthless heap of garbage who would never do anything right. But my feelings were wrong. I choose to believe God, not my feelings.

───

Figure 10–1

If Christian adult children do not have the habit of regular Bible study, counselors can have them begin by reading Ephesians. Explain the value of meditating or deeply dwelling upon the verses that tell them who they are in Christ.

7. *Introduce or reinforce thought stopping and substituting.* This procedure is outlined in chapter 8. Please take a moment to reread it if you are not familiar with this technique. You will recall that the word "stop" is written in large, capital letters on one side of a three-by-five-inch card. The new or substitute thought is written on the reverse side. Adult children can use the personalized summaries of verses from their accurate identity notebooks as substitute thoughts.

8. *Introduce the technique of thought focusing.* Thought stopping and substituting are used typically to counter specific misbeliefs. Thought focusing is actually meditating on scriptural truth and can be used daily to renew the mind in the area of personal identity.

Again, a three-by-five-inch card may be used. Have adult children write a summary of the biblical truths they have been learning. Perhaps they could summarize one chapter on each card. Or they might write a quotation from one of the biblically based books on self-image they have read. Figure 10–2 is an example of a thought-focusing card which could be titled "An Accurate Identity Affirmation."[25]

Thought-focusing cards may be kept on the bedside table to read before retiring and upon waking. They can be attached to the visor of a car with a rubber band or taped over the

An Accurate Identity Affirmation

Because I am in Christ I am fully pleasing to God. I no longer have to fear failure.

Because I am in Christ I am totally accepted by God. I no longer have to fear rejection.

Because I am in Christ I am completely forgiven and deeply loved by God. I no longer have to fear punishment or have to punish others.

Because I am in Christ I have been made brand new and complete. I no longer need to experience the pain of shame.

Figure 10–2

kitchen sink. Invite counselees to be creative in their use of these cards.

9. *Assign Step Four of the Alcoholics Anonymous Twelve-Step Program.* Alcoholics Anonymous uses its famous Twelve Steps as the foundation for recovery from alcoholism. Step Four is: "We made a searching and fearless moral inventory of ourselves."

If adult children are attending a support group affiliated with Al-Anon, it will be a Twelve-Step group. If they have done Step Four, discuss with them the results of assessing their strengths and weaknesses. Many adult children of alcoholics reel off lengthy lists of weaknesses but have great difficulty identifying their strengths.

All-or-nothing thinking allows only for a one or a ten— perfection or worthlessness. In part, the Step-Four process helps adult children recognize the "two-through-nine" aspects of themselves. Step Four encourages perfectionistic adult children to admit their sins and failures. And it encourages all adult children to acknowledge their positive traits.

10. *Assign Step Five of the AA Twelve-Step Program.* Step Five is: We admitted to God, to ourselves, and to another human being the exact nature of our wrongs.

This threefold confession process is founded solidly in Scripture. However, admitting sins and shortcomings to God, oneself, and others is difficult and humbling. Jeremiah 17:9 warns us that, "The heart is more deceitful than all else. . . ." Humanly, it is impossible for a deceitful heart to be honest about its sinful contents. Nevertheless, Christian adult children can be encouraged to trust the Holy Spirit of God to reveal to them their true selves.

Concerning our confession to God, Lamentations 3:40 instructs us all to ". . . examine and probe our ways, And let us return to the Lord." While 1 John 1:9 assures that, "If we confess our sins, He is faithful and righteous to forgive us our sins and to cleanse us from all unrighteousness."

Telling one's story to another person can be the most threatening part of Step Five. Many adult children of alcoholics have spent a major portion of their lives building defenses to prevent others from seeing their weaknesses. This defensive stance leaves adult children enmeshed in patterns of isolation and loneliness. "Step Five is our pathway out of isolation and loneliness. It is a move toward wholeness. . . ."[26] It is also biblical. James 5:16a encourages hurting Christians to ". . . confess your sins to one another, and pray for one another, so that you may be healed."

11. *Introduce the idea of treating oneself with realistic respect and* agape *love.* Realistic respect for others is the appropriate attitude for maintaining healthy interpersonal relationships. Realistic respect also is an appropriate and biblical foundation for relating to oneself.

Work with Christian adult children to help them understand that realistic respect includes an awareness of every Christian's inclination to sin coupled with the knowledge that every Christian bears God's image and is "his workmanship created for good works" (Eph. 2:10).

Adult children of alcoholics often disrespect and degrade themselves in words and deeds. To counteract this tendency, adult children could spend fifteen minutes two or three times a week recording in a notebook some behaviors, words, and thoughts that reflect either a respectful or a disrespectful attitude toward themselves. Discuss the results in light of their true identities as revealed in God's Word.

Ask adult children of alcoholics to begin changing one disrespectful item they've applied to themselves. Assign other item changes as previous ones diminish in frequency.

As earlier proposed, *agape* love is behaving toward someone with the goal of promoting increasing Christ-likeness. Adult children tend to treat themselves as enemies instead of friends. Typically, there is no self-application of agape love, especially when an adult child has disappointed himself or herself.

Verses four through seven of 1 Corinthians 13 describe the practical expressions of agape love in relationships. These verses also are a suitable guide for the relationship one has with oneself. Have counselees write paraphrases of these verses with applications to their relationship with themselves. Figure 10–3 shows one such paraphrase.

12. *Assess patterns of self-care.* Self-care is a broad concept. It includes elements of setting appropriate boundaries

Personalized Agape Application
Based on 1 Corinthians 13:4–7

───

I will treat myself with patience and kindness. Put-downs of myself are not pleasing to my Heavenly Father.

I will not be envious of others. I will not act boastfully and arrogantly to cover my feelings of worthlessness and shame.

I will not behave rudely and disrespectfully toward myself. Instead, I will learn to think, speak, and behave gently and respectfully toward myself.

I will not be so quick to criticize myself. I will stop mentally replaying all my wrong choices.

I will learn to be comfortable with my good and right choices rather than continue to believe I am doomed to repeat the old, wrong patterns over and over.

I will never give up on myself or think I am hopeless. I choose to believe that "nothing will be impossible with God" (Luke 1:37) including his change process in me.

I will never lose hope, and I will wait patiently to see the changes in me and in my relationships as I cooperate with the work of the Holy Spirit in my life.

───

Figure 10–3

and refusing to tolerate abuse. Some of these will be discussed in the next chapter.

Self-care also encompasses proper attention to nutrition and physical exercise. Rosellini and Worden have suggested that this is a problem for adult children.

> Children of alcoholics don't know how to live a healthy lifestyle because their parents didn't model healthy behavior. Hit and miss meals, emotional and physical exhaustion, and constant stress are normal components of homelife to adult children.[27]

The unhealthy lifestyle described above gets expressed in the self-care patterns of many adult children. These patterns often include irregular eating habits and constant dieting. They also may include inadequate exercise and relaxation time coupled with too much stress, caffeine, tobacco, alcohol, and other drugs.

The Bible clearly teaches respect for the physical body of every Christian. Adult children are no exception. In 1 Corinthians 6:19–20, Paul tells believers their bodies are temples of the

Holy Spirit who indwells them. Further, he declares that they do not belong to themselves but have been bought by God with a price, and as a result they are to glorify God, their Owner, in and through their bodies.

Christian adults from alcoholic homes must be confronted with the challenge to bring their self-care practices in line with this scriptural principle. They can be encouraged to take some steps toward that goal by switching to decaffeinated beverages, reducing the intake of sugar and fat, walking thirty minutes three times a week, and/or eliminating tobacco and all non-prescription drugs. Even prescription drugs like Valium may become a problem with prolonged use.

LOVING OUR NEIGHBORS AS OURSELVES?

The oft-repeated exhortation to love our neighbors as ourselves[28] is familiar to nearly all Christians and to most unbelievers as well. However, one wag has suggested that the problem with that principle is that we usually do!

How true. Our relationships with others often bear a striking resemblance to our relationships with ourselves. This chapter has focused on that relationship with ourselves; chapter 11 will spotlight our relationship with others.

CHAPTER ELEVEN

COUNSELING FOR RESPECTFUL RELATIONSHIPS

IN CHAPTER 10 WE SAW that a realistically respectful, biblically based relationship with ourselves is founded on learning to see ourselves as God sees us. In turn, healthy, biblically based relationships with others stand on two pillars of truth. The first is the accurate understanding of our true identities, which we examined previously. The second is the realization that God views all individuals as he views us: utterly fallen, yet the object of his love. The first pillar provides an appropriate basis for realistic *self-respect*. The second gives a solid foundation for realistically respecting *others*. Together, they undergird the construction of respectful relationships.

WHO ARE YOU, AND HOW DO WE
RELATE TO EACH OTHER?

As young children were learning to answer the question, "Who am I?" they also were discovering answers to, "Who are you?" and "How do we relate to each other?" These questions are first asked and answered in the informal classroom of the child's family.

Most of the relationship messages from alcoholic families translate into relational misbeliefs for the adults who were reared in those families. These adults did not learn about the traits of healthy, respectful relationships, because they rarely, if ever, saw them modeled.

Before examining the codependent and disrespectful relationships which adult children of alcoholics tend to have, we will look at the traits of respectful relationships.

RESPECTFUL RELATIONSHIPS

Janet Woititz summarizes healthy relationships in six, brief statements plus a "bottom line:"

1. I can be me.
2. You can be you.
3. We can be us.
4. I can grow.
5. You can grow.
6. We can grow together.

I accept you unconditionally, and you accept me unconditionally. That's the bottom line. It does not mean that changes in personality or actions are undesirable or impossible—it merely means that you begin by accepting your partner as he or she is.[1]

Woititz's description of healthy relationships focuses on issues of personal boundaries and unconditional acceptance. There are several other traits commonly found in healthy, respectful relationships.

Traits of Respectful Relationships

1. *Mutual respect.* When mutual respect characterizes a relationship, there will be shared esteem and consideration for

one another. With mutual respect, each person upholds the other's right to separate choices and opinions, and neither one attempts to control or manipulate the other. Respecting others requires that we allow them to be responsible for the consequences of their choices. Additionally, when we respect others, we assume God works in their lives as surely as he does in ours.

It was suggested earlier that respect must be balanced with realism to be most accurate. We respect others because they bear God's image and are the objects of his love. However, we face the reality that that image is marred by a sinful nature and that others may reject God's love.

2. *Agape love.* The words "agape love" can be read "love love," for *agape* is one of several Greek words for love. The word *agape* is unique to the New Testament, and was unknown in other Greek literature. This has been called "the characteristic word of Christianity."[2] Agape love can be part of any relationship, because it "is not an impulse from the feelings. . . ."[3] Agape seeks the best for the other person, and as previously suggested, this means relating to him or her in a manner that will promote movement toward Jesus Christ and increasing conformity with his nature.

3. *Mutual trust.* The basis of trust is the belief that we are psychologically and physically safe with another person. Trust develops slowly. It is not given immediately in healthy relationships. Trust is built on a track record of consistency, predictability, and reliability. And those qualities flow in both directions, because in healthy relationships, there is mutual trust. Further, trust of others is always tempered with an understanding that they will disappoint and fail us in some way at some time. Only God is totally trustworthy.

4. *Mutual honesty.* We can be honest about ourselves in healthy relationships. They provide a haven in which we may remove our masks of perfection and pretense. And when our faults are revealed, there is no fear of rejection. Respectful relationships also provide the freedom to be honest about our preferences, ideas, and opinions without fear of the other person's ridicule or rejection. Again, for the relationship to be genuinely healthy and respectful, both parties must feel the freedom to be honest, and both must choose to exercise that freedom.

5. *Realistic expectations.* In healthy relationships, one party does not expect the other to meet all needs, solve all problems, or relieve all pain. There are some things one can only do for oneself. There are more things only God can do for us. Also, in a wholesome, appropriate relationship, neither person expects the other to be a mind reader. This means there must be communication.

6. *Open communication.* When mutual respect and trust are part of a relationship, communication usually is open and honest. In relationships like these, it is safe to communicate feelings as well as thoughts. Clear and open communication includes both parties being skilled in listening as well as speaking. And when discussing problems, people in respectful relationships attack the issues, not each other.

7. *Social networks.* The healthiest relationships are more than "you and me against the world." They recognize that you and I live in a world of other people, and we have relationships with many of them. If parent-child relationships are healthy, both see the value of each having a life and social network outside of that relationship. Certainly this attitude typifies respectful relationships between single adults. Even in healthy marriage relationships, both partners recognize the other's need to have social contacts beyond their union. Appropriate, same-sex friendships at church, on the job, and in the community are an adjunct to these marriages, not a threat. And married couples will benefit from regular contact with other couples who also are in respectful marriages.

8. *Prompt forgiveness.* Because all relationships involve interactions between two sinful individuals, frequent forgiveness will be required. Forgiveness is neither forgetting nor excusing. It is releasing the wrong and moving on. Forgiving someone does not mean that person is not confronted with the request to change his or her behavior. To keep relationships healthy and respectful, forgiveness is best requested, received, and/or offered promptly. Forgiveness oils the machinery of well-running and respectful relationships.

9. *Increasing intimacy.* Intimacy in this case does not mean being sexual, and being sexual does not always mean being intimate. Intimacy is a mutual, balanced, and shared sense of unity.

It is a sense of "us" without the need to lose individuality. Intimacy grows naturally in healthy relationships when each of these other traits is present.

Certainly there are other traits of healthy, respectful relationships, but these nine represent the basic building blocks. Their balanced and mutual expression is the hallmark of these relationships. In contrast, codependent and disrespectful relationships lack this balance and mutuality.

Participants in respectful relationships display the capacity for interdependence which marks adults who view themselves and others with realistic respect. They are able to maintain clear and separate identities from others. At the same time, they recognize and are comfortable with their need for help and support from others, and they are able to get that help and support in appropriate, nondestructive ways. This is not true of disrespectful relationships.

DISRESPECTFUL RELATIONSHIPS

It was proposed in chapter 4 that, by their nature, codependent relationships always are disrespectful. Further, it was suggested that these relationships are characteristic of the interactions of adult children of alcoholics.

The remainder of this chapter describes the codependency misbeliefs, the major issues adult children face in codependent relationships, and counseling guidelines to promote respectful relationships.

As a reminder from chapter 4, a codependent person is defined as one who is being disrespected and controlled by someone he or she is disrespecting and attempting to control. Hence, a codependent, disrespectful relationship is marked by mutual disrespect and attempts to control the other's acts and/ or attitudes.

THE POWER OF CODEPENDENCY

What children must learn if they are to survive in dysfunctional families sets them up for codependent adult relationships. For children, the defensive roles and self-protective relationship styles served a purpose. For adults, these familiar maneuvers serve to isolate and create pain.

Codependency's Familiarity

The power of codependency is its familiarity. It feels safe, even though it feels miserable. Melody Beattie talks about "the Frog Syndrome" to describe the effects of codependency's familiarity.

> There is an anecdote circulating through codependency groups. It goes like this: "Did you hear about the woman who kissed a frog? She was hoping it would turn into a prince. It didn't. She turned into a frog too."
>
> . . . Some [codependents] become chronically attracted to frogs after kissing enough of them. Alcoholics and people with other compulsive disorders are attractive people. They radiate power, energy, and charm. They promise the world. Never mind that they deliver pain, suffering, and anguish. . . .
>
> If we don't deal with our codependent characteristics, probabilities dictate we will continue to be attracted to and kiss frogs. Even if we deal with our characteristics, we may still lean toward frogs, but we can learn not to jump into the pond with them.[4]

One adult child who recognized the pull of codependency's familiarity in her life exclaimed, "When Prince Charming does come along, I'll probably be down at the pond kissing frogs."[5]

Codependency's Foundation

The power of codependency is also its foundation: fear of abandonment. Codependency's roots are embedded in a child's early memories of absolute helplessness in the presence of inadequate, and sometimes abusive, caregivers.

Codependency is an adult condition. That is, children cannot correctly be called codependent. As noted above, children in alcoholic families learn what is necessary to survive. They also learn what is modeled. If no alternative is presented, no choice is possible.

Adults do have choices about how to relate to others. However, for adult children of alcoholics, their relationship choices often are veiled in a shroud of familiarity with codependency and lingering fear of abandonment. Their disrespectful relationships are characterized by several misbeliefs and major issues.

CODEPENDENCY MISBELIEFS

The following misbeliefs are prevalent among adult children of alcoholics. Counselors and other helpers will be more effective if they understand them, since these misbeliefs underlie the major issues and problems adult children experience in their codependent, disrespectful relationships.

1. *"My desires must dictate your appearance and behavior because you are an extension of me and I can feel good about myself only when others approve of both of us."* The first two misbeliefs illuminate the double-bind of codependency. They articulate the erroneous idea that we are controlled by others and that we have the right to control them. This concept exhibits disrespect both for ourselves and for others. In truth, others have the right to determine their own appearance and behavior. Then we have the right to choose our response.

2. *"Your desires may dictate my appearance and behavior because I am an extension of you and can feel good about myself only when you approve of me."* Many adult children of alcoholics have described feelings of despair and self-hatred over problems in even relatively casual relationships. These adults report that their self-respect can be destroyed if the other individual in the relationship expresses disapproval of them. As discussed in the last chapter, the truth is that self-respect and a healthy self-concept are not based on the approval of others. In reality, adult children can learn to maintain their good feelings about themselves whether or not others approve of them.

3. *"I can be happy only when you are happy."* When personal boundaries are unclear and there is no distinct sense of individual identity, a person may be unsure whose pain or happiness he or she is feeling. Many adult children of alcoholics report being unable to maintain their own positive attitudes and pleasant feelings if another person becomes upset. "How can I feel a sense of peace in the Lord when my mom is so angry at my dad for being drunk at work and losing his job again?" This question from a Christian raised in an alcoholic home expresses the I-can-be-happy-only-when-you-are-happy misbelief.

The truth is that one person does not have to automatically experience the emotions of another with whom he or she has a relationship. Adults can be compassionate, concerned, and helpful without actually experiencing the other person's anger, despair, or other distressing emotion.

4. *"If you really knew me you would discover I am not perfect, and you would abandon me."*[6] The familiar theme of pretending perfection to defend against abandonment is sounded here. Woititz suggests the truth is that adult children of alcoholics are not as good at pretending as they may believe. In addition, the people who care about them know they are not perfect—because no one is. And they still care anyway.

5. *"We will be as one, and we will do everything together."* Clearly, issues of personal boundaries are involved in this codependency misbelief. The truth is that even marriage partners, whom Scripture declares "become one flesh,"[7] retain individual identities. And, by necessity, friends and even married couples do not do everything together—nor should they.

6. *"We will always agree, and we will never criticize each other."* Most adult children of alcoholics believe there will be no conflict, and certainly no anger, in ideal relationships. Involved here is the "we-are-one" myth with its implication that we will have the same ideas, tastes, and opinions in every situation. Also, most adult children have little experience in conflict resolution in the context of a healthy relationship. In the real world, friends and couples disagree, argue, and are critical of each other's behavior from time to time.

7. *"You instinctively will anticipate my every need and desire."* With this misbelief, one expects spouse, friends, coworkers and others to be mind readers. Children in alcoholic homes learn that feeling unloved and having needs and desires unmet go hand in hand. They conclude it is less painful not to state or even to have expectations that needs and desires will be fulfilled.

In later relationships, adult children rarely state their expectations or identify their preferences. However, they may continue to link fulfilled expectations with being loved. For example, Anna shared in her support group that she was "crushed" that her husband failed to bring flowers on their first anniversary. Another member asked Anna if her husband knew she wanted flowers. "If I have to say something about it, it doesn't mean anything. Besides if he really loved me, he would know," Anna replied between sobs.

The reality is that even people who care about us are not mind readers. And if needs and desires are not clearly communicated, it is unlikely they will be fulfilled.

8. *"We will trust each other totally, automatically, and immediately."* Misbelief numbers eight and nine are polar opposites. This illustrates two extreme responses often seen in adult children of alcoholics. One extreme view of trust is seen in this misbelief. This concept of total, automatic, immediate trust is both unrealistic and unbiblical. The truth is that trust is built slowly in a healthy relationship.

9. *"Trusting and being vulnerable in a relationship always bring pain."* Here is the other extreme misbelief about trust, which underlies the adult child's determination to withhold trust and to control the other person(s) in the relationship. In reality, being open and vulnerable and trusting in a relationship sometimes has negative results and sometimes has positive results. But an eventual willingness to risk trusting another, appropriate person, and to risk being open and vulnerable are prerequisites to genuine intimacy.

MAJOR ISSUES OF CODEPENDENCY

What children experience in alcoholic families often leaves them with a sense of inner emptiness. As adults, they look outside themselves to relationships with others to feel fulfilled. However, the misbeliefs of adult children of alcoholics shape patterns of relating which are characterized by mutual disrespect and attempts to control. These patterns of relating are called codependency.

Five major issues are present in codependent, disrespectful relationships: fear of abandonment, trust, boundaries, control, and intimacy.

Fear of Abandonment

In chapters 2 through 4 we examined the physical, emotional, and spiritual precursors of fear of abandonment. The focus here is on the display of fear of abandonment and the defenses against it as they are expressed within relationships.

Fear of abandonment: the display. In codependent relationships, fear of abandonment is displayed in two major ways, by approval addiction and by a high tolerance for inappropriate behavior.

Approval addiction. The terminology of chemical dependency is selected purposely to emphasize the powerful pull of approval. When adult children of alcoholics feel liked and approved, they experience a temporary "fix" of safety and self-respect. But it does not last. These adults always are in search of the next "fix," and they become panicky if their current approval supplier threatens to end that relationship.

Most adult children of alcoholics lack an inner source of approval from God and themselves to provide a lasting sense of safety and realistic self-respect. Consequently, they pursue approval from others by being lovable and/or by being competent.

In pursuit of approval, adult children often relinquish their right to make their own choices. This is how Constance expressed it in her support group:

> I really wanted to see the new Meryl Streep film. I had been asking to go for two weeks. He was insistent we go to another Clint Eastwood movie, so that's where we went. It was no big deal—just a movie. But then I got thinking that we almost always do what he wants. Should I risk saying something? I sure don't want him to get mad. I can't stand it when we argue and he's angry.

Because Constance could not risk losing her current approval supplier, it never occurred to her that she could have gone to see the film of her choice either alone or with another friend. She even might have refused to go to yet another Eastwood movie.

It is disrespectful and inappropriate when one person in a relationship almost always determines what both parties do. However, inappropriate behavior is familiar fare to most adult children of alcoholics. Its tolerance displays fear of abandonment.

High tolerance for inappropriate behavior. If adult children of alcoholics are to maintain their approval suppliers, they must be prepared to tolerate inappropriate behavior that would motivate better-adjusted individuals to change or end the relationship. We have learned that the adult child has been prepared thoroughly to tolerate inappropriate behavior by growing up in an alcoholic family system.

Many adult children of alcoholics display this high tolerance for inappropriate behavior as Constance did in the example above. Because she valued her intense, romantic relationship and the feeling of approval it supplied, Constance could not bring herself to seriously question the appropriateness of her boyfriend's behavior. However, even adult children who seem to shun close, personal relationships sometimes display this outworking of fear of abandonment in relationship to their job performance. These aloof-appearing adults may tolerate inappropriate behavior associated with their employment, and it is not uncommon for them to work seventy or eighty hours a week to fulfill an employer's unrealistic expectations.

These two expressions of high tolerance for inappropriate behavior suggest there are two styles of defending against fear of abandonment.

Fear of abandonment: the defense. I have observed two coping styles or methods of defending oneself against fear of abandonment.[8] Some adult children are what could be called "porcupines." These "porcupine" adults, who are frequently— but not always—males, seem to avoid deep commitments and close relationships. It is as if they are sprayed with an invisible coating of Teflon. One can neither connect with nor cling to them, although there is another group of adult children who surely try.

Many women, and some men, raised in alcoholic families appear to relate to others as if they were vacuum cleaners. These "vacuum-cleaner" adult children attempt to pull everyone in their path into an immediate and fraudulent intimate relationship. It is as if these adult children are coated with an invisible layer of "super glue," and they try to bond with everyone they meet.

Pastors and counselors will recognize these defensive styles even in forms less dramatic and extreme than those described above. Both styles present special challenges to people helpers.

Both styles are expressions of codependency. And both styles are related to issues of trust.

Trust

The two contrasting concepts of trust described previously in misbeliefs eight and nine may be acted out at different times in the codependent relationships of adult children of alcoholics.

For example, adult children may trust someone so totally that at their first meeting they sit down and tell that person their complete life story. Often this is done without first assessing the other person's level of interest or respectfulness. "When this happens, the other person is likely to be overwhelmed by the onslaught of openness and will often 'bow out,' either gracefully or ungracefully, of the situation."[9] Usually adult children experience confusion, not insight, as a result of such an experience.

Often these adults will go to the opposite extreme in the next relationship and will neither trust at all nor share anything. In this situation, the other person may withdraw in response to an undercurrent of anger and mistrust in the adult child, who then feels rejected and hurt again. As with all-or-nothing thinking, it is as if there are only two extreme choices. Adult children may swing back and forth, trusting completely and inappropriately or not at all. "The adult child is engaging in a pattern of behavior which does not allow relationships to develop."[10]

Instead of moving to a middle ground, adult children of alcoholics tend to become fixed in one extreme or the other, as "porcupines" or "vacuum cleaners." Part of the recovery process is learning to find that "middle ground."

Boundaries

Adult children of alcoholics grew up in family systems where boundaries were very confusing. Sometimes the adults in the family behaved like parents and allowed the children to be children. Other times the adults behaved like children and demanded that their children become their parents. This inconsistent and confusing treatment received by children in alcoholic families gave unclear messages about their identity in relationship to others.

The chart in figure 11–1 summarizes the differences in personal boundary issues in interdependent, respectful relationships and codependent, disrespectful relationships.

Control

Repeatedly the struggle to maintain control of one's own emotions, general circumstances, and personal relationships emerges

Personal Boundaries

Codependent	*Interdependent*
I can fall in love with a new acquaintance.	I know that love is based on respect and trust; these take time to develop.
I talk at an intimate level at the first meeting.	I don't overwhelm a person with personal information. I allow trust to develop slowly.
I am overwhelmed by and preoccupied with a person.	I am able to keep my relationships in perspective and function in other areas of my life.
I let others define me.	I know who I am in Christ, and I am wary of people who want to remake me.
I let others describe my reality.	I believe my perception of reality is just as accurate as anyone's.
I let others determine what I feel.	I refuse to allow someone else to tell me, "You don't feel that way."
I let others direct my life.	I listen to opinions, but I make decisions for myself based on God's leading of my choices.
I violate personal values to please others.	I am not willing to "do anything" to maintain a relationship. I have values that are not negotiable.
I don't notice when someone else displays inappropriate boundaries.	I am wary of someone who wants to get too close to me too soon. I notice if someone has values and opinions.
I don't notice when someone invades my personal boundaries.	I notice when others try to make decisions for me, are overly helpful, and/or do not consult me about time commitments.

Figure 11–1

as a major issue for adult children of alcoholics. Control of those relationships is our current focus.

Healthy interdependence says, "I believe other adults have the capacity to make competent choices and be responsible for the consequences of those choices whether they are wise or foolish." In contrast, codependence cries, "I believe I can choose best for others, even unimpaired adults, and I will save them from experiencing the consequences of their own foolish choices. Others must think, behave, feel, and look the way I decide in order for me to feel safe."

Attempts to control relationships and the individuals in them create problems for adult children of alcoholics. Yet the alternative of relinquishing control can be frightening, especially if these adults care deeply about the other person. Letting go of control fosters independence in others. And this independence raises questions. Will the other person become so independent they will no longer need me? Will he or she leave the relationship and abandon me? Perhaps.[11] But the other person also could find someone else he or she "needs" more than the adult child of the alcoholic, and leave anyway despite the adult child's best efforts to control.

Clearly, the codependent approach to relationships is profoundly disrespectful. This attitude betrays the adult child's belief that God cannot guide and care for someone else the way he guides and cares for the adult child. In contrast to this attitude, God's Word encourages Christians to abandon judging whether others are competent to "stand or fall." Further, the Lord promises he is able to make other Christians stand.[12]

Intimacy

Genuine intimacy is a shared sense of openness. It is the ability to be who and what you are with another person—who is able to do the same. "The more you are able to be yourself, the more intimate you are . . . Self-disclosure is a hallmark of intimacy."[13]

This is a concept proposed not by contemporary mental health professionals, but by the Bible. In Romans 12:9, Paul exhorts Christians to let their love "be without hypocrisy." This expresses the idea of relating to others without wearing a mask to hide our sinful selves.[14]

The prospect of being maskless is terrifying for many adult children of alcoholics who are described as "intimacy-phobic." These adults enter relationships that cannot possibly last, because the risk of getting close enough to be seen realistically by another human being is too much of a gamble.

These intimacy phobics are actually the Teflon-sprayed "porcupines" described earlier. They experienced rejection as children, and now they reject themselves, and they expect to be rejected in all their relationships if they are seen for who they really are. Therefore, as a relationship begins to develop and require additional risks of self-disclosure, these adult children begin to panic and withdraw. In effect, these adults have given up their hope of ever being accepted and loved for themselves.

On the other hand, there are those adult children of alcoholics who keep trying to find someone to accept them just as they longed to be accepted as children. They could be called "intimacy phonies." Their attempts at intimacy are phony and strained because they continue to wear their masks while feigning openness. The "intimacy-phony" adult children are the super-glue-coated "vacuum cleaners" discussed earlier.

These adult children cannot tolerate being alone, because they need the approval of others to feel alive and safe. They try to rush relationships to an artificial level of pseudo-intimacy. As the relationships begin to develop, they begin to cling and clutch. Clutching at the other person in a relationship usually prompts him or her to back away, even if he or she cares about the intimacy-phony one. If these adult children of alcoholics continue to play out their intimacy-phony script, they set themselves up to experience their worst fear: abandonment.[15]

COUNSELING GUIDELINES

Pastors, counselors, and other helpers may feel overwhelmed by the magnitude of the counseling challenge presented by adult children of alcoholics, especially regarding relationships. The following suggestions may help:

1. *Identify and assess codependent, disrespectful relationship patterns.* Adult children of alcoholics usually identify with

these styles of interacting as they are described. Using a chart of personal boundaries (see figure 11–1) can be helpful because it allows adult children to see where they are currently and where they want to be in regard to their personal boundaries and codependent relating styles.

2. *Assign and discuss books that describe the present issues and connect the counselee to the past.* Woititz's *Struggle for Intimacy* is excellent.[16] It is not written from a Christian perspective, but is a valuable resource. *Healing for Adult Children of Alcoholics*[17] is a helpful volume written by a Christian; but it does not focus specifically on relationship issues as does the Woititz book.

Discuss what the adult child is learning about current relationships and past relationship models.

3. *Examine the adult child's use of others to fill his or her own sense of emptiness.* Examining childhood relationship models will spotlight the origins of the adult child's inner sense of emptiness. Some Christian adult children are overwhelmed with shame and guilt when they first see how they tend to use people as objects to make them feel good about themselves. Many have seen themselves as "givers," and may need encouragement to recognize that, in large part, their "giving" has been intended to gain approval from others.

Counselors can deal with the shame this realization may elicit by helping counselees recognize that their disrespectful relationship patterns are a natural outcome of their own sinfulness and the lessons they learned in childhood. Confessing their people-using tendencies to God and receiving assurance of his forgiveness and power to change will encourage Christian adult children at this point in their recovery process.

4. *Assign a Bible study on God as the satisfier of our deepest needs.* This will reinforce the adult child's shift from an outward focus to a Godward focus. These verses can be used to get started: Psalm 36:7–9, Psalm 107:8–9, Isaiah 55:1–2, Jeremiah 2:13, John 4:14, and John 7:37–38.

5. *Assign a search for new relationship models.* Have adult children of alcoholics begin noticing ways other people interact. Sometimes it is difficult to find healthy, respectful relationships being modeled within the adult child's circle of acquaintances.

Counselors may want to suggest appropriate relationship models whom counselees have not considered.

6. *Assign a study of the Gospels to identify Jesus' relating patterns.* Jesus was not codependent! He did not invade other people's personal boundaries (see John 5:6b where Jesus asked what the man wanted before he healed him). And he had well-established boundaries of his own (see Mark 6:31, where Jesus withdrew from ministering to his followers in order to rest, and exhorted his disciples to do the same). Jesus did not make decisions for other people (see Mark 10:17–22 where Jesus let the young man walk away from him even though he loved him and could have forced his will on him). And he did not let others make decisions for him (see Matthew 19:13–15 where Jesus' disciples try to persuade him to ignore the children). In this last example it is clear that Jesus does not see a child as a thing to be ignored, but as a person to be respected. Jesus consistently modeled healthy, respectful relationships.

7. *Reframe "abandonment."* Reframing is a kind of redefining which allows others to view an issue in a new light. This is one of the most significant things counselors and other helpers do for people.

Repeatedly, fear of abandonment has been identified as a core issue for adult children of alcoholics. The following reframing strategy is based on the reality that these individuals are no longer children living in danger of physical abandonment. Further, as Christians they have been assured that God will never forsake or abandon them.[18]

The truth is that adult children of alcoholics cannot be abandoned in the same way they could be abandoned as children. It is essential that they grasp this: *Adults can be left behind, jilted, stood-up, "dumped," forgotten, written-off, slighted, ignored, and even rejected, but they cannot be truly abandoned as they could be in childhood.* Why? Because adults have resources they did not have as children, when they could not leave their families and find new parents. But as adults they can find new, more respectful friends.

It is impossible to overemphasize the importance of reframing abandonment. Children will die if they are abandoned. Adults can survive rejection and loneliness, although they may be extremely painful experiences.

8. *Introduce the concept of responsibility discrimination.* Introducing the concept of responsibility discrimination seems to be second only to reframing abandonment in its impact on the way adult children of alcoholics think about relationships. Responsibility discrimination is the process by which an adult distinguishes between being responsible *for* and being responsible *to* another person. An understanding of the difference is instrumental in transforming disrespectful patterns of relating.

Each adult is responsible *for* very few other human beings. Parents are responsible for their children when the children are too young to take care of themselves. Once the children reach adolescence, parenting becomes a complicated relationship in which parents must work out the difference between being responsible *for* and being responsible *to*. However, this confusion is resolved when the children become young adults since then they are responsible for themselves.

Well-adjusted, interdependent, respectful adults may choose to assume responsibility for another person if that individual is mentally incapacitated or even extremely physically incapacitated. In the latter case it is more complicated again, since the physically impaired person should be encouraged to make his or her own decisions whenever possible.

Each mentally competent adult is responsible for his or her own choices and the consequences of those choices. Adults are responsible *for* themselves. As Christians, that responsibility is exercised under the lordship of Jesus Christ. But codependent adults assume responsibility for other mentally competent adults, often in the guise of "helping" or "Christian compassion." Many adult children of alcoholics have never thought of themselves as being responsible *to* other adults instead of being responsible *for* them.

The difference could be shown by a pastor, who is responsible *to* the congregation to proclaim the truth of God's Word and to minister to the needs of the people in an excellent manner as an undershepherd of Christ. However, the pastor is not responsible *for* making the congregants happy or winning their approval.

When pastors assume responsibility for controlling their congregations' responses, those pastors are in a codependent relationship in which they are being controlled. In such situations, pastors will work unreasonable hours, neglect their families, and injure their health all in an effort to control their congregations' responses and insure that they will gain approval. These are the kind of codependent adults of whom Jesus spoke in John 12:43 where he described them as loving the approval of men more than the approval of God. Surely, that same indictment can be made against Christian codependents today.

9. *Introduce the concept of the "necessary no" in personal choice.* This concept says that unless individuals feel the freedom to say "no" in a relationship, these adults have not *chosen freely* to say "yes." They said yes out of a compulsive and self-protective need to avoid conflict and get an approval "fix."

Christian adults raised in alcoholic homes frequently are overheard saying something like Carl's statement to his counselor: "I am going crazy trying to juggle all my obligations, and my wife and kids are complaining that I never have any time for them. But when Joe called and asked me to coach the church softball team—well, I couldn't say no." And without that "necessary no," Carl did not choose to say yes. Unless a person perceives at least two alternatives in a situation, there can be no element of choice.

Some adult children of alcoholics have said that grasping the concept of the "necessary no" gave them the freedom to make personal choices for the first time in their lives. Just because adult children learn to recognize and embrace the "necessary no" in situations requiring choices, it does not mean they must actually say "no." It just means they must realize they are free to say "no" if their "yes" is to be a freely chosen response.

10. *Use boundary-setting exercises.* Have counselees begin to establish personal boundaries and list them. Melody Beattie suggests the following as examples of boundaries common to recovering codependents:

> I will not allow anyone to physically or verbally abuse me.
> I will not knowingly believe or support lies.
> I will not allow chemical abuse in my home.

I will not allow criminal behavior in my home.

I will not rescue people from the consequences of their alcohol abuse or other irresponsible behavior.

I will not finance a person's alcoholism or other irresponsible behavior.

I will not lie to protect you or me from your alcoholism.

I will not use my home as a detoxification center for recovering alcoholics.

If you want to act crazy that's your business, but you can't do it in front of me. Either you leave or I'll walk away.

You can spoil your fun, your day, your life—that's your business—but I won't let you spoil my fun, my day, or my life.[19]

11. *Clarify need for realistic respect and appropriate trust.* As noted previously, realistic respect is a biblical position of relating to others with genuine respect tempered by an awareness of the other person's sinful nature.

This concept may be understood least by those Christian adult children who trust everyone totally, automatically, and immediately. Arlene was one of these adult children of alcoholics, and she was shocked when her Christian counselor suggested that it is not scriptural to trust in this manner. "But I thought Jesus told us to be like little children, and little children are so trusting," she responded.

Arlene's counselor pointed out that Jesus told his followers they must enter the kingdom of God with the trust of a child.[20] They could be like trusting children in their relationship to their Heavenly Father who is totally trustworthy because he is totally righteous and holy. However, in relating to other human beings, Jesus told his disciples to be "shrewd" or discerning, yet as harmless as doves.[21] That is, they were to recognize that other people (here Jesus called them "wolves") might want to harm them but they were not to harm others.

12. *Teach "share-check-share."* Share-check-share is a slow process in which adult children share a small part of themselves and then "check" the response from the other person. If that person is kind, interested, and respectful, it may be safe to share more at a later time. Gravitz and Bowden have suggested,

". . . fear of rejection is minimized because all of you cannot be rejected; only the very small part that was shared that first or second time."[22]

This intervention seems to enable the intimacy-phobic adult child to take small steps toward learning to trust appropriately. Building respectful relationships and increasing intimacy require adult children to risk self-disclosure. "Share-check-share" makes that prospect less threatening.

13. *Help establish goals and strategies for change.* As suggested above, a chart resembling figure 11–1 can help adult children of alcoholics establish goals for changing their codependent and disrespectful patterns of relating. Additional goals may be developed from examining healthy relationships.

With their all-or-nothing thinking patterns, adult children of alcoholics tend to declare all-out war on anything they want to change. They also tend to swing over to the opposite extreme behavior. I call this "the law of the pendulum." This law states that when relinquishing one extreme position, an individual tends to swing to the opposite extreme position before gradually finding a comfortable and appropriate middle position.

When adult children have determined their goals for change, counselors may need to assist them in establishing specific, reasonable, and non-reactionary steps for reaching these goals. For example, Warren, a Christian raised in an alcoholic home, was captivated by the concept of the "necessary no" in personal choices. He determined to begin choosing his responses rather than just reacting with an automatic "yes" to insure approval. When he discussed this with his counselor, it became apparent that Warren had substituted an automatic "no" for an automatic "yes." His counselor suggested that Warren reply to requests with the statement, "I want to think about that before I respond," instead of with an automatic anything. Christians are to be stewards of all their resources, including their time. Surely, it is fitting for Christian adult children of alcoholics to think and pray about requests for time commitments. Then they can determine if they are responding to the prompting of the Holy Spirit, the pull of their approval addiction, or the powerful reaction against it.

14. *Consider requiring withdrawal from codependent relationships.* Codependent relationships also have been described as addictive relationships. Individuals with relationship addictions use their total, life-dominating preoccupation with the other person in the same manner in which an alcoholic uses liquor. Both serve to anesthetize the pain of living.

Chemical-dependency recovery programs demand total abstinence and provide support during the process of drug withdrawal. These programs offer additional support and guidance to help the recovering addict face the pain of drug-free living.

Similarly, some counselors require total withdrawal from the addictive, codependent relationship for single adult children. It may be possible to resume the relationship when the adult child learns to relate interdependently, and if the other person adjusts to the changes that it brings.

If counselors request either temporary or permanent termination of a codependent relationship, they need to offer support and guidance as the adult child begins to cope with long-ignored personal pain. Counselors also will need to watch for the adult child's shift to other addictions such as overeating, overspending, or overworking. As many recovering alcoholics can attest, cigarette smoke is never thicker than at an AA meeting!

A Stranger in a Strange Land

Change can be frightening. And making changes in patterns of relating can be especially frightening. After working on relinquishing his codependent relationship style for several months, one adult child told his support group, "I feel like a stranger in a strange land. I don't know the language and I don't know if my map is right."

Christian people helpers can help adult children of alcoholics learn a new language and develop a more accurate map that will help them through the difficult process of changing their disrespectful relationship patterns. Nowhere is this help needed more than in the special relationships of marriage and parenting, to be discussed in chapter 12.

CHAPTER TWELVE

COUNSELING FOR HEALTHY MARITAL AND PARENTING RELATIONSHIPS

ADULT CHILDREN OF ALCOHOLICS grapple with the major issues of codependent and disrespectful relationships in every area of interpersonal contact: at school, on the job, in the church, and within the neighborhood. However, codependency issues are intensified in marital and parenting relationships.

Surely it is reasonable to expect that growing up in an alcoholic home would affect an individual's adult relationships with spouse and children. Consider the adult child's earliest models of these relationships. Without access to healthier relationships than those displayed in alcoholic homes, adult children face their own marriages unprepared for the challenges of such intensely intimate interactions. Later, as parenting tasks are added, many adult children of alcoholics report feeling overwhelmed with their inadequacy.

All the codependent issues examined previously are magnified in marital and parenting relationships. In addition, each of these relationships has distinct challenges of its own.

MARRIAGE AND COMMITMENT

God designed marriage to be the union of a man and woman in a relationship of such complete emotional, spiritual, and physical intimacy that Scripture speaks of the two as "one flesh." To approach such an ideal, men and women must be capable of maintaining healthy, interdependent relationships which are marked by mutual respect and the other traits discussed in the last chapter.

Beyond that, successful marriage partners are required to demonstrate a level of commitment to each other expected in no other adult interaction. This "for-better-or-for-worse" pledge translates into, "I choose to maintain this union even if you don't meet all my needs."

Unrealistic Expectations and Relational Demands

Adult children of alcoholics often harbor unrealistic expectations that others will fill their personal emptiness and meet their needs. And often they may come to believe that the marriage commitment is one they cannot fulfill. In my research with evangelical Christian adult children of alcoholics, 32.8 percent reported having been divorced, compared with 9.7 percent of Christians from nonalcoholic homes.

Counselors and authors have noted that unrealistic expectations cause problems in all marriages. Some adult children seem to bring relational demands rather than expectations to their marriages. These demands place a spouse under the heavy burden of anticipating and meeting all of the adult child's previously unmet needs. Many marriages collapse under the weight of this burdensome, codependent demand.

MARRIAGE AND CODEPENDENCY ISSUES

When many adult children of alcoholics whisper, "I do," they may actually mean, "I do agree to let you spend the rest of your life making me feel good about myself and making up to me for what I didn't have in my childhood." These adults bring themselves "on empty" to this most intimate and challenging of relationships, and often see marriage as one long opportunity for a"fill-up." This unrealistic, relational demand is expressed in the major codependency issues as they become magnified and intensified in marriage.

Each of the codependency issues examined in chapter 11 is displayed distinctly within marital relationships. Certainly this is true when considering fear of abandonment.

Fear of Abandonment

"I can't tell you how disappointed I am," Virginia told her counselor. "When I entered this marriage, I really believed I had finally found the person I'd been looking for all my life. I thought to myself, *at last—at last I've found someone who will really love me for just being me. Someone who will be there for me, someone who will really care about my happiness.* But now I realize he's just like all the others."

When Virginia entered marriage, she brought more than shower gifts and her grandmother's silver. Virginia's dowry included a deep fear of being emotionally abandoned as she had been by her two alcoholic parents. Virginia expected to experience in marriage the unconditional love and acceptance that assured her she would be safe from feelings of abandonment.

In marriage, fear of abandonment may be exhibited through unrealistic demands for total devotion and undivided attention from a spouse. A husband or wife's appropriate involvement with work, friendships, personal activities, and even children can be experienced as rejection and abandonment by adult children of alcoholics. One wife of an adult child described this reaction in her husband.

"He just seems to want my full attention all the time. No matter what I do it's not enough. I planned a romantic weekend away, hired the sitter, booked the hotel and everything. He was fine while we were gone, but as soon as we got back and I had to tend to the kids and plan for work, he started saying I neglect him. I know I'm not perfect. I guess I could do more, but honestly I have tried and it just never seems to be enough to make him feel loved."

What this wife described might be called the "Chinese food syndrome." The old cliché about eating Chinese food says you get full, but an hour later you're hungry again. Adult children who receive a spouse's frequent attention and displays of affection often have difficulty *retaining* the safe feelings of being loved. Almost immediately they are starved for attention and affection once more.

In addition, the normal disagreements in marital relationships alert adult children to the threat of perceived abandonment. To prevent conflicts, they may employ their familiar self-protective maneuver of denying feelings. This defensive strategy erects barriers, not bridges, between marriage partners. Still other adult children face more than normal disagreements within their marriages.

Clinical evidence and research findings suggest that adult children of alcoholics frequently marry individuals addicted to work, gambling, alcohol, and/or other chemicals. The inappropriate behavior accompanying these addictions is familiar to adults raised in alcoholic families. Any suggestion or thought of requesting changes or leaving the marriage activates fears of abandonment in many of these adult children. And it may be these fears, rather than religious convictions, that bind adult children to spouses who even become violently abusive and/or sexually promiscuous.

These marriages launched with such lofty hopes and unreachable goals may crash at the feet of adult children of alcoholics when dreams are dashed and trust is shattered—for trust is always a core issue in marriage as well as in codependency.

Trust

In the last chapter it was suggested that adult children of alcoholics may take one of two extreme positions regarding trust. Initially, they may vacillate between the two extremes as they attempt to initiate adult relationships, but eventually they tend to be characterized by either automatic distrust or automatic trust. Both are inappropriate and unbiblical, as we have seen.

Even distrusting "porcupine" adult children marry, although they may have lower expectations of receiving the unconditional love that makes them feel safe. They may even *expect* to be abandoned eventually. But these less-trusting adult children hope, at the very least, their pervasive sense of loneliness will be diminished within a marital relationship. However, distrusting adults fear the self-disclosure necessary to attain the genuine intimacy which can reduce these feelings of loneliness. Further, as a spouse's natural selfishness or addictive behaviors contribute to conflict in the marriage, the distrusting adult child's tentative expectations are relinquished. Then loneliness returns, and the resulting disappointment eventually turns to anger and resentment. This experience serves to reinforce in these adult children the belief that no one should be trusted.

For the ever-trusting "vacuum" adult children, the marital journey begins at a different point, but eventually reaches the same destination. Those adult children of alcoholics who typically trust totally and immediately enter marriage with exuberant expectations that cannot be met by any mere mortal. These adults again experience their worst fear—abandonment— when spouses fail to fulfill their idealized roles of demonstrating unconditional love through undivided attention. Then the fear of abandonment resurfaces, followed by deep disappointment. In time, the disappointment hardens into anger and resentment.

Whether the adult child is distrusting or all-trusting, his or her marriage is often characterized by smoldering anger punctuated by occasional flashes of rage. The anger may be expressed overtly, which is more characteristic of the less-trusting spouse, or covertly. And unacknowledged anger may be displayed by withholding sex, money, and/or approval and affirmation.

Whichever trusting style adult children of alcoholics employ, they begin marriage with unrealistic, hidden agendas which omit the fact that spouses have their own, separate ideas. Coping with separate ideas, or separate anything, raises the core issue of boundaries in codependent and disrespectful marriages.

196

Boundaries

The first codependency misbelief examined in chapter 11 addressed personal boundaries. This misbelief stated, "My desires must dictate your appearance and behavior because you are an extension of me and I can feel good about myself only when others approve of both of us." If this is true of relationships in general, it is especially true in marriage.

It is as if codependent adult children of alcoholics look at their spouses and tacitly declare, "You *really* are an extension of me because you reflect my ability to make wise personal choices and I can feel good about myself only when others approve of both of us." Furthermore, an adult child tends to see a spouse as an example to the world representing the worth or quality of individuals who would choose the adult child as a marriage partner. The implication is that the adult child is a person of similar worth or quality.

When personal boundaries are weak and unclear, a spouse's success is perceived by the adult child of an alcoholic as enhancing his or her own worth. Conversely, a mate's failure or disgrace is experienced as diminishing the adult child's personal value. In reality, neither a spouse's success nor a spouse's failure is a statement about the other spouse's own intrinsic worth.

In addition to the problems caused by unclear personal boundaries between adult children and their mates, there may be unresolved boundary issues between adult children and their parents. Some adults raised by alcoholic and co-alcoholic parents report believing that if they stopped concentrating on rescuing their parents, the family would disintegrate and it would be their fault. So these adults never cease parenting their parents, and they relate to them as though the parents were children rather than adults who are responsible for the consequences of their own behavior. These adult children are unable to focus appropriately on nurturing their own marriages because they are too busy attempting to control their parents' lives. However, they are not too busy to work at controlling spouses too, since control is a major issue in all codependent relationships.

Control

By extending the codependency misbelief about boundaries, we see how adult children's intense efforts to control their spouses makes sense. The expanded version of the misbelief is: "You really are an extension of me because you reflect my ability to make wise personal choices and I can feel good about myself only when others approve of both of us. Therefore it is essential for me to control you so that I will feel good." But there may be more than boundary issues involved in the frequently noted control orientation of adult children of alcoholics.

When many adult children of alcoholics marry, they do not commit to a romantic partnership so much as they contract for a renovation project. These adults often marry someone they want to "fix." To change and "fix" a spouse, the spouse must relinquish responsibility for his or her own life and transfer that responsibility to the "fixer." In other words, the "fixer" must be able to control the "fixee" to complete the renovation project.

These attempts to control and "fix" may have as a goal the elimination of drug use, prevention of angry outbursts, or improvement in clothing selection. Each goal is treated equally as a life-and-death issue. Adult children of alcoholics often are surprised and confused by the intensity of their desires to control and change their spouses. Counselors and others can help adult children connect their urgent need to control situations and people with the lack of control that prevailed in their chaotic childhoods. This realization reduces their confusion, and gives the adult child a context for his or her own change. This understanding helped Carl see how he had been disrespecting his wife by attempts to control her.

"Sue moved out two weeks ago," Carl told his support group. "I've been thinking about the discussion last week on our need to control to feel safe. God has really convicted me of what I have been doing in my marriage. It is as if I failed when I was a kid. I mean I failed to make a difference in my family as my dad's drinking got worse and everything hit the skids. I guess all this time I've been thinking my marriage was a second chance to make a difference in someone's life—you know, to change them for the good. Plus, I just feel better when I know what's going to happen and when Sue acts right. As Sue began to get under more pressure at work, she gained weight and started to have a drink now and then to relax. I got scared and kept hiding her wine and all the sweets she likes. I don't know; maybe I thought she was going to turn into a drunken slob like my dad. I was after her constantly about it. Really, I drove her away with my criticism and lack of love."

Carl's counselor helped him learn the difference between *influence* and *control*. It is not disrespectful to attempt to influence another's decisions by encouragement, discussion, education, prayer, and other appropriate means. This is what pastors, counselors, and other professional and nonprofessional helpers do all the time. An influencer may grieve over and pray about the self-destructive choices of another adult; but he or she will not take over responsibility for preventing those choices or for mopping up the messes caused by them. In effect, Christian influencers, whether spouses or counselors, acknowledge God as the sovereign Controller in their own lives and in the lives of others.

Clearly, Carl's attempts to control his wife's behavior disrespected her. Clearly also, it damaged the potential for intimacy in their marriage.

Intimacy

In marriage, intimacy is expressed both sexually and nonsexually; and because communication patterns and sexual functioning are both reflecting the couple's level of intimacy, both are affected when intimacy is impaired.

A couple's communication pattern is the clearest non-sexual expression of marital intimacy. The level of this non-sexual intimacy can be measured by each spouse's belief that he or she is free to disclose true thoughts and feelings without fear of personal rejection. This atmosphere of freedom and acceptance contributes to a growing sense of shared unity or intimacy.

Considering the codependent elements found in many marriages of adult children of alcoholics, it is no surprise that they experience little true intimacy, as is often displayed openly in the marital communication.

Communication Problems. Rosellini and Worden suggest that in alcoholic families, people talk *at* each other rather than *with* each other. What appear to be dialogues are actually double monologues:

> Dad spouts off his demands and rationalizations. Mom waits for him to pause for breath and when he does, she launches into her own agenda, her own demands and rationalizations. They are like debate opponents vying for advantage, seeking to score points. The purpose of these conversations is to . . . browbeat, manipulate, guilt-trip and generally convince the opposition to act right.[1]

Since this is the marital communication taught in most alcoholic families, this is the pattern the children learn. When these children marry, they tend to adopt the communication style learned from Mom and Dad.

Adult children of alcoholics usually lack basic communication skills such as empathic listening and use of "I" statements, which facilitate healthy communication. Additionally, most adult children are committed more to subtly controlling rather than to openly communicating. They have a greater emotional investment in self-protection than in self-disclosure. Yet open communication and self-disclosure are the building blocks of genuine intimacy.

Sexual Dysfunction. It comes as no surprise that the intimacy problems of adult children, which are expressed in the living room by shouts or sullen stares are revealed in the bedroom by sexual dysfunction.

Children in alcoholic families seldom see their parents displaying spontaneous, tender physical affection in ways that are both respectful and appropriate. Instead, children may see the co-alcoholic parent frequently repelling the sexual advances of the intoxicated parent. In recent years, many parents have objected to schools teaching sex education classes because they want to teach their children about sex at home. In reality, parents *always* teach their children about sex at home. Alcoholic and co-alcoholic parents usually teach their children that sex is dirty, degrading, and embarrassing, and that it should be avoided except for the purpose of procreation.

In addition to poor parental modeling, some adult children of alcoholics bring memories of sexual abuse to their marriages. These memories may intrude on the marriage bed, leaving the abused adult child of an alcoholic parent nonorgasmic or impotent. The bedroom also may be filled with distrust, anger, and attempts to control. All limit the couple's capacity to fully celebrate the sexual expression of intimacy.

Clearly, marital relationships present unique problems to typically codependent adult children of alcoholics. Parenting also offers its own unique challenges.

PARENTING PROBLEMS

Problems in both marriage and parenting are related to the fact that adult children of alcoholics must guess at what constitutes normal family living. These adults are in this position because they did not have healthy parental role models. Most feel they are parenting without adequate guidelines, and they acknowledge they have problems. These problems occur in two major areas: unrealistic expectations and inappropriate boundaries.

Unrealistic Expectations

First, adult children of alcoholics have unrealistic expectations of themselves. They do not want to be *good* parents; they want to be *perfect* parents. Although they had inadequate parenting models, they expect themselves automatically to be perfect parents. Instead, most adult children find themselves repeating the despised parenting practices learned in childhood, including placing unrealistic expectations and demands on their children.

Because of their unusual childhoods most adult children are unaware of normal human development and may find natural childhood behavior confusing and unacceptable. Many adult children were extremely compliant; many remember that at age seven or eight they were cooking, caring for younger siblings, and/or cleaning up after an alcoholic parent. These adult children see their own offspring engaging in more normal and age-appropriate behavior and think, "I would not have done that." They forget that their criteria for what is normal are their own abnormal childhoods.[2]

Certainly, adult children of alcoholics regret the loss of their childhoods and resent parental expectations which required that they be adults at birth. At the same time, many of these adult children expect their own offspring to be mature beyond their years. Pastors and counselors will need to help the adult child learn about age-appropriate expectations for children. These counselees also may need to work through resentment that their own children are experiencing a quality of family life that was unavailable to the adult child. That was Leslie's parenting challenge.

She covered her face with one hand and dabbed at tears with a tissue in the other. "You can't imagine how ashamed I am of these feelings," Leslie stammered. "I am actually jealous of my two girls because of how much time their dad spends with them. Oh, Bill spends time with me, too; that's not what I mean. I mean when I see him playing with the girls or helping them with their homework, I think about my dad. He was either working or drunk. I don't ever remember him really looking at me or talking to me, let alone ever playing with me. I'm happy for my girls, but it makes me realize what I missed and I resent it."

Robert Ackerman suggests that having children of their own always raises unresolved issues for adult children of alcoholics. In relating to his or her own children, Ackerman tells the adult child to, "remember this is their childhood, not yours."[3]

Some unrealistic expectations seem to be related to the gender of the child. For example, adult children of alcoholics may tend to disregard the needs and feelings of a same-sex child more than those of an opposite-sex child. This is especially true if the adult child is distanced from, and disregards, his or her own needs and feelings. If an individual perceives himself or herself as a "rock" with no needs and feelings, there may be a tendency to view all of one's gender as "rocks." This may even extend to one's children.

In contrast, daughters of alcoholic fathers frequently appear to overindulge their sons and expect less of them than is age-appropriate. This may be related to a childhood belief that "You have to take care of men." It seems to be difficult for adult children to maintain clear boundaries between expectations regarding their parents, themselves, and their children. As always, the boundary issue is a knotty one.

Inappropriate Boundaries

The troubling boundary issue is most intense for codependent adult children of alcoholics in their relationships with their own children. More than any other person in any other relationship, one's child is seen as an extension of oneself.

Two major aspects of the boundary problems are experienced by adult children in their parenting. There are problems in setting boundaries for the children, and there are problems in establishing boundaries between the adult child and his or her children.

Establishing Boundaries for the Children. The Scriptures reveal that parents are responsible for training their children. Part of this training involves setting boundaries to separate what is acceptable from what is unacceptable. God's Word also describes a child's heart with the word "foolishness" in Proverbs 22:15. When setting boundaries requires correction, what reactions might parents expect from children with hearts of foolishness? Proverbs 9:7–8 declares the reaction will be anger or even open hostility.

This can be a major problem for parents who are adult children of alcoholics. They look to their children to provide the total love and acceptance found in no other relationship. In infancy, children fill this need for unconditional love, and that almost seems to make up for the adult child's past rejections and disappointments. As their children develop, parents need to establish boundaries for the children's behavior. At these times, the children often react with anger and/or by withdrawing from their parents. This can be agony for the adult child who cherishes times of closeness with his or her children.

Watching their children relax and even smile when they give in to them can be a tremendous relief to some parents. It's almost as if they go underwater when their children become angry with them and they're finally able to come up for air! Children quickly learn how dependent their parents can become on their good graces, and they can hold their parents hostage by withholding their love when they want to avoid a rule.[4]

Children are able to "hold their parents hostage" because insecure and codependent parents, such as adult children of alcoholics, may be concerned more about maintaining their children's approval than in developing their children's character. In their efforts to establish appropriate boundaries for their children, adult children of alcoholics are hampered by their approval addiction which requires them to concentrate less on controlling their children's behavior than on controlling their children's attitudes toward them.

Approval addiction is rooted in fear of abandonment. And the codependent issues of fear of abandonment and control figure prominently in the second major boundary problem:

Establishing Boundaries between Parent and Child. Sometimes one parent fails to set clear boundaries between the other parent and the children by using children as confidants and making them "little spouses." Friel and Friel suggest that when codependent parents lean on their children for support and share their deepest problems with them it is a form of emotional incest.[5]

Emotional incest. When there is conflict in marriage, or after divorce, adult children of alcoholics may relate to their children in this emotionally incestuous manner. At those times, an adult child experiences a sense of abandonment and may use his or her children to fill the emotional role of the spouse.

Pastors, counselors, and others can help adult children of alcoholics understand the boundaries between adults and children within family systems. Parents are to look to each other as sexual partners, confidants, and best friends. To use another adult outside the marriage to fill these roles is physical or emotional adultery. To look to children within the family to fill them is physical or emotional incest.

Both forms of incest are destructive boundary violations that force children into inappropriate adult roles. In contrast, the other major challenge of establishing boundaries between parents and children involves forcing maturing children to remain in inappropriate childhood roles.

Releasing. Parenting can be viewed as a gradual process of releasing control and responsibility. At birth, the child has 0 percent of both control and responsibility and the parents have 100 percent. By approximately age twenty-one, the parents should have 0 percent of the control and responsibility while the young adult child has 100 percent.

Considering their codependent struggles with the need to control and the tendency to be over-responsible, it is not surprising that adult children of alcoholics have difficulty releasing their own children at nearly every developmental stage. The major releasing crises typically occur when the child is a toddler, in adolescence, and when leaving home.

Dr. Michael Yogman, a pediatrician with the Infant Health and Development Program at Boston Children's Hospital, was quoted in a newspaper article as recommending, "that parents who are frustrated by their toddlers take a closer look at their own need to be in control of every situation. 'What kinds of ghosts from your past are shaping those feelings?' he asked."[6]

Earlier chapters examined the "ghosts" that shaped the need to be in control—a characteristic of many adult children of alcoholics. This control orientation will produce stress and even panic in an adult child when his or her own children push away to develop separate identities. Dr. Yogman believes that a parent's intense need to control a child increases the stress of parenting. And many adult children of alcoholics tackle the uncertainties and stresses of parenting by becoming even more rigidly controlling.

Seixas and Youcha describe one adult child's codependent parenting battle with overcontrolling.

"The rules were always changing in my family. I never knew what to expect or what was expected of me," one mother put it. Now she is determined that her own children will behave according to clear, strict standards. In reacting to her own concern about control, she has been making unrealistic demands on her children, insisting on rigid curfews, homework every night from 7:00 to 9:00, and very little time for relaxed fun.[7]

As their offspring enter adolescence, adult children of alcoholics may tighten their controlling grip. Psychologist Laurence Steinberg has found that, "the stronger the need to control the child, the more likely the parent is to feel a lot of stress during the child's adolescence."[8] In contrast, less-controlling parents who enjoyed their teenagers looked forward to adolescence because they would no longer have to tell their children what to do all the time. These less-controlling parents welcomed the changes in their children and the release of some parental control and responsibility.

In well-functioning families, there is a comfortable fit between the child's developmental capacity to handle additional responsibility and the parents' willingness to release control and responsibility. Ideally, as children continue to mature, parents reciprocate by relinquishing additional control and responsibility to their children. This process culminates as the children leave their parents' homes and control to assume full responsibility for themselves.

Many adult children of alcoholics find this child-launching phase extremely stressful. This is especially true if they have been absorbed in the lives of their children in lieu of facing personal or marital problems. When boundaries are weak between adult children and their offspring, a child's development and departure from the home is experienced as a deep personal loss rather than as a sign of growth. And the adult children may seek to bind their offspring to them with the same imprisoning loyalties with which their alcoholic and co-alcoholic parents bound them. Thus the intergenerational, codependent patterns are perpetuated. Without intervention this pattern will continue unto the third and fourth generation and beyond.

COUNSELING GUIDELINES

Pastors and counselors can intervene in this codependent cycle to assist adult children of alcoholics in changing their marital and parenting relationships. The following suggestions offer some practical guidelines:

1. *Review and apply counseling strategies from chapter 11.* All the counseling guidelines for respectful relationships are applicable to the special marital and parenting relationships.

2. *Assign books on marriage and/or parenting.* Many excellent books on marriage and parenting have been written from a Christian perspective. Some of these volumes cover specific marital issues such as communication and sexual satisfaction. There are also books offering guidelines to parents of young children, and others that deal with parenting adolescents. Your local Christian bookstore may offer some excellent selections.

3. *Refer to a marriage and family therapist as needed.* Many readers will be trained and experienced in working from a family-systems perspective in counseling. Others may be overwhelmed at the prospect. When marital and parenting conflicts are the major problems faced by adult children of alcoholics, they will benefit from working with a marital and family therapist who understands the intergenerational dynamics of an alcohol-dominated home.

4. *Offer hope for change.* As adult children begin to realize they are repeating marital and parenting patterns learned in their childhoods, most are filled with a sense of hopelessness. They may feel they and their present families are trapped forever in codependent, dysfunctional interactions.

Christian adults from alcoholic homes need to be reminded that because of his great mercy, the God and Father of our Lord Jesus Christ, "has caused us to be born again to a living hope through the resurrection of Jesus Christ from the dead."[9] There is a valid basis for the Christian's hope in the resurrection of our Savior. The same power that brought Christ out of the tomb operates in his followers. That power is available to bring forth into new life those individuals and families entombed in old, unhealthy, and disrespectful relationships.

5. *Counter guilt with truth.* Most adult children of alcoholics experience guilt when they recognize that their attitudes and actions have damaged relationships with their spouses and/ or children. These adults worry especially about destroying their children's self-concepts and hopes for well-adjusted lives.

Typically, adult children berate themselves for not being better parents.

The truth is that nearly all spouses and parents do the best they *know*. However, it is not accurate to say they do the best they *can*, because they *could* have done better if they had *known* what "better" was. This truth gives adult children the sure hope that now that they *know* more about being wise and loving spouses and parents, they *can* do more about being wise and loving spouses and parents.

An additional truth is that adult children of alcoholics may need to repent of sinful behaviors related to marital and parenting responsibilities. Pastors and counselors will need to compassionately confront the necessity for renouncing such practices, for confessing them as sin to God and to the offended party, and for receiving forgiveness from both. If this behavior includes any form of child abuse, helpers must face the issue of mandatory reporting.

All fifty states require reporting any type of child abuse. "Those who report are generally given immunity from liability and can remain anonymous, as long as the report was made in good faith," notes Grant Martin in the Resources for Christian Counseling volume entitled *Counseling for Family Violence and Abuse.*[10] Martin states that some pastors seem to resent government interference with their role as spiritual confidants. However, Martin correctly observes:

> Clergy confidentiality is intended as part of a process to help a person overcome personal problems so as not to cause further harm to self or others. Confidentiality is not intended to protect offenders from being accountable or from getting help. Protecting abusers from the consequences of their actions will deny them the opportunity for spiritual repentance and a chance to change.[11]

Further, it is suggested that Scripture has always supported the responsibility of the believing community to protect those who are most defenseless and vulnerable. Surely abused children are numbered in that category. "Maintaining an effort of confidentiality for secrecy's sake while ignoring the pleas of victimized children contradicts the entire message of Jesus Christ."[12]

The message of Jesus provides a third life-changing truth which can deal with guilt: "If we confess our sins, He is faithful and righteous to forgive us our sins and to cleanse us from all unrighteousness," declares 1 John 1:9. And two verses earlier, God's Word says, ". . . the blood of Jesus His Son cleanses us from all sin." These verses announce the gracious truth that *all* sinful acts can be forgiven on the basis of Jesus Christ's atoning death. Even child abuse is included. But the abusing parent must not only repent and receive forgiveness, he or she also must enter treatment. Pastors, counselors, and other helpers should refer this parent to a professional trained in the treatment of abuse offenders.

6. *Seek healthier marriage and family models.* Adult children of alcoholics and their spouses can talk with and visit couples who have healthy, respectful marital relationships. Adult children also can watch other parents to see how they set limits, resolve conflicts, and talk with their children. This is one of several strategies designed to re-educate adult children about the traits of well-functioning families.

7. *Attend seminars and classes on marriage and/or parenting.* Many churches offer biblically based seminars or classes on the characteristics of a Christian home. In addition, the YMCA or mental-health center in most communities offers courses covering basic skills in communication and conflict resolution with spouse and children. Pastors and Christian counselors can supplement the secular courses with scriptural guidelines for developing Christ-centered homes.

8. *Teach parents to "release their arrows."* The psalmist describes children as "arrows" and declares," blessed is the man whose quiver is full of them."[13]

Ancient warriors knew their arrows needed to be polished to remove irregularities that would prevent the arrows from accomplishing their purposes. Arrows also need to be balanced so their flight is straight and true. Arrows need to be polished and balanced; but they also need to be pointed in the right direction. Obviously, tragedy can result when arrows are directed in the wrong path. But even when arrows are polished, balanced, and pointed in the right direction, one thing remains to be done: *Arrows must be released.*

Like a diligent warrior with his arrows, healthy parents "polish" their children with discipline. These parents also "balance" their children with affirmation and encouragement. Then, good parents point their children in the right direction for life by instilling biblical values and by consistently exposing them to the message of God's redeeming love. But adult children of alcoholics and other codependent parents may find it difficult to release their children. Counselors can help these parents see that, like arrows, children must be released to accomplish the tasks for which they were created.

9. *Address the issue of an alcoholic spouse.* If the adult child is married to an alcoholic, there are several specific steps to take.

a) If there are children in the home, get help for them immediately. Call the local Alcoholism Council to locate Alateen or Alatot groups. Alateen is a self-help organization for adolescents who have a relative or close friend who is an alcoholic. Alatot groups are for young children of alcoholics and are led by trained adults. (Unfortunately, Alatot is not as widely available as Alateen.) Also look for books written for children and adolescents who have an alcoholic parent. Several are listed in Appendix A. It is essential for children to get help as early as possible to break the intergenerational cycle of codependency.

b) Encourage the adult child of an alcoholic to attend Al-Anon meetings. Al-Anon is a self-help group for spouses and other adults close to alcoholics.

c) Consult with a trained alcoholism counselor about the possibility of doing an intervention with the alcoholic spouse. An intervention is a loving confrontation in which the alcoholic is told about the harmful effects of alcohol-induced behavior on himself or herself and loved ones. The alcoholic is also confronted with the consequences of continuing an alcoholic lifestyle. Finally, the alcoholic is asked to enter a treatment program. Those who participate in the intervention need to attend one or more preparation meetings with an alcoholism counselor.

d) Pastors, counselors, and other helpers will benefit from reading *Counseling for Substance Abuse and Addiction*, which is volume 12 in the Resources for Christian Counseling series. Two physicians, Stephen Van Cleave and Walter Byrd, and a registered nurse, Kathy Revell, co-authored this informative book.

10. *Make Jesus Christ the center of the home.* If there is an alcoholic spouse in the home, he or she may be the primary focus for the adult child spouse. The patterns sketched in chapter 2 will be enacted once more. Even if there is no drinking problem, the adult child's past pain and current codependency may dominate the home.

One aspect of recovery from the effects of parental alcoholism involves reordering priorities. Many adult children of alcoholics learn to turn their lives over to their "Higher Power" rather than to their alcoholic and co-alcoholic parents. For Christian adults from alcoholic families, recovery hinges on making Jesus Christ the *Highest* Power in their lives and homes. In reality, this is both a one-time decision and an ongoing process.

HOPE AND HISTORY

This book is intended to offer hope for change and new beginnings to adult children of alcoholics. The focus in this chapter has been on hope for changing marital and parenting relationships—hope for new family life.

Plutarch said, "My family history begins with me." Plutarch captured the adult child's hope for new beginnings. But even as the recovering process moves forward, part of the adult child's earlier history tags along: parents. The next chapter addresses the adult child's challenge to manage this old relationship in new ways.

CHAPTER THIRTEEN

COUNSELING FOR NEW FAMILY ROLES

"I KNOW IT'S SILLY, BUT I wish God would give me a magic pencil with a huge eraser on it." Betty Lou flashed a tear-sprinkled smile as she sat in her counselor's office. "I'd erase my past and rewrite it, and I'd start with my folks. I'd rewrite my parents completely—starting with no booze." Betty Lou's counselor invited her to accept and forgive her parents while she also scripted a new relationship with them using the instrument of choice.

Betty Lou and other adult children of alcoholics are learning that, although they cannot change their parents, they can make new, healthier choices about their relationships with their parents. These adult children do not have to play out the roles assigned to them in childhood. As adults, they now can make choices they could not make as children. And as Christians, adult children of alcoholics, and all believers, have the promise that old things—including parent-authored "life-scripts"—have passed away, and new things—including God-directed choices—have come.[1]

However, even Christian adult children may remain trapped in denial and the enactment of parentally prescribed roles.

PRE-RECOVERY PREOCCUPATION

If adult children of alcoholics do not move out of denial and into thinking, feeling, and telling the truth about their parents' alcoholism, they will never see the possibilities of choosing new family roles. They will maintain their preoccupation with alcoholic and co-alcoholic parents. Stephanie Brown suggests that this preoccupation can be consuming especially for young adult children of alcoholics.

> Some are so preoccupied with their families immediately after leaving home, they are unable to concentrate as students, unable to be committed to career training or first jobs. To focus on themselves is to run the risk that a calamity will occur in their family and they will not have done all that they could to avoid it. Such children feel abandoned and are constantly frightened about the loss of one or both of these parents.[2]

> Once more, the familiar theme of abandonment is sounded. These young adult children of alcoholics may have already experienced abandonment because they left their parents' homes. By remaining preoccupied with their parents and families, they minimize the painful feelings of further abandonment.

Chapter 5 examined the effects of this parental preoccupation on the lives and marriages of unrecovered adult children of alcoholics. We saw that in the alcoholic family the "tie that binds" is more like a chain that chokes.

If adult children break free of their families' denials of parental alcoholism, they begin to see that life has been shaped by distortion of truth and constricting childhood roles. But familiar, childhood roles and patterns of relating change slowly. Even when adult children begin recovering from the effects of parental alcoholism, they may remain preoccupied with their alcoholic families. The preoccupation may take the form of a fantasy.

EARLY RECOVERY RESCUE FANTASIES

Gravitz and Bowden suggest that some adult children of alcoholics greet the emergent awareness of early recovery with a "flight into parental salvation."[3] These authors use "salvation" without any religious connotation, but as a synonym for rescuing. They believe this parental rescuing can be a way adult children avoid dealing with their own problems. However, there may be other reasons for the rescue fantasies embraced by many initially recovering adult children.

Their codependent patterns of controlling and taking responsibility for others predisposes adult children of alcoholics to these rescue fantasies. Besides, the self-focus of early recovery feels strange to adult children who grew up learning that the needs of their alcoholic and co-alcoholic parents always came first.

Still more strange—and painful—for adult children is the feeling of being disloyal to the family and the accompanying sense of parental abandonment experienced as they begin their recovering process. As adult children break out of the family denial of alcoholism, they stand alone in the warm light of emerging truth. Once the sunrise of recovery has begun, adult children cannot return to the night of distortion and denial with their families. The sense of parental abandonment and isolation from the family drives many adult children to undertake a frantic effort to drag their families into the light of their own recovery processes.

Friel and Friel tell a delightful fable about "The Littlest Gosling" who struggled with rescue fantasies. This gosling lived on a little pond with his parents, Mr. and Mrs. Gander, and his gosling siblings. Gradually the Littlest Gosling became aware that something was wrong with the pond as he noticed a peculiar odor and spotted more and more dead fish. His family just called him a silly goose for worrying. But as the Littlest Gosling began to feel sick, he went to his parents again to warn them, and again they told him he was foolish.

Finally, the Littlest Gosling was so worried, he dared to break the family rule. He flew away from the pond to a large, clean lake where he met many geese who believed his story about the pond. They told him the pond was poisoned and that some geese had died because of the pond. Immediately, the littlest gosling went to warn his family.

"Dad! Mom!" he shouted. "I know I'm not supposed to leave the pond, but I just had to get away. I was feeling so sick. And I was so curious. Anyway, I talked to some geese in a lake near here, and the Eldest Gander there said that the water in this pond is poison, and that he lost two goslings because of it. We need to get out of here right away!" he said excitedly.

Mr. Gander looked sternly at his son and said, "We told you never to leave this pond until we are all ready to fly south for the winter. You have broken our most important rule. We are very disappointed in you. Now go back to the nest and don't leave there until we tell you to!"

The Littlest Gosling was heartbroken and terrified. He didn't know what to do. He loved his family, and he wanted to be a good gosling, but he didn't want his family to die either. He began to return to the nest. When he was almost there, he suddenly turned, looked up into the sky, recalled the words of the Eldest Gander, and then flew off toward the big lake.[4]

We will come back to the Littlest Gosling later. But already we can see some striking similarities between his experience and those of many adult children of alcoholics. For example, parents and other family members may resist the adult child's rescuing efforts just as Mr. and Mrs. Gander did with their littlest gosling.

Counselors can help adult children of alcoholics understand that their efforts to recover from the effects of growing up in alcoholic homes may be too threatening for their parents to accept. The adult child's new awareness of truth will usually be experienced by parents as an accusation of total failure. The guilt of even *recovering* alcoholic and co-alcoholic parents may render them deaf and blind to the concerns of their adult children.

Siblings of adult children of alcoholics frequently do not see themselves as adult children. It is not unusual for only one adult child in an alcoholic family to recognize and discuss openly the effects of parental alcoholism. The recovering adult child may be labeled a "disloyal liar" as was a counselee named Tony. His brother and three sisters refused to include him and his wife in family activities after he told them he was learning about the impact of their father's alcoholism. Tony's siblings never told their actively alcoholic father about Tony's "disloyalty," because they said they did not want to upset their father. But they told their mother, and she also withdrew emotionally from Tony.

Sometimes, the unrecovering siblings will look to the recovering adult child to "handle" the alcoholic parent. Joan's brothers were not interested in facing the effect on their own lives from growing up with two alcoholic parents; but they did recognize their parents' declining mental and physical health. Joan reported to her support group that her brothers told her since she was the one "worrying about the family's alcoholism" she should be the one to "take care of Mom and Dad."

Joan's counselor worked with her to see that she could not cure her parents' alcoholism anymore than the Littlest Gosling could force his parents to leave the poisoned pond. Joan and all recovering adult children of alcoholics must accept the difficult truth that their own recovery is not going to make their parents automatically recover. This truth is enmeshed with painful, codependent issues of controlling, unclear personal boundaries, and fear of abandonment.

Joan also learned about differentiating between control and influence. Her counselor helped Joan see that she only set herself up for failure and disappointment when she took responsibility for something she could not control. Joan was not responsible for her parents' alcoholism and she was not responsible for their recovery. However, Joan is responsible for her own recovery. She can control her ongoing pursuit of truth in thinking, feeling, and relating to God, herself, and others.

Adult children of alcoholics need to learn that the best thing they can do for their parents and families is to work on their own recoveries. Relinquishing rescue fantasies enables adult children to focus on their own healing processes which, in turn, move them toward accepting and forgiving their parents. As the adult child continues to move beyond the past's bondage and bitterness, someone else in the alcoholic family system may want to join him or her. Or perhaps he or she will remain the only member of the alcoholic family to choose truth over lies.

Even if adult children do not formally declare to the entire family that they have begun a process of recovering from the effects of parental alcoholism, they will disturb the family equilibrium. Recovering adult children will begin to talk and behave differently. They will want to lay aside their confining childhood roles and develop their own, valid identities. These adult children will begin to be less tolerant with outrageous alcoholic behavior. The family will notice and someone will ask, "What's gotten into you?" Whether the adult child chooses a brief or detailed description of his or her recovery, there will be one of two responses from the family. And either response presents additional challenges to the recovering adult child of an alcoholic.

Figure 13–1 is a flow chart depicting the choices facing adult children as they progress in their own recoveries and interact with their families. The capitalized words describe the adult child's choices or those in which he or she participates. The broken horizontal lines indicate positive changes which can occur after initial, unhealthy choices by the alcoholic, the family, and/or the recovering adult child.

NEW ROLES IN THE BEST-CASE FAMILY SCENARIO

The right side of figure 13–1 displays what could be called the best-case family scenario in response to changes in a recovering adult child. As shown, others in the family forsake their denial of parental alcoholism and enter their own recovery processes. The family dynamics begin to change. Perhaps the

Personal and Family Recovery Choices

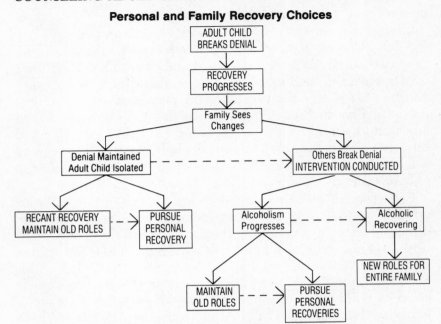

Figure 13-1

recovering family members agree to stop enabling the alcoholic parent(s). They may participate in a well-planned family intervention with the alcoholic. The best possible result, of course, is for the alcoholic to enter treatment and maintain his or her sobriety. This best-case scenario includes the co-alcoholic parent entering recovery also. But even then, the family's situation is not paradise.

Less than Paradise

Counselors and other helpers need to know, and help adult children understand, that just because a parent is sober and actively recovering the family will not be transformed into a problem-free paradise. Old relational patterns are difficult to change. If the entire family is recovering, everyone will be struggling with unfamiliar new roles. Each member of the family may need to pursue his or her own recovery through participation in suitable support groups such as Alcoholics Anonymous, Al-Anon, Alateen or Adult Children of Alcoholics. In addition, recovering families will benefit from counseling with professionals experienced in the dynamics of recovering alcoholic family systems.

Counselors also will need to help adult children of alcoholics adjust their expectations to the duration of their parents' sobriety. Relating to a newly sober parent is very different from interacting with one who has maintained sobriety for years. As parents continue to recover from alcoholism they will become more rational, more reasonable, and more willing to assume responsibility for their own lives.

Understandably, adult children panic when recovering parents slip back into drinking after a period of abstinence from alcohol. Seixas and Youcha report that Dr. Terence Wilson of Rutgers University School of Alcohol Studies believes it is most helpful to view a slip as "a mistake, not a failure."[5] When the slip occurs, parents need to be encouraged to resume sobriety rather than made to feel guilty. And recovering adult children may need to remind themselves that they are not responsible for their parents' recoveries.

Obviously, the very best situation would be for alcoholic parents to begin recovery immediately and maintain sobriety perfectly. But adult children rarely find such ideal responses from their alcoholic families.

NEW ROLES IN LESS-THAN-BEST-CASE FAMILY SCENARIOS

Few adult children witness a smooth progression from their own personal recovery to that of their siblings and parents. Even when the alcoholic eventually enters recovery, there may be lengthy and painful detours in route to complete family recovery.

The left side of figure 13–1 depicts an initial detour which may occur when one or more family members first notice changes in the recovering adult child of an alcoholic, and perceive that adult child as defecting from the family. If so, the family will staunchly maintain denial and close ranks, thereby isolating the "defector."

The adult child is confronted with a choice to pursue his or her personal recovery or play out the old family-assigned role. Both choices bring pain.

Old Roles and Simulated Denial

If an adult child recants the professed recovery with its new, reality-based view of the family, he or she enters a charade of simulated denial. These adult children are not free to pursue their own personal recoveries. And they are not comfortable pretending they do not see the family organized around alcohol.

"It was crazy. I felt like I was trapped in the story of the 'Emperor's New Clothes.' I was like the little kid who saw the truth and no one else would acknowledge it," a support group member recalled. "At first I didn't have the guts to stick to the truth. But eventually I decided I would go crazy if I continued to play my family's game. God gave me the strength to choose his truth instead of my family's denial of it. But I feel completely alienated from my family and it still hurts."

This young man chose to pursue his personal recovery after his own brief detour into simulated denial and old roles. But choosing new roles has its own challenges.

New Roles and New Choices

When alcoholic parents continue drinking, adult children must make new choices if they are to progress in their own recovering process. The middle paths in figure 13–1 illustrate two possibilities for choices when parents are actively alcoholic. First, the recovering adult child may stand alone against the denial of the entire family, as did the young man described above. Or, some other family members also may break out of denial and join the adult child in recovery. Either way, those individuals in the family who are recovering from the effects of parental alcoholism will be required to make some new choices and establish some appropriate limits.

Setting Limits

Whether adult children of alcoholics stand alone or with some of their family, difficult new choices must be made.

When the Adult Child Stands Alone. To relate in new, respectful ways to alcoholic and co-alcoholic parents and to play new, healthier roles in the family, adult children must establish some personal limits which reflect new attitudes and choices. Before setting limits on any interaction with drinking parents, such as loaning them money, adult children must clarify their purposes.

Clarifying purposes. Chapter 2 explored the fact that dysfunctional, alcoholic families often fail to provide safety, security, and stability for children. As adults, these children can make choices that contribute to their own safety, security, and stability and that of their offspring. Preservation of physical and emotional well-being for adult children and their loved ones is one purpose for setting limits with alcoholic parents. For example, just because adult children of alcoholics grew up riding with an intoxicated parent driving the family car, they don't have to continue to expose themselves and their own children to that danger. Adult children can make new choices. They can establish limits.

The recovering adult child's desire to relate to his or her parents with a new attitude of realistic respect is another reason for making new choices and establishing limits with alcoholic parents. As counselors continue to lead adult children to examine their codependent relationship patterns, the need to choose new ways to relate to parents will become obvious.

Much of the limit setting will be to clarify the boundaries of responsibility that are blurred or nonexistent in most alcoholic families. It is disrespectful to assume responsibility for another adult's life or for protecting that adult from the consequences of his or her own behavior. When this is done for alcoholics, it is called "enabling."

Enabling. Enabling is a kind of protecting and "mopping-up" behavior that actually enables the alcoholic to avoid facing the consequences of his or her alcoholism. This enables the alcoholic to continue denying that drinking causes problems, which in turn enables him or her to continue drinking alcoholically. In reality, enabling sabotages the sobriety adult children long to see their alcoholic parents achieve.

221

From a biblical perspective, enabling actually promotes the mental, moral, spiritual, and physical destruction of the alcoholic. In contrast, Scripture tells believers to think about how to stimulate others to produce loving attitudes and good actions.[6] Christian adult children of alcoholics need to acknowledge that their enabling is an aspect of their codependency. They also may need to repent of it as sin.

When recovering adult children of alcoholics begin to adopt attitudes of realistic respect toward others, they will have to learn to establish boundaries with their parents. Pastors, counselors, and others can provide the direction and support that adult children will need.

Determining specifics. Each adult child will have unique limit-setting challenges to face based on the dynamics of his or her own particular family. The following general areas are some in which adult children of alcoholics will need to seek answers and make new choices about what is and is not appropriate and tolerable.[7]

1. *Finances.* Will adult children lend money to parents or borrow from them? Will they pay drinking parents' rents, thus freeing money for liquor? If parents drink up their Social Security and/or retirement incomes, will adult children rescue them? Will adult children pay for their parents' medical care? Will adult children pay fines or bail for their parents?

Healthy, respectful answers to these questions will lead to setting limits which acknowledge alcoholic parents as responsible for their choices and the consequences of those choices.

2. *Visits to parents' home.* Must adult children of alcoholics visit their parents whenever parents expect a visit? Must adult children stay as long as the parents expect? Will adult children visit when parents are drinking? What are the reasons for terminating a visit?

Early in their recovering process, some adult children of alcoholics find it impossible to visit their parents' homes if parents are actively alcoholic. Later, these adult children may visit infrequently for short periods of time. This is the case especially for adult children who are recovering from their own alcoholism.

In many alcoholic family systems, use and abuse of alcohol is the common social bond. When an alcoholic adult child is recovering from the effects of personal and parental alcoholism, visits home can be extremely difficult. George described it this way: "Me and my brother and dad use to booze it up together real good. I mean the three of us could drink the rest of the family under the table. But now that I have been sober a couple of years and have started going to the ACA [Adult Children of Alcoholics] group I feel like 'the odd man out.' My dad and brother are still real close, but I don't go over as often anymore."

The holidays often mean a visit home is expected. And in alcoholic families, the holidays often signal increased alcohol consumption and inappropriate behavior. Again, many adult children find it necessary to celebrate the holidays in their own homes, either omitting or severely limiting visits to their parents' homes.

3. *Visits by parents in adult children's homes.* Will adult children permit parents to drink when visiting the adult children's homes? What are the reasons for asking parents to leave? Will parents visit anytime or must they notify their children first?

Adult children of alcoholics tend to feel more comfortable setting limits regarding visits in their own homes. Often alcoholic parents will refuse to visit the homes of children who do not allow them to drink. The co-alcoholic parents may continue to visit their children or they may support the position of their alcoholic spouses.

4. *Grandchildren.* Will adult children allow their parents to babysit? At whose home and for how long? Will adult children allow their own children to ride with their drinking parents? How long must a parent be sober before it is safe to let grandchildren ride with him or her? What will the adult children tell his or her own children about the alcoholic grandparent's problems?

Christian adult children of alcoholics often feel trapped between two biblical mandates. These Christian adults know they are to protect their children and train them to value truth.

They also know the Scriptures command them to honor their parents. Counselors can provide guidance and encouragement as Christian adult children learn for themselves and then teach their children to love, realistically respect, and forgive alcoholic grandparents.

There are other areas that will require limit setting. For example, will adult children accept collect calls from drinking parents? Will they continue a conversation if it becomes evident the parent is intoxicated? Some adult children have a policy of stating to the rambling, slurring parent, "Dad (or Mom), I cannot understand you now. Call back when you are speaking more clearly." And they hang up. This allows the adult child to set an appropriate limit without getting into an argument about whether or not the parent is drunk. Arguing with an intoxicated alcoholic is frustrating and futile.

All these limit-setting procedures can be handled by a recovering adult child without any support from other family members. However, setting limits with an alcoholic parent obviously will be more effective with additional family members participating.

When the Family Stands Together. The right and middle-right sides of figure 13–1 show a possible progression of actions which begins with other family members breaking denial and conducting a family intervention. However, this is not the "best-case scenario," because in this instance the alcoholism continues to progress after treatment is refused. At that point the family members can choose to maintain their old roles and continue to "enable" the alcoholic parent, or they can pursue their own recoveries. If they choose the latter course, they will need to establish new limits with the alcoholic parent.

Planning a family contract. Seixas and Youcha suggest that family members need to establish a written family contract which will eliminate enabling of alcoholic behavior. The effectiveness of this contract will depend on the family's consensus regarding the need for such an agreement and their commitment to carry it out.

These authors recommend that the family meet together and include the sober alcoholic so he or she will fully understand the content of the family contract. They also say that grandchildren should be informed about the provisions of the contract if they are old enough to understand. If they are informed about the contract, grandchildren will not be left guessing about what is happening in the family, and they will be more able to cope with any resulting stress. Seixas and Youcha note that in some situations the contract will have to be formulated by the family and presented to the alcoholic parent as a "fait accompli."[8]

The sample family contract in figure 13–2 is adapted from one developed by Seixas and Youcha.[9]

Sample Family Contract

Parents: Mary D. Jones, Bill Jones

Children: Peter Jones, Rhonda J. Smith, Stuart Jones

Others: Robert Smith (brother-in-law); Alice D. Johnson (mother's sister); Albert Johnson (mother's brother-in-law); Robert Smith, Jr. (grandchild).

1. We will not pretend that no one knows about the drinking. Everyone knows, and we know everyone knows.
2. We will make no excuses to those in authority—courts, police, and others.
3. We will never make excuses to bosses about absenteeism, tardiness, errors, or other alcohol-related problems.
4. We will not speak to our parent on the phone if we detect that that parent has been drinking.
5. We will never buy alcoholic beverages for our parent.
6. We will not clean or fix up messes that are consequences of too much drinking. ("Messes" include broken furniture, banged-up cars, spilled food or drink, and/or burns.)
7. We will not ride in any kind of vehicle or allow our children to ride with anyone who has had so much as one drink.
8. We will not allow any child-care or baby-sitting, day or night, unless our parent has been sober for at least two years.
9. We will not get involved in discussions about financial needs and alcohol-related accidents or fights.
10. We will remain calm about complaints about each other, friends or neighbors, and about hangovers and other health matters related to drinking.

We agree that the above statement is fair and reasonable and further agree to follow its terms and conditions. (At the bottom of the contract is space for the signatures of all those named in it. All are expected to sign.)

Figure 13–2

Spontaneity versus safety and sanity. Some families who use contracts like this post them on bulletin boards or on refrigerators so everyone can refer to them easily. These families acknowledge that such structured family interactions can reduce spontaneity; but they know they also reduce chaos. Ellen reported to her counselor that she and her sisters felt awkward and uncomfortable establishing such a family agreement; but they believed they had to do it to preserve both their sanity and the safety of their children.

To be able to establish personal and family boundaries with an alcoholic parent, adult children will have to be able to lovingly detach from assuming responsibility for the alcoholic.

Loving detachment. Detachment is a phrase heard often in Al-Anon meetings. To detach from an alcoholic means to relinquish control and let the alcoholic face the consequences of his or her drug-induced behavior. Detachment means forsaking relational patterns that serve to "enable" the alcoholic.

Al-Anon promotes detachment with love. Clearly, God's Word supports the need for genuine *agape* love to undergird all interactions. Detachment meets the agape criterion of promoting the alcoholic's movement toward Christ because it allows alcoholics to experience their neediness. Detachment removes the artificial "cushion" that softens the alcoholic's fall into deterioration.

It is important to remember the significance of the broken horizontal lines shown in figure 13–1. They represent positive, second choices that can be made after an unhealthy, initial choice. As figure 13–1 depicts, alcoholic parents may choose to enter recovery after rejecting their families' earlier attempts to promote sobriety. This move from "alcoholism progresses" to "alcoholic recovering" is not likely to occur if family members choose to maintain their old, enabling roles. However, if families can lovingly detach, establish appropriate limits, and pursue their own personal recoveries, alcoholics will be forced to face their drinking problems. Often, that is the beginning of the journey to sobriety.

This chapter has focused on new choices for adult children as they relate to their alcoholic parents. However, that is not the whole story.

RELATING TO CO-ALCOHOLIC PARENTS

We have examined several possible family scenarios. Each scenario presents choices to alcoholics, their unrecovering families, and their recovering adult children. There is an additional consideration that needs to be addressed: relating to nondrinking, co-alcoholic parents.

Not all alcoholic parents are violent and abusive. Children often perceive a sober alcoholic parent as kind, playful, and generous. Perhaps some are "on good behavior" when sober because they feel guilty about getting drunk. In contrast, children may experience their nonalcoholic parent as uncaring, angry, and overwhelmed.

Many adult children of alcoholics report having warmer, more loving feelings toward the alcoholic than toward the co-alcoholic parent. These adults often feel guilty about their negative feelings toward their nondrinking parents since these parents may have brought some measure of stability to families.

Genuine recovery for an individual or a family includes examining the dynamics between adult children and their nondrinking parents. Ultimately, adult children must face the need to forgive both alcoholic and co-alcoholic parents. Chapter 15 will elaborate on the necessity of forgiveness.

At this point, we will focus on some interventions that will assist adult children of alcoholics find new, respectful roles in their families.

COUNSELING GUIDELINES

Pastors, counselors, and others undoubtedly realize by now that nearly all of the counseling strategies recommended thus far have some application to counseling adult children of alcoholics for new family roles. Therefore, a review of previous counseling suggestions is the best place to begin.

1. *Emphasize some previous counseling strategies.* Reading about and discussing the origins of their family roles can assist adult children of alcoholics gain perspective and give them a context for change.

Also, when an adult child is the only recovering member of a family, the powerful pull to renounce recovery and return to misbeliefs must be resisted continually. Counselors and others will need to provide support and encouragement to these adults as they repeatedly recommit to truth.

2. *Help with setting limits and making new choices.* Counselors can ask adult children to prepare what could be called a "bottom-line" list. That is, the adult child determines his or her limit or "bottom line" for what is appropriate behavior on the part of alcoholic parents. Even if the rest of the family members refuse to participate, the adult child can prepare a written statement of personal limits similar to the sample family contract shown in figure 13–2.

Counselors should encourage adult children to share their statement of personal limits with their families, including their alcoholic parents. This is difficult to do if the recovering adult child is the only family member out of denial.

If the adult child has children old enough to understand, it is important for those children to know they are protected by their parent's statement of personal limits. Adam told his counselor that his eight-year-old daughter had the courage to refuse her alcoholic grandmother's insistence that the child accompany her when she drove to a market.

"I'm sure Jenny would have gone with my mother if she hadn't known that my wife and I told mother about our new limits. And as it turned out, my mom had been drinking quite heavily that afternoon and hit another car in the parking lot of the grocery store. It could have been worse, and Jenny could have been with her." Although none of Adam's siblings joined him in loving detachment and limit setting with his mother, he was able to provide some stability for his own family and safety for his daughter.

3. *Balance limit setting with the need to honor parents.* Christian adult children of alcoholics may need guidance to reconcile loving detachment from alcoholic parents with the biblical directives to honor those parents. Pastors and counselors may find the following material helpful in providing this needed guidance:

From the Book of Proverbs, Smalley and Trent list biblical instructions on honoring parents.[10] The following instructions are applicable particularly to adult children in their efforts to relate to alcoholic parents with agape love and realistic respect.

a) Proverbs 27:11 says parents are honored when they see their children acting wisely. Coming out of denial and entering a recovery process is one of the wisest things an adult child of an alcoholic could do. That process focuses on choosing to replace lies with truth—a very wise choice.

b) Proverbs 15:30 says that sharing "good news" with parents (or anyone) can bring "health to their bones." When a recovering adult child tells an alcoholic parent that alcoholism can be overcome through abstinence and participating in a recovery program, that is good news. Truly, it can bring health to an alcoholic parent if he or she will heed it.

c) Proverbs 30:17 warns that mocking and scorning parents dishonors them. The preceding verses in Proverbs 30 set the mocking and scorning of parents in the context of a "haughty spirit," and saying one is "pure" when he or she is not. How pertinent to recovering adult children in their relationships with alcoholic and co-alcoholic parents! Pastors and counselors may need to help adult children examine their attitudes and actions to prevent or eliminate "haughty," self-righteous, and disrespectful attitudes toward their parents. Even when parents are enmeshed in alcohol addiction, it is possible to relate to them with agape love and realistic respect which will honor them.

4. *Introduce the concept of "hurtproofing."* Many adult children of alcoholics report they are always upset and disappointed after a conversation or visit with their alcoholic parents. Frequently this occurs after family celebrations and holiday visits.

Rhonda had high hopes for the Christmas visit with her alcoholic father and co-alcoholic mother. As usual, she was deeply disappointed, hurt, and depressed after her visit. When Rhonda shared her experience in the adult children's support group after the holidays, nearly everyone present had similar stories.

When Rhonda told her counselor about the disappointing Christmas visit, the counselor taught Rhonda about "hurtproofing." As the two discussed Rhonda's expectations for the visit, it was apparent that she cherished the "this-time-it-will-be-different dream" common to adult children. Rhonda learned that it was her unrealistic expectations that set her up to be disappointed and hurt. "Hurtproofing" is simply the adoption of hopeful realism as the adult child's prevailing expectation during every parental interaction. An attitude of hopeful realism "hurtproofs" because it says, "I expect my folks will be basically the way they have always been. I am hopeful that the changes in me will make the relationship better; but I am not expecting them to be different."

"Hurtproofing" is not pessimistic resignation. As a Christian, Rhonda knew she was to continue to pray for changes in her parents while she sought God's will and power for continued changes in herself. "Hurtproofing" is closely related to loving detachment; both stand in contrast to codependent, disrespectful relationship patterns.

5. *Introduce the concept of "truth breaks."* Both "hurtproofing" and "truth breaks" are strategies designed to help adult children cope with the distress and emotional pain connected with visiting their parents.

In chapter 8, counseling strategy number eleven suggested that adult children reconstruct and write out their family story based on the new truths they were learning. To use "truth breaks," adult children must have with them a copy of that truth-based family history when they go to visit their parents. This is how Ray, a recovering alcoholic son of an actively alcoholic father, used a "truth break" after his counselor described the idea.

"My wife and kids and me went to visit my folks as usual during spring vacation. I was fine the first day—really keeping my thinking straight and able to see all the crazy stuff that goes on to keep the big secret about my dad. By the second day, I was beginning to enter into all the craziness. I went upstairs to our room and read over my 'True Family History' as I call it. I had to do this a couple times a day. Finally my wife and I decided we'd leave a day early. I called those time-outs my 'sanity breaks' instead of 'truth breaks.'"

6. *Face the "death of the dream."* When pastors, counselors, and others help adult children of alcoholics face the "death of the dream," they actually are engaged in a special form of bereavement counseling. The dream referred to here is the adult child's dream that he or she will one day have the perfect, loving family that's always longed for and sought. The dream includes parents who are not only addiction-free but also wise,

godly, and able to love unconditionally. The dream depicts a family like the Cleavers (of "Leave It To Beaver") or "The Waltons" living on their idyllic mountain!

But the dream remains only a dream, even when alcoholic parents enter recovery and maintain their sobriety. When parents are unrecovering, the dream mocks reality. Adult children of alcoholics need to be supported and encouraged with the Scriptures as they grieve the idealized parents they never had. At the same time, these adults can be encouraged to honor and realistically respect their parents for who they are.

7. *Find healthy, surrogate "families."* Most Christian adult children of alcoholics can find many of the elements of a healthy family in their churches. Pastors and counselors can encourage adult children to find an older couple in the church to whom they could minister and from whom they could receive support and encouragement. Christ-centered support groups often become substitute families for adult children of alcoholics. But remember that these surrogate families are intended to supplement, not supplant, the adult child's biological family. Involvement in a support group or caring church is not a license for the adult child to reject his or her parents.

8. *Emphasize the importance of prayer and hope.* Throughout this chapter there has been an emphasis on having reality-based attitudes toward alcoholic and co-alcoholic parents. This must not be understood as a renunciation of hope or belief in the power of prayer.

Counselors can use figure 13–1 to help adult children visualize hope for change in their parents and families. Have the adult children locate themselves, their parents, and families on figure 13–1. Then point out the broken, horizontal lines which represent hope for positive changes.

Remember "The Littlest Gosling"? His parents and sibling goslings finally corrected their initial, self-destructive choices and joined the Littlest Gosling on the big lake.

It took a lot of courage on their part, but once they were settled into their new home, Mr. and Mrs. Gander called a meeting of all the flocks.

As a hush settled over the lake, Mr. Gander put his wing

around the Littlest Gosling and said, "This is my Littlest Gosling. For a while I thought he was a Bad Little Gosling. I thought he was a Selfish Little Gosling. I thought he was a Silly Goose. But he wasn't. We were the Silly Geese. And the Littlest Gosling saved our lives. We are proud of him."[11]

Unfortunately, all families do not respond this way. When parents and/or siblings continue to deny the destructive impact of alcoholism, counselors will need to encourage adult children of alcoholics to commit their parents and families to God. As adult children increasingly realize they cannot change their parents or others, they may recognize that their parents' futures are determined by their own responses to the Lord. God's Word declares that he is patient and is "not wishing for any to perish but for all to come to repentance."[12]

"YOU CAN'T GO HOME AGAIN"

Novelist Thomas Wolfe once said, "You can't go home again." Adult children of alcoholics know that when they begin recovering from the effects of parental alcoholism, their views of "home" will never be the same. Beyond that, the recovering process requires relinquishing the fantasy of a perfect home. In place of this fantasy is the truth about oneself and one's family, and the hope for changes in all.

PART FIVE

COUNSELING SPIRITUAL PROBLEMS

GROWING UP IN AN ALCOHOLIC FAMILY affects every dimension of life. Thus far we have examined the impact of parental alcoholism on personal, relational, and spiritual problems, and counseling suggestions have been offered for the first two problem areas.

But recovering from the effects of growing up in an alcoholic home also includes recovering from the scars of "spiritual abuse" that were described in chapter 6. The spiritual abuse of children by alcoholic and co-alcoholic parents results in distorted concepts of God, which the children carry into adulthood. Chapter 14 provides guidelines for helping Christian adult children of alcoholics learn to look past their parents and gaze upon the face of the living God as he is revealed in his Word and in his Son.

Chapter 15 discusses the necessity of forgiveness, which is the capstone of the recovering process. Genuine forgiveness is rooted in an awareness of having been forgiven, which in turn is based on an accurate understanding of God. Hence, we begin Part V with a discussion of how to counsel for a biblical view of God.

CHAPTER FOURTEEN

COUNSELING FOR BIBLICAL GOD-CONCEPTS

WHEN HELEN KELLER WAS TWO YEARS OLD, a nearly fatal illness left her both deaf and blind. As a result, she was unaware of her parents' love during her formative years. Almost daily, "her mother would stand over her crib saying, 'Oh, Helen, how your mother loves you! How she wants to tell you of her love! But she cannot make you understand. Your eyes are closed, and your ears are stopped.'"[1]

How like Helen's mother is our loving Redeemer God. He longs to have all mortals see and experience his love. Yet some individuals, including many adult children of alcoholics, possess spiritual ears and eyes that have been damaged by neglect and abuse at the hands of severely impaired parents.

Throughout her life, Helen Keller struggled to overcome the sensory impairment which separated her from her parents' love. Her affliction had lifelong effects. She needed specialized help to transcend it; it was not something she could "outgrow." Similarly, Christian adults from alcoholic homes do not "outgrow" distorted concepts of God. These distortions do not automatically evaporate like fog in the warm light of Christian conversion. They must be renounced and put away.

PUTTING AWAY CHILDISH GOD-CONCEPTS

In his fine book, *Putting Away Childish Things*, Dr. David Seamands includes distorted concepts of God as one of the "childish things" that the apostle Paul put away (see 1 Corinthians 13:11). Dr. Seamands writes, "Childish things don't simply fall away by themselves as dead leaves fall from a tree. We have to put them away, *katargeo* them, and be 'finished with childish things.'"[2] *"Katargeo"* is a strong Greek verb translated "put away" (KJV) or "did away with" (NASB). *Katargeo* means "to abolish, wipe out, [or] set aside something."[3] Clearly, this verb pictures not a casual, automatic occurrence, but a purposeful, energetic endeavor.

This putting-away endeavor includes both identifying childish distortions as lies about the character of God, and replacing them with the truth. This process is the pivotal element of recovering journeys by adult children of alcoholics. Without an accurate understanding of God, Christian adult children will have neither the hope, the wisdom, nor the power necessary to pursue biblical mind renewal through which their lives and relationships will be transformed.

But how do adult children of alcoholics begin to recognize and relinquish their distorted God-concepts? Just as Helen Keller required assistance to overcome her sensory impairments, adult children benefit from help in overcoming their spiritual impairments. However, I submit that Christian helpers must offer more than is available in typical recovery programs and support groups for adult children of alcoholics.

MORE THAN A "HIGHER POWER"

All secular approaches recognize a spiritual dimension in the process of recovering from alcohol-dominated childhoods. Step Three of the Alcoholics Anonymous Twelve-Step Program offers the secular approach to meeting recovering individuals' spiritual needs: We made a decision to turn our will and our lives over to the care of God as we understood him.

Christian counselors, pastors, and other helpers surely realize that a nebulous "Higher Power" concept of God "as we understand him" is inadequate. One of the major problems for adult children of alcoholics is their understanding of God, or, more correctly, their misunderstanding of God. As repeatedly noted, their concepts of God are distorted as a result of childhood experiences.

It is not enough for concerned helpers to stand by hoping the distortions will disappear inevitably. To be most helpful, pastors and counselors must concentrate on correcting false concepts of God throughout their work with adult children of alcoholics. Simply allowing adult children to relate to the distorted deity they "understand" is counterproductive. But helping them see God as the Scriptures reveal him undergirds their efforts to learn to see themselves accurately, to trust others appropriately, and to forgive and move beyond the bondage of their pasts.

PRESCRIPTION: TRUE KNOWLEDGE
OF GOD

Chapter 6 reported the results of my investigation into what were called "religious problem areas" in a group of evangelical adult children of alcoholics and a group of evangelical adults from nonalcoholic families. Figure 14–1 displays some of these results. The percentages represent the proportion of Christian adults in each group that reported they had problems experiencing God's love and forgiveness, trusting God's will for their lives, and believing biblical promises about God's care for them. All percentage differences between groups were statistically significant. (See figure 6–1 for complete results and statistical data.)

Chapter 6 concluded that these findings support the logical assumption that Christian adult children of alcoholics are

Subjects' Religious Problem Areas Reported in Percentages by Group

Religious Problem Areas	Adult Children of Alcoholics	Adult Children of Nonalcoholics
Experiencing God's Love & Forgiveness	44.8%	4.8%
Trusting God's Will	53.7%	11.3%
Believing Biblical Promises	43.3%	4.8%

Figure 14–1

damaged spiritually by their distorted concepts of God. What is the prescription for their spiritual malady? True knowledge of God.

To Know Him Is to Trust Him

A review of the "religious problem areas" reveals that, at their root, all deal with the issue of trusting God. The Scriptures clearly articulate the truth that to know God rightly is to trust him completely. Of course, both the capacity to know and to trust are constrained by the sin-tainted limitations of our humanity.

Psalm 9:10a states, ". . . those who know Thy name will put their trust in Thee. . . ." In Scripture, God's name represents his person and character. Perhaps Moffat's translation expresses this concept most clearly. It reads: "Those who know What Thou art can trust in Thee. . . ." Adult children need pastors and other Christian people helpers to point them beyond their distorted understanding of deity to the true God of Scripture to learn what and who he is. Clearly, relating to God "as we understand him" will not heal the adult child's impaired capacity to trust God to be and do all that his Word promises. And I suggest that it will bring only a counterfeit serenity.

COUNTERFEIT SERENITY OR CHRIST-CENTERED PEACE?

Most secular recovery programs for alcoholics and their family members seek to help their adherents achieve personal "serenity" founded on acknowledging their powerlessness and turning their wills and lives over to the care of God as they understand him. It could be argued that promoters of these programs are like the false religious leaders denounced by the prophet Jeremiah.

False Leaders and Spiritual Deception

In Jeremiah 6:14, the prophet of Jehovah God accused Judah's false religious leaders of proclaiming a counterfeit peace to the people. Those who adopted the idolatrous worship practices promoted by the false priests were provided with only superficial healing of their spiritual brokenness. By clinging to the illusion of right relationship with God through wrong religious practices, the deluded Hebrews failed to seek the true and living God by the means he provided.

To understand their acts of spiritual deception, we must examine the attitudes of the false religious leaders. They rejected the word of the Lord and substituted their own spurious wisdom (see Jeremiah 8:9b). Jeremiah 9:3 describes this bogus spiritual insight as follows:

". . . Lies and not truth prevail in the land; For they proceed from evil to evil, And they do not know Me," declares the Lord. And later, this further indictment is added: "Your dwelling is in the midst of deceit; Through deceit they refuse to know Me," declares the Lord. (Jer. 9:6)

Jeremiah wept day and night, he was so heartbroken by the people's refusal to know the true and living God, and by the sure destruction such refusal would bring (see Jeremiah 9:1) Well might pastors, Christian counselors, and others also grieve the current deception which rejects the Word of God and substitutes spurious, human wisdom. This prevalent, humanistic wisdom promotes a nonspecific, self-shaped "higher power" as the source of spiritual healing and personal serenity.

KNOWLEDGE OF CHRIST: GRACE AND PEACE

The written Word of the Old Testament foreshadowed the Living Word revealed in the New. The more complete New

Testament revelation concerning true knowledge of God and its results in believers' lives is summarized in 2 Peter 1:2: "Grace and peace be multiplied to you in the knowledge of God and of Jesus our Lord." Again, knowledge of God, as he is revealed— not as he is imagined—is the source of redeeming grace and genuine peace.

Throughout the New Testament it is clear that the path to a life-giving relationship with God leads one to acknowledge Jesus Christ as Lord, for we cannot embrace the Father while rejecting his Son.[4] John 1:17 proclaims that Jesus Christ is the One who brought us the saving grace of God and the clarifying truth about his character. That is, the clearest revelation of God's truth is found in knowing Jesus Christ. Therefore, when we counsel with adult children of alcoholics for a biblical God-concept, we must point them to Jesus Christ. Further, it could be argued that since spiritual truth is discerned solely by those who are spiritually alive (1 Cor. 2:14), only those who have received God's grace in Christ can hope to have an accurate, biblical concept of God.

But knowledge of God and of Jesus our Lord multiplies not only grace to believers, it is the source of peace in their lives, according to 2 Peter 1:2. Christian adults raised in alcoholic homes often are characterized by a lack of peace in their spiritual lives. My research findings support that observation. When pastors and counselors help these adults gain knowledge about God and his Son, we are enabling them to experience the "multiplied" peace which will strengthen them for every step along their recovery paths.

As noted previously, much of the missing spiritual peace seems to center on Christian adult children's difficulty trusting God. And they have difficulty trusting God because they do not know who he really is, according to Psalm 9:10. So as counselors guide adult children into more accurate and biblical concepts of God, these adults will increase their capacity to trust God and experience genuine peace.

COUNSELING GUIDELINES

Certainly, there are differences in individuals' trust in God and their accurate knowledge of him. In adult children of alcoholic parents, these differences seem to be related to the varying levels of neglect and abuse experienced in childhood. However, all adult children of alcoholics will benefit from gaining a more accurate and biblical concept of God. The following suggestions are designed to promote that goal and assist adult children to *katargeo,* i.e., do away with, their damaging distortions of God.

1. *Identify beliefs and misbeliefs about God's character.* Have counselees prepare a list of the attributes of God as they understand them. Encourage them to annotate the lists with explanations of how the attributes affect them personally. This process establishes a baseline for counseling with adult children to promote biblical God-concepts by identifying counselees' existing distortions.

2. *Assign Bible studies on the attributes of God.* As we have seen, accurate knowledge of God comes not from human reasoning but from divine revelation. Adult children can use an exhaustive concordance to do a topical study on attributes of God such as his holiness, grace, lovingkindness, mercy, and many others.

Also, The Navigators publishes an excellent Bible study guide designed for individual and/or group use: *Experiencing God's Attributes.*[5] This workbook is described as, "a personally enriching, application-centered study and meditation on the Person of God." This resource could be used by individual Christian adult children or by a group of adult children who acknowledge Jesus Christ as their Highest Power.

3. *Assign a Bible study on God as the perfect parent.* As noted in chapter 6, many Christians raised by alcoholic parents have great difficulty relating to God as a Heavenly Father. This is true especially if their fathers were violent and abusive. It is essential for these adult children to recognize that God, their Heavenly Father, is entirely different from their earthly fathers and mothers. A study of the Scriptures will highlight this liberating truth.

For example, Psalm 103:13–14 describes God as a compassionate Father who has compassion or pity on his children because he perfectly understands their true natures and limitations. What a contrast from alcoholic and co-alcoholic parents who often exhibit only self-pity and are too emotionally unavailable to really know their children individually. As a result, these parents usually have unrealistic expectations of their children.

Be creative in this study and encourage counselees to be creative, also. For example, the Scriptures declare that God the Father is love, and Robert McGee suggests applying this truth to a rewording of 1 Corinthians 13:4–8a. An exercise like this focuses creatively on the love and kindness of our Heavenly Father. Figure 14–2 is an adaptation of McGee's concept.[6]

The Bible also speaks of God with maternal characteristics. In Isaiah 66:13, God tells Israel that in the future he will comfort his people as a mother comforts her children. And in Isaiah 49:14–16, the Lord declares that he is even more mindful of his children than a nursing mother is of hers. Again, these aspects of God's character are very comforting to adult children of alcoholics. These adults' mothers may have been too distracted by their own alcoholism, or that of their spouses, to give attention and comfort to their children.

4. *Assign a Bible study on God's attitude toward orphans.* Many adult children of alcoholics describe feeling like orphans. Even if both their parents are living, these adults may experience an emotional abandonment that leaves them feeling parentless. The Bible repeatedly describes God's tender compassion for the "fatherless" and orphans.

My Father's Character

My Father is very patient and kind.
My Father is neither envious nor boastful.
My Father is not arrogant.
My Father is neither rude nor self-seeking.
My Father is not quick to take offense, but is longsuffering.
My Father keeps no score of my forgiven sins.
My Father does not gloat over my sins, but always delights
    when I choose truth.
My Father knows no limit to his endurance, no end to his trust.
My Father is always hopeful and patient.
My Father's good purposes never fail.

Figure 14–2

God is presented as "A father of the fatherless" in Psalm 68:5a. He also is pictured as helping (Psalm 10:14b) and supporting the fatherless (Psalm 146:9) and having mercy upon orphans (Hosea 14:3).

Many Christian adult children of alcoholics find Psalm 27:10 particularly comforting because they have experienced being forsaken by their fathers and mothers. This verse reads: "For my father and my mother have forsaken me, But the Lord will take me up."

5. *Assign books about the attributes of God.* Two classics on this subject are *Knowing God* by J. I. Packer (Intervarsity Press, 1973) and *The Knowledge of The Holy* by A. W. Tozer (Harper and Row, 1961). Both are excellent resources. Tozer's book is the shorter and perhaps the less intimidating of the two.

While adult children of alcoholics read an assigned book, they could also keep journals in which they record personal reflections. For example, they could write about how their lives would be different if they really believed and acted upon the truths they are learning about God's character.

Throughout this aspect of the counseling process, pastors and counselors will want to encourage adult children to recommit themselves to their pursuit of truth. Nowhere is forsaking lies and embracing truth more crucial than in the area of understanding the character of God.

6. *Confront confusion of life's circumstances and God's character.* For adult children of alcoholics who have experienced parental neglect and/or abuse, it is difficult to separate the physical reality of this world from spiritual reality. Often the reasoning is: If God is kind and just, then life ought to be kind and just. And the corollary to this is: Since life has been cruel and unfair to me, God must be cruel and unfair.

Philip Yancey reports a conversation with a physically disabled but faith-filled friend who challenged Yancey to read again the story of Jesus whenever he pondered life's inequities. This Christian friend said, "How 'fair' was life to Him? For me, the Cross demolished for all time the basic belief that life is supposed to be fair."

After reflecting on this man's comments, Yancey concluded:

The Cross exposed the world for what it is: a breeding ground of violence and injustice. And that dark Friday can only be called Good because of what happened on Easter Sunday.

Good Friday demolished the instinctive belief that this life is supposed to be fair. But Easter Sunday gives a bright and startling clue to the riddle of the universe. Someday, God will restore the physical reality of planet Earth to its proper place under His reign. The miracle of Easter will be enlarged to cosmic scale. It is a good thing to remember, when disappointment with God hits, that we live out our days on Easter Saturday.[7]

Wise and sensitive pastors and counselors will recognize that they need to do more than spew religious clichés at hurting and confused Christian adult children of alcoholics. We must not offer easy answers to imponderable questions. It is a deep and disturbing consideration that the sovereign, loving God of the universe has chosen to let sin run its destructive course for this time. Truly, we believers strain breathlessly to see the dawn of that coming, cosmic Easter.

WORKING WORSHIPERS

Worship is always a choice. It has been suggested that worshipers may be divided into three categories: wandering, willing, and working.[8] The differences between them may be explained, in part, by variables such as childhood experiences, past decisions, and present circumstances and choices. Their common denominator is a basic, sinful nature.

Wandering worshipers are those who give God a passing glance, at most, then choose to wander away to their own pursuits. *Willing worshipers* seem to be on a smooth path headed straight for God from their earliest years. Their hearts embrace him eagerly. Then there are the other believers who embrace God—but warily. These are the *working worshipers*.

Many Christians raised in alcoholic homes could be categorized as working worshipers. As we have seen, their childhood experiences may have predisposed them to view God as cruel, demanding, unforgiving, and/or disinterested. Pastors and counselors may need to encourage these worshipers to continue their work of replacing old distorted deities with accurate, biblical knowledge of the true and living God.

When these working worshipers learn more about God as he is revealed in his Word and through his Son, they will come to see him as forgiving. They will also come to see his expectation that they forgive others as they have been forgiven. This is the counseling challenge we now examine: counseling for forgiveness.

CHAPTER FIFTEEN

COUNSELING FOR FORGIVENESS

FORGIVING IS HARD WORK—especially for those who feel unforgiven.

In my research comparing evangelical Christian adult children of alcoholics and nonalcoholics, there were statistically significant differences between those groups of subjects on questions relating to forgiveness. I asked all the evangelical subjects to identify problems in four areas of their spiritual lives, including problems feeling forgiven by God and problems forgiving others. Among Christian adult children of alcoholics, 44.8 percent said they have problems feeling forgiven by God, compared to 4.8 percent of Christians from nonalcoholic families. And 40.3 percent of the Christians raised by alcoholic parents reported having problems forgiving others, while only 14.5 percent of the evangelicals from nonalcoholic homes reported the same problem.[1]

Increasingly, even secular mental health professionals are recognizing the therapeutic effects of forgiveness. One noted non-Christian psychiatrist is reputed to have said, "If I were a preacher, I would preach repentance and forgiveness, for nothing I know of brings such release and deep, lasting peace."[2] Nevertheless, forgiveness—genuine, life-changing, biblically-based forgiveness—is primarily a spiritual issue. And counseling for forgiveness is an appropriate topic to conclude a discussion of spiritual problems faced by adult children of alcoholics.

This chapter will examine both the spiritual foundation and the basic elements of forgiveness. We will explore also the barriers to forgiveness and its breadth. Then we will look beyond forgiveness to reconciliation. And finally, we will conclude with specific suggestions on counseling for forgiveness.

THE BASIS OF FORGIVENESS

In secular writings, the basis of forgiveness is self-aggrandizement and personal enhancement. "Forgiveness is a gift of love to yourself," trumpets a secular self-help book.[3] In contrast, the Bible portrays forgiveness as a gift of grace to us from our loving God.

In the Scriptures, forgiveness speaks of complete cancellation of debts. Colossians 2:13–14 paints the scene at Calvary where the sum of our sin-debt was nailed to the cross and stamped "paid in full." Of course our sin-debt was owed to God, because all sin is ultimately against God (see Psalm 51:4). What a remarkable thought: The Holy One to whom the debt was owed is also the Gracious One who paid the debt.

The basis of human forgiveness is personal acceptance of this divine forgiveness. When that foundation is laid, forgiveness is facilitated by knowledge of the basic forgiving characteristics.

THE BASICS OF FORGIVENESS

The topic of forgiveness is rife with misunderstanding. Forgiveness often is confused with explaining, justifying, and/or excusing. Many of those who misunderstand refuse to consider forgiving because they erroneously believe that to forgive is to say what the other person did was not wrong or was "no big deal." As adult children of alcoholics, and other hurting Christians, learn both what forgiveness is not and what it is, they will have fewer misunderstandings and be more motivated to face the need to forgive.

What Forgiveness Is Not

Forgiveness is not excusing. One of the loveliest biblical portraits of genuine human forgiveness is seen in the story of Joseph, and in Genesis 50:20 we see that he sought neither to minimize nor to justify his brothers' behavior.

Forgiveness is not a "quick fix." It requires more than just a single, sincere declaration of desire.

Forgiveness is not amnesia. Apart from suffering some organic brain dysfunction or sustaining significant brain trauma, human beings probably do not forget in the traditional sense of forgetting. Joseph had not forgotten his brothers' past betrayal of him according to Genesis 50:20.

Forgiveness is not humanly possible. Certainly, more and more secular mental-health professionals tell their clients about the personal benefits that come from forgiving. However, other counselors and helping professionals negate the *necessity* of forgiveness. I submit, first, that benefit-based forgiveness will not produce the personal, relational, and spiritual results of grace-based forgiveness. Second, the spiritual results of this forgiveness are not produced by human effort.

While it is useful to know what forgiveness is not, it also is necessary to understand what forgiveness is.

Forgiveness Is Attributing Personal Responsibility

Joseph could have blamed his brothers' actions on their father's favoritism and poor judgment or on his own immaturity and tactlessness; but Joseph didn't. Instead, he recognized that neither his own nor his father's actions determined his brothers' wrong responses. They were responsible for their own sinful choices. "You meant evil against me," Joseph acknowledged in Genesis 50:20. That statement places the responsibility squarely on the brothers.

Pastors, counselors, and other helpers may need to help adult children of alcoholics attribute responsibility to their parents and others who hurt them. This realistic attribution of personal responsibility paves the way for adult children to face their own responsibilities to choose forgiveness.

Forgiveness Is an Event and a Process

My husband and I live on a tiny lake north of Cincinnati, and we have a small sailboat that is well suited to the lake's dimensions. Forgiving is a little like sailing from our dock to the end of the lake. It begins with an act of the will, but reaching the goal involves a process of continual recommitment.

The concept of "setting your sail for forgiveness" has proven helpful with Christians committed to forgiving. Adult children do not have to be sailors to understand that reaching a certain destination involves an initial decision to set the sail. But even after that original commitment, storms may come which temporarily blow the sailor off course. However, when the storms subside, the sailor will reach his or her destination if the sail remains set for that goal.

Throughout the entire process of recovering from the effects of parental alcoholism, adult children need to be challenged to choose new responses. As children, most of them felt powerless. But as adults, no one can take from them their right to choose how they respond to those who hurt them. Forgiveness begins with an initial choice—one of the most significant, life-giving choices any individual can ever make. Forgiveness begins with a purposeful commitment—an act of the will which "sets the sail."

But even after that sincere commitment, many forgivers can be blown temporarily off course by painful memories and other violent emotional "storms." During the "storms," these adults often become confused, discouraged, and guilty because they doubt the sincerity of their commitment to forgive. Pastors and counselors can help struggling forgivers understand the need to recommit to forgiving during and after the emotional storms. Adult children of alcoholics will be better prepared to negotiate the stormy seas of forgiveness if they understand that forgiving involves both an initial commitment and an ongoing recommitment process.

Forgiveness Is "41:51 Forgetting"

It was suggested previously that a sincere forgiver does not automatically become an amnesiac. However, our biblical forgiver, Joseph, did mention forgetting in Genesis 41:51. That verse tells of Joseph naming his firstborn son Manasseh, which means "one who causes to forget." Joseph explained his choice of the name by saying, "God has made me forget all my trouble and all my father's household." Now we know from subsequent verses that, in fact, Joseph did not have the actual recollection of the painful childhood events removed from his memory. What was removed? What was he caused to forget? Perhaps the next verse gives a clue to the answer.

In Genesis 41:52, Joseph named his second son Ephraim, which means, "God has made me fruitful in the land of my affliction." Joseph could not have had such a clear sense of God's abundant blessing in his life if he had been filled with resentment and bitterness about injustices experienced at the hands of his brothers. Apparently the painful past events could be recalled, but the soul-wrenching sting had been removed from the memories. This is a very special kind of forgetting. It could be called "41:51 forgetting," referring to Genesis 41:51; it frees the forgiver from the bondage of the past.

Forgiving Is a Supernatural Work of God

Look again at Genesis 41:51 and at Joseph's explanation for the change in him that led to a sense of fruitfulness. "God has made me forget all my trouble and all my father's household." God did it, not Joseph. It was a supernatural work, not the result of human effort alone.

Forgiving is not natural to human beings. We are more in tune with an "eye for an eye and a tooth for a tooth." As a result, many of us go through our lives and our relationships blind and toothless! Mortals are never more like God than when they extend to others the forgiveness they have received from him through Jesus Christ. The idea of forgiving originates with God, and the power for forgiving emanates from God. In truth, we love because he first loved us, and we also forgive because he first forgave us.

There are many more facets to forgiveness, but these few basic elements suggest its richness and power. Even when the basics of forgiveness are understood, there are barriers to forgiveness that must be recognized and removed.

THE BARRIERS TO FORGIVENESS

Forgiving is never easy. However, there are three barriers to forgiveness that challenge even the most sincere and informed forgiver: the need to blame others, the desire to "balance the scales," and the power of "pain addiction." If adult children of alcoholics are helped to see and circumvent these barriers, the course of their forgiving will proceed more smoothly.

The Need to Blame Others

Two secular writers, Joy Miller and Marianne Ripper, have noted in adult children of alcoholics a pervasive tendency to blame parents not only for childhood patterns of living but also for their adult lives. These authors suggest that adult children of alcoholics need to learn the following:

1. Our parents did the best parenting they knew;
2. Our parents parented through their own experiences from their parents (as we are parenting or would parent without changes);
3. Our parents did not set out to hurt us intentionally; and
4. *We cannot continue to blame our parents for what we continue to do. Instead we need to take responsibility for ourselves.*[4]

In their last suggestion, I believe Miller and Ripper get to the heart of the need to blame. Blaming allows adult children of alcoholics to shift the responsibility for their present lives from themselves to their parents. Blaming is second nature for adult children of alcoholics who were raised in families where other things and people—including themselves—were blamed for alcoholism.

Sean spent most of his adult life playing the blame game. Learning about issues confronting adult children of alcoholics just made him a more skillful player. "If only my dad hadn't been a drunk and a rotten husband and father, my life would be completely different now. I've been married three times and

251

have kids I never see scattered all over the country. At least I'm able to hold my liquor!"

Sean's counselor tried to help him recognize that his life was being shaped by his own choices although many of those choices were influenced by his childhood and his father's example. His counselor also told Sean that unless he gave up blaming his father and took personal responsibility for his own choices, he would not be able to see the possibility of making different, healthier choices.

Blaming alcoholic parents chains Sean, and other adult children, to their painful pasts with crippling fetters of unforgiveness. Blaming blinds people to the possibility of taking personal responsibility for new choices. When blaming kept him focused on his father, Sean was not able to see any hope for more responsible living.

Forgiveness is necessary for adult children to continue recovering from their alcohol-dominated childhoods. Blaming blocks forgiveness. In fact, blaming appears to be the most formidable obstacle to forgiveness, and the other two barriers are related to blaming.

The Desire to "Balance the Scales"

Human beings seem to possess a strong desire to "balance the scales" of right and wrong. Most of us do not suffer injustice lightly. This characteristic may be especially pronounced in adults raised in shame-based, alcoholic families where blaming was the most popular participation sport.

David Seamands suggests that all individuals possess an automatic, built-in debt-collecting mechanism, and he points out that the words "owe" and "ought" come from the same root.[5] When someone important, like a parent or a spouse, *ought* to have done good and appropriate things but did not, this leaves the offended child or adult with a sense that the parent or spouse *owes* a debt.

In volume six of the Resources for Christian Counseling series, Dr. Grant Martin discusses the forgiveness problems faced by victims of family violence and abuse.[6] Martin has observed that a battered wife wants a "pound of flesh" from her husband. He believes that against this desire for payment, Christ's atoning death on the cross forms a practical foundation for breaking free from bitterness and unforgiveness.

Isaiah 53:10–11 is the crucial passage in understanding this concept. These remarkable verses describe God's pleasure when Christ was "crushed and put to grief" at Calvary. The source of the Father's delight in the suffering of the Son was his satisfaction that justice had been served and sin's penalty had been paid. The scales had been balanced. The substitutionary, atoning, sacrificial death of the Righteous One balanced the scales for all the hopelessly unrighteous who would accept his payment.

Pastors and counselors can help Christian adult children see that Christ atoned for the parents and/or other individuals who offended them. The adult child's desire to have the scales balanced has been realized at the cross. Adult children are free to stop trying to make their parents pay the debt they owe because of all the things they ought to have done but failed to do. They can abandon blaming. They are free to forgive.

The Power of Pain Addiction

Personal and relational pain seems to be addicting for many adult children of alcoholics. And blaming is a necessary part of the pain "fix." Blaming parents focuses on the pain and misery of growing up in an alcoholic family. Misery fuels the bitterness which fans the flames of more pain and misery.

Some recovering adult children describe themselves as "pain junkies," because they recognize their penchant for self-destructive behaviors and relationships. They actually seem to feel most energized and alive in a state of "excited misery." This misery may not be comfortable; but it is familiar. The emotional turmoil of "excited misery" is reminiscent of frightening and painful childhood experiences.

As noted previously, if adult children of alcoholics forgave their parents and were free from the bondage of the past, these adults would be faced with the possibility of choosing healthier, less painful patterns of living and relating. The powerful pull of pain addiction becomes a barrier to that forgiving and freeing process.

If pain addiction and the other forgiveness barriers can be

overcome, adult children of alcoholics face the issue of whom to include in their forgiving. The question they must answer is: What is the breadth of forgiveness?

THE BREADTH OF FORGIVENESS

The most simple answer to the question is: Forgive everyone. That is also the biblical answer. And surely, with their troubled childhoods and their tendencies to get into painful adult relationships, most adult children of alcoholics will have many individuals to forgive. However, the present discussion of adult children of alcoholics will focus on the varying dynamics in forgiving the alcoholic parent, the co-alcoholic parent, and the adult child himself or herself.

Forgiving the Alcoholic Parent

The alcoholic parent is the most obvious target for forgiveness. Forgiving is never easy, but forgiving this parent seems to be easier if he or she is involved in recovering from alcoholism.

Forgiving the Recovering Alcoholic. If alcoholic parents are recovering and involved in Alcoholics Anonymous, they are working on admitting their wrongs and making amends whenever possible. Obviously, it is easier for adult children to forgive these parents when they see them accepting personal responsibility for their alcoholic and irresponsible behavior and its effects.

Although having an alcoholic parent in recovery may facilitate the adult child's forgiving, it is never pain free. This is true especially if there is a history of physical and/or sexual abuse by this parent. In these cases, recovering family members usually require professional assistance to heal the wounds caused by such abuse. This assistance may take the form of both individual and family therapy. Pastors and lay counselors should refer to trained professionals.

Forgiving the Unrecovering Alcoholic. Unrecovering alcoholic parents are still enmeshed in denial. Not only do they refuse to take responsibility for their alcoholic behavior and its effects on their children, these parents often continue to blame these children for many of their own problems.

Counselors need to help adult children of unrecovering alcoholics stay focused on their need to choose to forgive regardless of their parents' behavior. The basis for forgiving is God's grace in the life of the Christian adult child, not the attitudes and acts of his or her alcoholic parent.

In some cases, unrecovering alcoholic parents may never know they have been forgiven by their adult children. This is true when parents have severed relationships with their families, have deteriorated mentally, or have died. Even if these parents fail to experience the release that comes from receiving forgiveness, their adult children can enjoy the freedom that results from extending it.

Forgiving the Co-alcoholic Parent

Many adult children of alcoholics report it is more difficult to forgive nonalcoholic than alcoholic parents. There is a tendency to rationalize the alcoholic's hurtful behavior because he or she was "under the influence." But the nonalcoholic parent does not benefit from that excuse.

Learning the basic dynamics of codependency will enable an adult child to see his or her co-alcoholic parent as impaired in ways similar to the alcoholic parent. The latter was addicted to alcohol, and the former to the alcoholic. As counselors and others teach this perspective of codependency, they are increasing the adult child's understanding of both parents and facilitating the forgiving process. During this part of the adult child's recovering process, it is helpful to reinforce the fact that neither alcoholism nor codependency relieves parents from their personal responsibilities. Both parents need to be forgiven, not excused because of their impairments.

Again, the challenge to forgive an unrecovering co-alcoholic parent will be greater than if that parent is out of denial and working toward healthier relationships. And again, the adult child may have to be lovingly confronted with the need to forgive in obedience to God's call and not in response to a parent's change. Adult children also may need to be confronted with what often is their greatest forgiving challenge: receiving forgiveness from God and forgiving themselves.

255

Forgiving the Adult Child

Hurt people hurt people.

The unaccepted become unaccepting; the unloved become unloving. Most wounded adult children leave a trail of wounded victims in their wake. This is human and understandable. It also is sinful and needs to be forgiven.

Spiritually, all sin is against God and against God only. Practically, adult children of alcoholics are most apt to sin against their parents, spouses, and children. They also sin against themselves by dishonoring their bodies with substance abuse and sexual promiscuity.

Forgiving Sexual Sins. Many adult children of alcoholics reach out to fill their inner emptiness with sexually promiscuous and self-debasing relationships. This pattern of behavior often contributes to other sins like abortion and divorce. Daughters of alcoholic fathers may have experienced the "father loss" frequently associated with vulnerability to inappropriate sexual relationships. And sons of male alcoholics often saw sexual promiscuity modeled as "normal" adult male behavior.

Their sexual sins haunt Christian adult children—especially those sins committed after they asked Jesus Christ into their lives. To experience all the freedom forgiving can bring, adult children must not only receive forgiveness from God, they must be willing to extend it to themselves as freely as they offer it to others.

Although Christian adult children experience deep regret about promiscuity and/or divorce, their greatest guilt appears to be related to the way in which their behaviors influence their own children.

Forgiving Parenting Sins. "I feel like I've ruined their lives. I see them fight the same battles I've fought all my life, and I know it is all my fault. I see it so clearly now, but I never knew what I was doing all those years. I don't know if I can ever forgive myself for what I've done to those precious girls." Jo, a Christian adult child of an alcoholic father, was learning about her unbiblical self-concept and her performance orientation to life. She was also beginning to see how she had passed those traits on to her three daughters.

Jo grieved her two failed marriages; but her deepest regret and sense of guilt involved her parenting failures. After Jo received God's forgiveness and finally forgave herself, her counselor encouraged Jo to admit her parenting shortcomings and sins to her daughters and ask for their forgiveness. She did, and her two younger girls responded with immediate forgiveness. Jo and her daughters began family therapy with a Christian counselor, and a few months later Jo was reconciled with her oldest child.

Jo, and most other adult children of alcoholics, face their own parenting sins with the common cry, "I love my kids and never meant to hurt them." This recognition that sinful human beings hurt the people they love—even innocent children—provides a context in which adult children can understand their own alcoholic and co-alcoholic parents.

Understanding is not excusing. Understanding recognizes the limitations of sinful people without relieving them of personal responsibility for the consequences of their choices. This is true whether or not the sinful person is a parent. Pastors and counselors can provide some direction as adult children take responsibility for making new parenting choices. Chapter 12 offered some suggestions. Pastors and counselors also can offer guidance as adult children face the need to receive forgiveness for years of debt collecting.

Forgiving the Debt Collecting. Charles was shocked to hear his pastor suggest he needed to be forgiven for years of disrespectful and dishonoring attitudes toward his alcoholic and co-alcoholic parents.

"How can you possibly say I need to ask God to forgive me for my past actions toward my parents? That really blows me away! I am just beginning to come to grips with God's demand that I forgive them. Now you tell me I need to be forgiven. I've got to tell you that I really feel like whatever I've said or done to them was perfectly justified considering what complete failures they've been as parents."

Charles was a Christian; but he was extremely bitter about his childhood, and he had not yet forgiven his parents. His bitterness kept him mired in blaming and unforgiveness. Charles's dishonoring behavior toward his parents was a way of telling them, "You ought to have been better parents. You failed and now you owe me." And Charles had developed some subtle, yet hurtful, methods of debt collecting.

All bitter and unforgiving adult children are debt collectors. Law and unforgiveness say "you owe me; now pay up." Grace and forgiveness say "you can never pay; now I release you from the debt." Charles was a Christian, but he had no grace-consciousness. His life bore the scars of that destructive root of bitterness which flourishes when believers come short of under-standing grace (see Hebrews 12:15).

In Hebrews 12:15, God warns unforgiving Christians that their bitterness "defiles" many. Charles had defiled his parents with neglect and verbal abuse for years. He also defiled his chil-dren as he taught them to dishonor their grandparents. And with-out realizing it, Charles was failing to model the very forgiveness of parents which he hoped his children would extend to him.

Writing from a secular perspective, Rosellini and Worden suggest that adult children experience healing when they stop blaming and start forgiving their parents. These authors have developed "The Adult Child's Golden Rule: Live in such a way so that you can expect the same amount of love, acceptance and forgiveness from your children as you showed your parents."[7] Adult children of alcoholics who forgive their parents find this "Golden Rule" a blessing. For Charles it had become a curse.

Dishonoring and debt collecting for unpaid parental "oughts" have a high price tag. Both Old and New Testaments prom-ise that life will be longer and more satisfying for those who honor their parents.[8] Debt collecting inevitably dishonors. Many mental-health professionals believe that unresolved anger and unforgiveness toward parents may predispose an individual to develop anxiety, phobias, depression, and functional illness as an unconscious means of self-punishment. All these conditions re-duce the quality of life and may even shorten it.

The solution to self-punishment. Forgiveness is the only solu-tion to self-punishment for dishonoring and debt-collecting atti-tudes toward parents and others, including oneself.

In fact, we cannot stop self-punishment until we know how to obtain forgiveness. We must learn to trade our self-punishment for God's forgiveness. . . . We must not let our failures continue to cast a dark shadow of guilt across our freedom and happiness, since we can receive the ultimate of all forgiveness. To punish oneself is to make a mockery of the Cross.[9]

Many Christian adult children of alcoholics have distorted and inadequate concepts of God which extend to inadequate concepts of forgiveness. Pastors and Christian counselors can point these adults to the biblical passages that assure them of God's forgiveness. Then Christian adult children may need to be confronted with their need to agree with (literally, to confess) what God has said about their sins: They are forgiven.

We have surveyed the breadth of forgiveness, which must include oneself as well as others. When this wide expanse of forgiveness is in place, it may be possible to move beyond it to reconciliation.

BEYOND FORGIVENESS TO RECONCILIATION

The biblical basis for reconciliation is mutual acceptance of truth. The Scriptures clearly present the cross as the means of reconciliation between a holy God and a sinful people (see 2 Corinthians 5:18–21). And when an individual accepts God's truth about the cross—namely, that it is the only source of salvation, then that person is reconciled to God.[10]

Without an individual being willing to agree with God, there is no mutual acceptance of truth and no basis for reconciliation. It could be said that God offers the possibility of reconciliation to all; but possession of reconciliation is limited to those who agree with God's truth about their need of it.

The Longing for Reconciliation

Forgiveness is a prerequisite to reconciliation between two individuals; but mutual acceptance of truth is still necessary for completely bridging the relationship gap. In a sense, reconciliation between humans and God is less complicated because we always know which party has the truth. This is not the case with two, selfish, sinful individuals—even when one has forgiven and longs for reconciliation.

Most adult children of alcoholics report the desire to have close relationships with their parents. When recovering adult children's alcoholic and co-alcoholic parents are in their own recovery, these parents are more willing to acknowledge the truth the adult children have been learning. As both the parents and the children accept responsibility for their own wrong choices, and as they extend and receive forgiveness, reconciliation becomes a reality.

But what about reconciliation with unrecovering parents? Are there any situations where even limited reconciliation is impossible?

The Limits of Reconciliation

Limited reconciliation is possible with unrecovering parents who are nonabusive. The mutually accepted truth can be the fact that the parents and children love each other and recognize they have divergent views about the effects of alcohol on the family. Clearly, this is not an ideal or complete reconciliation, but it is the limited reconciliation experienced by many adult children.

The desire for reconciliation should never become an invitation to abuse. In Ephesians 5:11, Christians are told to "not participate in the unfruitful deeds of darkness, but instead even expose them." When parents are physically and/or sexually abusive, adult children need to "speak the truth in love," protect themselves and their offspring, and report abuse to appropriate authorities.

Pastors and counselors can provide support and encouragement as adult children choose this courageous, biblical, and painful response. The alternative is to promote a parent's sinful behavior. The actively abusing parent may choose to deny the facts and sever the relationship with his or her adult child as a result. But this parent has been faced with his or her sin and given the opportunity to repent and get help. If these parents seek help, stop their abusive behavior, and take responsibility for their acts, reconciliation is possible.

It is clear that forgiveness and reconciliation are related but separate issues. Forgiveness is unrestrainable and unilateral. In other words, nothing can deter an individual from choosing to forgive, regardless of what the other person does in response. In contrast, one of the individuals needing forgiveness can block reconciliation by refusing to acknowledge the truth about his or her sinful behavior.

COUNSELING GUIDELINES

Counseling adult children of alcoholics for forgiveness is both a great challenge and a high privilege for Christian people helpers. As we do so, we stand in the priestly tradition of those who plead, "Be ye reconciled to God." We also offer adult children hope for reconciliation with others. The following suggestions offer practical guidelines for this task.

1. *Assign Bible studies on God's forgiveness.* These scriptures can be useful: 1 John 1:9, 1 Peter 1:18–19, Ephesians 1:7, Isaiah 43:25, Jeremiah 31:34, and Psalm 103:12.

2. *Meditate on God's forgiveness.* Charles Swindoll recommends that believers desiring to forgive others begin to "focus fully on God's forgiveness. . . ."[11] Swindoll suggests Christians get very specific about God's mercy just as the psalmist did in Psalm 103:2–5 and 10–12.

3. *Assign books on forgiveness.* There are many excellent books on forgiveness by Christian authors.[12] As with previous reading assignments, counselees could keep a journal of their thoughts and feelings as they read.

4. *Emphasize the intergenerational benefits of forgiveness.* Frequently adult children of alcoholics will commit to needed changes in their lives primarily for the sake of their children. Constance expressed it well: "I didn't care enough about myself to come for counseling. But when I began to see what was happening to my kids, I decided we needed help— especially me."

Pastors and counselors can share thoughts on "The Adult Child's Golden Rule: Live in such a way so that you can expect the same amount of love, acceptance and forgiveness from your children as you showed your parents."[13] This adaptation of the scriptural "Golden Rule" expresses one of the intergenerational benefits of forgiving parents. The torch of family pain does not have to be passed on to the next generation if adult children of alcoholics will choose to forgive.

5. *Assign a study of the parents.* Have adult children talk to aunts and uncles, grandparents, and other family members who knew the alcoholic and/or co-alcoholic parents when they were young. It is especially helpful to get photographs of the parents when they were children, adolescents, and/or young adults.

This assignment is designed to let adult children see their parents as complex individuals who existed beyond their roles as alcoholic and co-alcoholic parents. This perspective increases understanding of parents as weak and needy human beings who usually do the best they know how to do with their personal limitations. Again, it cannot be overstressed that increasing understanding is not used to excuse parents from personal responsibility for their choices. It simply allows adult children to see some of the forces that shaped those choices. Many adult children resist this assignment at first, only to inform their counselors later that it was extremely valuable.

6. *Introduce a "forgiveness contract."* Appendix D contains a forgiveness contract developed by Christian psychologist Richard Walters. Pastors and counselors could use this contract, or something similar, to provide structure for the difficult and often lengthy task of forgiving alcoholic parents and others.

7. *Encourage confession and repentance of past bitterness and "debt collecting."* The previous six counseling guidelines were designed to increase the motivation of adult children for the hard work of forgiving and to provide some structure and a means to determine progress. With the present suggestion, the hard work of forgiving begins in earnest.

Have adult children make a list of what they need to confess and encourage them to be as specific as possible. It usually is most effective to have adult children pray through their list in the presence of their pastors or counselors. These fellow Christians can provide assurance of forgiveness based on the authority of God's Word. This emphasis on the truth of verses such as 1 John 1:9 is especially needed in counseling adult children of alcoholics who may have more difficulty than other Christians in experiencing God's forgiveness.

Stress the truth that whether or not their confession and repentance improves relationships with their parents, it assuredly will improve their fellowship with God. Emphasize also that genuine repentance is always followed by changed behavior.

8. *List parental acts that need to be forgiven.* The "forgiveness contract" in Appendix D can be copied and distributed to counselees, to be used for listing injustices that need to be forgiven. Encourage adult children of alcoholics to be specific and honest in preparing their lists. This may be an emotionally distressing exercise since memories of parental injustices are infused with painful feelings.

9. *Assign the "confronting and forgiving" exercise.* With the list of parental injustices in hand, and in the presence of his or her pastor or counselor, the adult child should symbolically "confront" and specifically forgive both parents.

During the confrontation phase, counselees can pour out the emotions connected with each hurtful and unjust act as they speak to an empty chair where the parents are seated symbolically. Often it is useful to place a parent's recent photograph in the chair. After each act has been described and the emotions expressed, adult children should state their sincere desire to forgive and release the parent.

It is important for pastors and counselors to witness adult children's initial decisions to forgive parents. These helpers serve as witnesses to help keep adult children on course for forgiveness when "emotional storms" later arise. For this same purpose, it is useful to have adult children initial and date the forgiveness contract beside the "I-have-forgiven-the-person" statement.

10. *Pray for healing of painful memories.* God stands willing to do for all adult children of alcoholics what he did for Joseph: remove the stinging pain from childhood memories.

11. *Introduce the concept of "setting your sail for forgiveness."* As noted previously, most adult children of alcoholics seem to be able to readily grasp this analogy of the forgiving process. This imagery gives counselees a way of identifying and describing the inevitable "emotional storms" that temporarily may blow them off course.

FROM BITTERNESS TO BLESSING

The thick, powerful root of bitterness damages fellowship with God and pushes its way up through the broken lives of the unforgiving. Only the miracle of grace-based, blood-bought forgiveness can free adult children of alcoholics from the bondage of bitterness. Those so freed raise their voices with the psalmist to sing:

> Bless the Lord, O my soul;
> And all that is within me, bless His holy name.
> Bless the Lord, O my soul,
> And forget none of His benefits. (Ps. 103:1–2)

PART SIX

FINAL THOUGHTS

MANY OF THE GENERAL ISSUES and specific counseling needs of adult children of alcoholics have been examined and addressed during the first fifteen chapters of this book. What more could be offered?

Chapter 16 offers some final thoughts on three potential problems as well as the promise and privilege facing Christian helpers who care about adult children of alcoholics.

CHAPTER SIXTEEN

PROBLEMS, PROMISE, AND PRIVILEGE

IT MAY BE WISE to conclude our learning and helping enterprise with an examination, first, of three potential problem areas: unhelped helpers, New Age thinking, and the limitations of labels. And finally, we will consider an encouraging promise and an awesome privilege.

PROBLEM ONE: UNHELPED HELPERS

Recently, on the campus of one of America's largest seminaries, a group of theological students formed a support group for adult children of alcoholics. The response was far greater than anyone expected.[1] These evangelical people helpers recognized their need for mutual support and personal assistance. What about those who do not?

Many sincerely concerned and committed Christians are in the category of what I call "unhelped helpers." These pastors, counselors, and others have never faced their own personal struggles and scars from childhood experiences in dysfunctional families. They are less helpful helpers because of their own misbeliefs, inaccurate identities, disrespectful relating patterns, and distorted God-concepts. Often their own bitter unforgiveness underlies critical, unaccepting, and judgmental attitudes which blast rather then bless those who seek their counsel.

These unhelped helpers will help less. So it is essential for Christian helpers to be honest about their needs for wise counsel and/or professional therapy once they have recognized their personal brokenness. Then they must be humble enough to actually seek it.

During a period of depression more than two decades ago, God used six months of therapy with a secular psychiatrist (the only kind available at the time) to begin a process of emotional healing in my life. At that time, God also graciously supplied an older, Christian woman to provide the spiritual side of my counseling process. A childhood in an alcoholic family, coupled with my own sinful and self-protective choices, led to the depression that often accompanies misbeliefs and codependent relational patterns. Although that was one of the most painful periods of my adult life, certainly God was using it as necessary preparation for a helping ministry.

David Seamands beautifully paints a portrait of Jesus as the "Wounded Healer" who totally identifies with our human weaknesses and infirmities. Seamands quotes the Phillips translation of Hebrews 4:15 which says, "We have no superhuman High Priest to whom our weaknesses are unintelligible—He Himself has shared fully in all our experience."[2] When Christians realize that God cares about and fully understands their struggles and feelings, they go into his presence without shame and fear.

There is no shame in admitting that we helpers are broken and needy people too. But it is tragic when we refuse to acknowledge our wounds and seek the Wounded Healer, Jesus Christ, who stands ready to comfort and help.

PROBLEM TWO: NEW AGE THINKING

When the Twelve Steps of Alcoholics Anonymous were first formulated, America was influenced more distinctly by a traditional Judeo-Christian image of God. It probably never occurred to the AA founders that the "Higher Power" concept of God "as we understood Him" would open the door decades later to an influx of Eastern mysticism and what is commonly called New Age thinking. However, it appears that door has been flung open and some leaders and participants in the adult children of alcoholics movement have passed through it.[3]

One popular book, subtitled "Twelve Steps of Recovery for Adult Children," says:

> God, as I understand God is the life that lives through me. I look within. I see God in the images which speak to me: Guides. Special settings I visit either in imagination or in reality. I find God at the beaches of the California North Coast and on Maui, and in the mountains behind Big Sur, or out among the redwoods and the high views across the ridges of the coast Range and Sierras. . . .
>
> I like to see God (and visualization is important to me as a means of enhancing healing) as a woman wearing white or pale turquoise, or as a rangy dark-haired man who is my lover and my mate.[4]

Another, even more widely read book for adult children of alcoholics proposes that the highest level of recovery consists of a "commitment to a power beyond one's self and beyond the visible, observable world, [but] it does not require participation in a particular, organized religion."[5] Unfortunately, some of the powers beyond the visible, observable world are those "rulers, . . . world forces of this darkness, . . . [and] spiritual forces of wickedness in the heavenly places" which Christians are warned to fight in Ephesians 6:12.

The lack of discrimination regarding the origin or nature of spiritual powers "beyond one's self and beyond the visible, observable world" apparently denies the reality of Satan and the existence of evil. Anything from the mystical and spiritual realm is viewed as equally valuable. In fact, the suggestion that judgment and discrimination are necessary is greeted with accusations of dogmatism and self-righteous narrow-mindedness.

This failure to discriminate between sources of "wisdom" and spirituality is reflected in a popular book of daily meditations for adult children. It gives equal weight to quotations from Vince Lombardi, Shakespeare, Buddha, Carl Rogers, the Tao, Machiavelli, the Bible, Garfield the cartoon cat, and others.[6] In these books, and in all volumes that refer to the Twelve-Step Program, authors talk about "God's will," and they speak repeatedly about "spirituality." However, the "spirituality" of the Twelve Steps is not distinctly biblical in nature.

The Twelve-Step Program was never intended to save souls. It was begun to save the lives and sanity of alcoholics. The founders of Alcoholics Anonymous recognized that alcoholism destroyed people physically, emotionally, and spiritually. They borrowed the concept of the Steps from the Oxford Movement in England and purposely "de-Christianized" the program to reach *all* alcoholics. In time, Twelve-Step Programs were extended to scores of other groups of people seeking to recover from problems that left them feeling out of control, e.g., Alanon (for families of alcoholics) and Overeaters Anonymous.

Christian adult children of alcoholics have no difficulty understanding that Jesus Christ is their "Higher Power." Therefore, in their recovery from the effects of parental alcoholism, they benefit from the structure provided by Twelve-Step type programs. Nevertheless, there is concern that some immature and uninformed Christians may become caught up in the nebulous, and often New Age, "spirituality" permeating some writings and Twelve-Step groups for adult children.

A thoroughly Christian alternative to the Twelve Steps is shown in figure 16–1. Dr. Gary R. Sweeten has prepared the "Twelve Steps of Wholeness" to provide a distinctly Christ-centered program for recovering Christians. The Twelve Steps of Wholeness openly acknowledge that Jesus Christ must be embraced not only as a teacher and healer but as Savior and Lord. This focus upon Christ may appear narrow-minded, but it is consistent with biblical truth (see John 14:6).

The Twelve Steps of Wholeness

Distributed by the Christian Information Committee, Inc.

Following a tradition of the early church and the Wesley revival, the Oxford Group systematized a series of "steps" as a process of cleansing one's inner life. These "steps" were later adapted by Alcoholics Anonymous, with much of the Christian basis ignored. They are here re-adapted emphasizing this great Christian base so integral to the wholeness sought. Here the center of wholeness is recognized as the Lord Jesus Christ. The "steps" have also been changed to conform to other principles of discipleship and Christian growth. If a Christian will vigorously apply these principles, and make these decisions, that person will move toward "Teleios"—Wholeness in Christ.

1. I now see that I, of myself, am powerless, unable to control (manage) my life by myself.
   Romans 7–8   Romans 7:18–19   Psalm 32:3–7
                          Romans 3:9–10, 23

2. I now realize that my Creator, God the Father, Son, and Holy Spirit, can restore me to wholeness in Christ.
   Psalm 27:4–5   Mark 10:26-27   Philippians 2:13
   Romans 8:9   Ezekiel 36:27

3. I now make a conscious decision to turn my entire will and life over to the care and direction of Jesus Christ as Teacher, Healer, Savior and Lord.
   Joshua 1:8–9   Jeremiah 29:11–14   Jeremiah 32:27
   John 14:6   John 10:30   Mark 10:27
                          Matthew 28:18, 20b

4. Having made this decision, I now obey God's call in Scripture to make a fearless, ethical, moral, and scriptural inventory of my entire life in order to uncover all sins, mistakes, and character defects, and to make a written list of every item uncovered.
   Psalm 139:23–24   Lamentations 3:40   Jeremiah 23:24
                          Romans 8:26–27

5. After completing this inventory I now will to "walk in the light, as He is in the light" by admitting to myself, to God, and to at least one other person in Christ the exact nature of these wrongs.
   1 John 1:7   Ephesians 5:13–14   Psalm 119:9–11
   1 Timothy 1:15   Acts 13:38–39   James 5:13–16
   Hebrews 9:14   Acts 2:37–38

6. Having agreed with God about my sinful behavior, I now ask His forgiveness through Christ and openly acknowledge that I am forgiven according to the Scripture.
   1 John 1:8–9   James 4:10   1 John 2:1–2
   Psalm 27:13–14   Psalm 118:18, then 17

7. I now repent (turn away) from all these behaviors in thought, word, and deed and ask God to remove each besetting sin, through Jesus Christ.

John 5:14	John 8:10–11	Job 11:13–19
Ezekiel 18:30–32	Romans 5–6	Romans 12:1–2
1 John 2:3–6	2 Corinthians 10:5	Colossians 3:17

8. I now make a list of all persons I have harmed in thought, word, and deed, and a list of all persons I believe have harmed me, and will to make amends to all of them.

Ephesians 4:29–32	Hosea 11:1–4	Ephesians 5:1–2
Luke 6:31	Matthew 5:43–44	Matthew 18:15
Leviticus 19:17–18	Mark 12:31	Matthew 5:9

9. I now go directly to these persons to forgive and to seek forgiveness, reconciliation, restitution, or release whenever and with whomever possible, unless to do so would cause further harm.

Matthew 5:23–24	Isaiah 1:18–20

10. I now consciously and prayerfully continue to "walk in the light" by unceasingly taking personal inventory of all my temptations and sins, and by keeping a constantly open relationship with God, myself, and other persons.

Matthew 26:41	James 1:13–15	Matthew 6:11–13
Colossians 3:13	Proverbs 30:8–9	Ephesians 5:15–18
Psalm 4:3–5	Psalm 55:22	1 Peter 5:6–7
	Ephesians 4:22–28	

11. I now continue in regular Scripture, study, prayer, worship and fellowship to increase God's will in my life.

Acts 2:42	Mark 12:28–33	Matthew 6:33
Psalm 89:15	Joshua 1:8	1 Kings 8:56–61
	Colossians 3:12–17	

12. Recognizing the impact of God in my life, I now intentionally share these principles and their effect with others as God's Spirit leads, and will to practice these principles in all areas of my life.

Micah 6:8	Ephesians 5:8	Psalm 40:8–10
Galatians 5:1	Revelation 12:11	2 Corinthians 3:17
	Ephesians 6:10–18	

Prepared by Dr. Gary R. Sweeten & Hal B. Schell
©1989 Christian Information Committee, Inc.
P.O. Box 24080 • Cincinnati, Ohio 45224

Figure 16–1

PROBLEM THREE: LABELS

Labels serve a purpose. They are a kind of verbal shorthand. Labels can summarize a vast body of knowledge, for example about the complex disorder of paranoid schizophrenia, with a word or phrase: "paranoid schizophrenic." But labels are limiting and simplistic when applied to complex human beings. They smooth over the uniquely shaped variations in each individual's personal topography. This is true whether the human beings are labeled "paranoid schizophrenics" or "adult children of alcoholics."

Throughout this book, the verbal shorthand "adult children of alcoholics" has been employed to summarize the information presented in the first few chapters as it is lived out by thousands of unique individuals. While that may be useful, it can also be dangerous if pastors, counselors, and other helpers begin to see these adults as solely identified and personally limited by this label.

Christians raised in alcoholic homes must be seen as more than just "adult children of alcoholics." Of foremost importance, they are children of God through faith in Jesus Christ; and that relationship is the basis of their identities and their hopes. To work most effectively with these adults, we must guard against pasting labels over their unique, God-given, experience-shaped strengths and struggles.

AN ENCOURAGING PROMISE

The process of recovering from the effects of parental alcoholism has been presented as one aspect of the entire sanctification process of conforming Christians more and more into the image of God's Son. That perspective holds an encouraging promise for pastors and Christian counselors.

We are not out there trying to pull this off by ourselves. As we prayerfully, patiently persist in the counseling process, our efforts are energized by the Holy Spirit of God. We are instruments in the hand of the Great Physician who is performing his "open-heart surgery" on all sin-sick Christians, including those raised by alcoholic and co-alcoholic parents. Our responsibility is to be personally clean and professionally sharp instruments. Yet there is more.

273

"'Not by might nor by power, but by My Spirit,' says the Lord of hosts," in Zechariah 4:6. If pastors and Christian professional and lay helpers truly believed that, we would spend as much time praying for ourselves and our congregants, clients, and counselees as we do reading books like this. And we would trust God's adequacy more than we fear our own inadequacy. This is not an apologetic for incompetent counseling; it is a promise of God's undergirding power when our most skillful efforts seem insufficient for the task. And it is the awesome nature of the task that renders its participation such a privilege.

AN AWESOME PRIVILEGE

The division of labor is clear: God supplies the power and direction, yet he calls us to participate in the process of applying that power to specific needs in hurting Christians' lives. A dramatic prototype of this co-laboring relationship is found in John's Gospel, chapter eleven.

Never before or since has there been a graveside service like the one by those hill caves near Bethany. Jesus had come, but Lazarus had been dead four days. In a foreshadowing of his coming triumph, Christ cried out to wrest life from death, "Lazarus, come forth" (verse 43).

And he did.

Now here is the remarkable part, and here is where we enter the scene. Lazarus came forth all right, but he was still bound in the trappings of death. So Jesus told concerned bystanders to, "Unbind him, and let him go" (verse 44). God the Son supplied the power and the direction, but he sovereignly chose to use human helpers to participate in the unbinding process.

He still does.

Did God "need" help to complete the unbinding task? I seriously doubt it.

Did Lazarus fail to be spiritually mature enough to set himself free? I don't know, but clearly that was not God's plan for him.

Did those Bethany helpers realize their awesome privilege when they were called to be co-laborers with Christ to free his child from the residual bondage of sin?

Do we?

274

God still uses human participants in the unbinding process. Pastors and Christian counselors are the concerned Bethany helpers of today. As God provides the power and direction, we participate in the process of freeing Christians still swathed in the bindings of childhood injustices. What an awesome privilege to know that, "we are labourers together with God. . . " (1 Cor. 3:9 KJV).

APPENDIX 1

RESOURCES

SECULAR RESOURCES

Books for and about Adult Children of Alcoholics

Robert Ackerman, *Let Go and Grow* (Pompano Beach, Fla.: Health Communications, 1987). This well-researched volume reports findings from the author's study of more than one thousand adult children of alcoholics.

Claudia Black, *It Will Never Happen To Me!* (Denver: M.A.C., 1981). This is one of the "classics" in this field. Black describes how parental alcoholism affects children and adult children and offers suggestions for helping.

Gayle Rosellini and Mark Worden, *Taming Your Turbulent Past* (Pompano Beach, Fla.: Health Communications, 1987). This helpful and well-written volume covers the usual adult children issues but emphasizes the importance of forgiveness.

Judith Seixas and Geraldine Youcha, *Children of Alcoholism: A Survivor's Manual* (New York: Harper & Row, 1985). The authors give a clear picture of adult children's struggles along with coping and changing ideas.

277

Sharon Wegscheider, *Another Chance: Hope and Health for the Alcoholic Family* (Palo Alto, Calif.: Science and Behavior Books, 1981). This is another classic in the field, by one of the pioneers in working with adult children of alcoholics.

Janet Woititz, *Adult Children of Alcoholics* (Pompano Beach, Fla.: Health Communications, 1983). Perhaps the most widely read book on this topic, this "classic" describes the characteristics of adult children and offers suggestion for coping.

Books for and about Young and Adolescent Children of Alcoholics

Claudia Black, *My Dad Loves Me, My Dad Has a Disease* (ACT, P.O. Box 8536, Newport Beach, CA 92660: 1979). Black pioneered work with young children of alcoholics, and this workbook is designed for that population.

Cathleen Brooks, *The Secret Everyone Knows* (San Diego: Operation Cork, 1981). This is forty pages of easy reading for teenagers when "alcohol is a problem in your home."

Edith Hornik, *You and Your Alcoholic Parent* (New York: Associated Press, 1974). Teenagers will learn about parental alcoholism and how to cope with it in this very readable book.

Eric Ryerson, *When Your Parent Drinks Too Much: A Book For Teenagers* (New York: Facts On File, 1985). As the subtitle states, this book is designed to tell teens how to understand and cope with parental alcoholism. An excellent resource.

Magazines

Changes is a bimonthly magazine for and about adult children of alcoholics. It can be ordered from Health Communications, Inc., 3201 S.W. 15th Street, Deerfield Beach, FL 33442. A one-year subscription costs $18.

FILMS

"Alcoholism, A Family Problem" (13 minutes, 1978). This film presents a dramatization of the three stages of alcoholism as it affects family members. It also explores the feelings and behaviors typical of each stage. Available from Health Sciences Consortium, 200 Eastone Drive, Suite 213, Chapel Hill, NC 27514.

"Another Chance" (30 minutes, 1983). Sharon Wegscheider works with a woman from an alcoholic family who experiences the process of family exploration and "reconstruction." Available from Health

Communications, Inc., 3201 S.W. 15th Street, Deerfield Beach, FL 33442. Health Communications distributes many films on this topic; request a catalog.

"Children of Denial" (28 minutes, 1984). Claudia Black speaks about youngsters, adolescents, and adults as children of alcoholics, with emphasis on the "rules" of "don't talk," "don't trust," and "don't feel." Available from A.C.T., 30100 Town Center Drive, Suite 0-211, Laguna Niguel, CA 92677.

"Soft is the Heart of a Child" (30 minutes, 1980). This is a dramatization of the effects of alcoholism on a family, especially the children. The focus is on the trauma of the children and the help offered by a school counselor. Available from Gerald T. Rogers Productions, 5225 Old Orchard Road, Suite 6, Skokie, Ill. 60077. Ask for a catalog of other films on the subject.

Videotapes

"Adult Children of Alcoholics" (35 minutes, 1985). Janet Woititz discusses insights into problems confronting adult children of alcoholics. This is a valuable resource for adult children and those working with them. Available from Alcoholism Counselor's Continuing Education Services, 3901 Meadow Drive, B-1, Indianapolis, IN 46205.

"That's Marilyn" (28 minutes, 1980). This is a dramatization about the trauma of growing up in an alcoholic home. It is designed for teen and adult audiences. Available from Aims Media, Inc., 626 Hustin Avenue, Glendale, CA 91201. Request a catalog of other videos and films on the subject.

"The Children of Alcoholics" (15 minutes, 1980). Claudia Black discusses the effects of parental alcoholism on children and adults and examines treatment programs. Available from Health Communications, Inc., 3201 S.W. 15th Street, Deerfield Beach, FL 33442.

AGENCIES AND ORGANIZATIONS

Al-Anon/Alateen Family Group Headquarters, Inc.
Madison Square Station
New York, NY 10010
212-683-1771

Alcoholics Anonymous World Services, Inc.
468 Park Avenue South
New York, NY 10016
212-686-1100

Children of Alcoholics Foundation, Inc.
23rd Floor, 540 Madison Avenue
New York, NY 10022
212-351-2680

National Association for Children of Alcoholics (NACOA)
31582 Coast Highway, Suite B
South Laguna, CA 92677
714-499-3889

National Council on Alcoholism
12 West 21st Street, 8th Floor
New York, NY 10010
212-206-6770

National Clearinghouse for Alcohol Information
P.O. Box 1908
Rockville, MD 20850
301-468-2600

National Institute on Alcohol Abuse and Alcoholism
5600 Fishers Lane
Rockville, MD 20857
301-443-2403

CHRISTIAN RESOURCES

Books

Sara Hines Martin, *Healing for Adult Children of Alcoholics* (Nashville: Broadman, 1988). Martin covers the basics presented in other volumes, but does so from a subtly Christian perspective.

Janet Ohlemacher, *Beloved Alcoholic* (Grand Rapids, Mich.: Zondervan, 1984). This book is sensitively written by an adult daughter of an alcoholic mother. It provides a strong Christian perspective and lots of valuable, practical information.

Anderson Spickard and Barbara Thompson, *Dying for a Drink* (Waco, Tex.: Word, 1985). This volume focuses more on alcoholism and alcoholics, but also touches issues of children of alcoholics.

Jeffrey VanVonderen, *Good News for the Chemically Dependent* (Nashville: Thomas Nelson, 1985). This valuable resource is written by a pastoral counselor who is also a recovering alcoholic and a certified chemical dependency counselor. Like the previous volume, this one focuses on the alcoholic. Nevertheless, it has some excellent chapters on codependency, shame, and intergenerational effects of alcoholism.

Biblically Based Twelve-Step Literature

The following two publications incorporate the Scriptures with the Twelve-Step process. Both refer to Jesus Christ as well as God, although neither presents a clearly evangelical perspective. However, they are the "most Christian" Twelve-Step materials currently available.

The Twelve Steps for Christians can be ordered from Recovery Publications, 1201 Knoxville Street, San Diego, CA 92110, 619-275-1350. This book is intended for Christians from addictive and other dysfunctional families.

The Twelve Steps—A Spiritual Journey is a workbook-style publication intended for the same readership described above. It can also be ordered from Recovery Publications.

Organizations

Alcoholics For Christ
1316 North Campbell Road
Royal Oak, MI 48067
419-782-1684

Liontamers
2801 North Brea Boulevard
Fullerton, CA 92635-2799
714-529-5544

Substance Abusers Victorious
One Cascade Plaza
Akron, OH 44308
216-253-5444

Overcomers Outreach, Inc.
2290 West Whittier Boulevard
La Habra, CA 90631
213-697-3994
This organization is the only one which addresses the needs of adult children.

APPENDIX 2

C.A.S.T.

Please check the answers below that best describe your feelings, behavior, and experiences related to a parent's alcohol use. Take your time and be as accurate as possible. Answer all 30 questions by choosing either "Yes" or "No."

Sex: Male _____ Female _____ Age: _____

Yes	No	Questions
_____	_____	1. Have you ever thought that one of your parents had a drinking problem?
_____	_____	2. Have you ever lost sleep because of a parent's drinking?
_____	_____	3. Did you ever encourage one of your parents to quit drinking?
_____	_____	4. Did you ever feel alone, scared, nervous, angry or frustrated because a parent was not able to stop drinking?
_____	_____	5. Did you ever argue or fight with a parent when he or she was drinking?

_____   _____   6. Did you ever threaten to run away from home because of a parent's drinking?

_____   _____   7. Has a parent ever yelled at or hit you or other family members when drinking?

_____   _____   8. Have you ever heard your parents fight when one of them was drunk?

_____   _____   9. Did you ever protect another family member from a parent who was drinking?

_____   _____   10. Did you ever feel like hiding or emptying a parent's bottle of liquor?

_____   _____   11. Do many of your thoughts revolve around a problem-drinking parent or difficulties that arise because of his or her drinking?

_____   _____   12. Did you ever wish your parent would stop drinking?

_____   _____   13. Did you ever feel responsible for and guilty about a parent's drinking?

_____   _____   14. Did you ever fear that your parents would get divorced due to alcohol misuse?

_____   _____   15. Have you ever withdrawn from and avoided outside activities and friends because of embarrassment and shame over a parent's drinking problem?

_____   _____   16. Did you ever feel caught in the middle of an argument or fight between a problem-drinking parent and your other parent?

_____   _____   17. Did you ever feel that you made a parent drink alcohol?

_____   _____   18. Have you ever felt that a problem-drinking parent did not really love you?

_____   _____   19. Did you ever resent a parent's drinking?

_____   _____   20. Have you ever worried about a parent's health because of his or her alcohol use?

_____   _____   21. Have you ever been blamed for a parent's drinking?

_____   _____   22. Did you ever think your father was an alcoholic?

———— ———— 23. Did you ever wish your home could be more like the homes of your friends who did not have a parent with a drinking problem?

———— ———— 24. Did a parent ever make promises to you that he or she did not keep because of drinking?

———— ———— 25. Did you ever think your mother was an alcoholic?

———— ———— 26. Did you ever wish you could talk to someone who could understand and help the alcohol-related problems in your family?

———— ———— 27. Did you ever fight with your brothers and sisters about a parent's drinking?

———— ———— 28. Did you ever stay away from home to avoid the drinking parent or your other parent's reaction to the drinking?

———— ———— 29. Have you ever felt sick, cried, or had a "knot" in your stomach after worrying about a parent's drinking?

———— ———— 30. Did you ever take over any chores and duties at home that were usually done by a parent before he or she developed a drinking problem?

———— Total number of "Yes" Answers

[C1: ——— C2: ——— C3: ——— C4: ——— C5: ——— C6: ———]

The *Children of Alcoholics Screening Test* (C.A.S.T.) may be ordered from:

Camelot Unlimited
5 North Wabash Ave., Suite 1409
Chicago, IL 60602
(312) 938-8861

APPENDIX 3

CHRISTIAN CHILDREN OF ALCOHOLICS GROWTH GROUP FORMAT

Appendix 3 contains a format that can be used by groups of Christian adult children of alcoholics who do not want to follow a Twelve-Step Program. The format is structured so that any member of the group can lead. During the fifteen-minute "Scripture Focus," the leader shares Bible verses on a theme he or she has selected, e.g., forgiveness, or dealing with anxiety. Appendix 3 also includes "I Am a Christian with a Challenge" which describes common characteristics of adult children of alcoholics. A copy of "I Am a Christian with a Challenge" is given to each group participant.

Opening (10 minutes)

Welcome and Introductions: Leader introduces him/herself and welcomes everyone to this growth group for Christian adult children of alcoholics, i.e., adults who have committed themselves to Jesus Christ as Savior and Lord. Leader asks others in group to introduce themselves.

Opening Prayer: Leader prays briefly, committing the meeting to the guidance of the Holy Spirit.

Group Objectives: (Note: Before beginning to read, the leader can ask specific group members to read the scripture passage(s) that accompany each objective.) Leaders says: *The objectives of this group are based on the acrostic H-O-P-E taken from 1 Peter 1:3, which reads: "Blessed be the God and Father of our Lord Jesus Christ, who according to His great mercy has caused us to be born again to a living hope through the resurrection of Jesus Christ from the dead." Our objectives are:*

H—Healing of painful childhood memories.
". . . I am still not all I should be but I am bringing all my energies to bear on this one thing: Forgetting the past and look-ing forward to what lies ahead, I strain to reach the end of the race and receive the prize for which God is calling us up to heaven because of what Christ Jesus did for us" (Philippians 3:13–14 TLB).

"'For I will restore you to health And I will heal you of your wounds,' declares the Lord, 'because they have called you an outcast. . . .'" (Jeremiah 30:17).

O—Open sharing of feelings and emotions.
"Share the joy of those who are happy and the grief of those who grieve" (Romans 12:15 MLB).

P—Prayer.
"Admit your faults to one another and pray for each other so that you may be healed. The earnest prayer of a righteous man has great power and wonderful results" (James 5:16 TLB).

"The Lord is near to all who call upon Him, To all who call upon Him in truth" (Psalm 145:18).

E—Encouragement toward spiritual growth, responsible living, and a healthy self-concept based on God's love as re-vealed in his Word. "Therefore encourage one another, and build up one another just as you also are doing" (1 Thessaloni-ans 5:11).

"And I pray that Christ may be more and more at home in your hearts, living within you as you trust in him. May your roots go down deep into the soil of God's marvelous love; and may you be able to feel and understand as all God's children should, how long, how wide, how deep, and how high his love really is; and to experience this love for yourselves, though it is so great that you will never see the end of it or fully know or

understand it. And so at last, you will be filled up with God himself" *(Ephesians 3:17–19 TLB).*

Scripture Focus: (15 minutes)

The leader guides in the reading and discussion of verses on a topic he or she selects.

Sharing: (40 minutes)

Leader reads the following guidelines for sharing in this group:

The meeting is now open for general discussion. Please limit your sharing to three to five minutes. We ask that you speak only in the "I," that is, focusing on yourself and not on someone who is not in the group, or even on someone else present in the group.

Please refrain from criticizing others who share, and offer advice sparingly and only after much prayer. Remember we are not here to be responsible for solving each other's problems; we are here to share common concerns and to support each other as we learn to take responsibility for our own lives under the Lordship of Jesus Christ.

Finally, we ask you to remember that anything shared here must remain in this room and is not to be discussed with anyone, even other members of the group, after this meeting ends.

Praise and Prayer: (20 minutes)

1. Leader asks for sharing of answered prayer and other reasons to give God praise.

2. Leader requests and records tonight's prayer requests.

NOTE: Be sure to leave time to actually *pray* about these requests.

I AM A CHRISTIAN WITH A CHALLENGE

(NOTE: Ideally, "I Am a Christian with a Challenge" would appear on one page.) I am a Christian facing the challenge of overcoming the effects of parental alcoholism. But *I am much more than just an adult child of an alcoholic. Of foremost importance, I am a child of God through faith in Jesus Christ, and this relationship is the basis of my identity and my hope.* As God's child, all my sins are forgiven (Ephesians 1:7) and nothing can ever separate me from his love (Romans 8:38–39).

Growing up with the chaos of parental alcoholism caused me to develop certain ways of protecting myself from emotional pain. These self-protection patterns developed in childhood often cause problems in adult life. Here are some of the personal and relational problems noted in many adults like myself.

1. We usually feel different from other people. We may also feel that God relates to us differently than he relates to other people— that he loves us less or punishes us more.

2. We are usually unsure of what constitutes normal family functioning, and as a result, we often have a high tolerance for inappropriate and disrespectful behavior.

3. We often have difficulty trusting people appropriately. We may also have difficulty trusting God and biblical promises about his love and provision for us.

4. We usually judge ourselves without mercy and treat ourselves disrespectfully.

5. We usually take ourselves (and life) very seriously and have difficulty (and may feel guilty) when we try to relax or have fun.

6. We tend to be "approval addicts," i.e., we are constantly seeking affirmation.

7. We usually have difficulty identifying, feeling, and/or expressing emotions.

8. We are often terrified by angry people and personal criticism.

9. We usually attempt to control circumstances and relationships, and we tend to overreact to changes over which we have no control. (We may not like surprise parties even when they are for us!)

10. We often feel trapped, doomed, victimized, and helpless, i.e., unaware that we have choices now as adults.

11. We are often self-blaming, guilt-prone, and over-responsible— we take responsibility for people and situations over which we have no control and blame ourselves when things go wrong.

12. We are usually terrified of abandonment and will do anything to hold on to a relationship to avoid the pain of abandonment. We also confuse love with pity and tend to "love" people we can pity and rescue.

13. We may also tend to have difficulty following a project through from beginning to end, as well as have difficulty with impulsivity and lying. We also tend to become addicted to excitement and crises.

Parental alcoholism may have caused me to "stumble" as a child (Matthew 18:6) in developing distorted thinking patterns; but I am not "doomed" to remain crippled forever. God calls all Christians to a lifelong process of transformation by renewal of our minds (Romans 12:2) because sin distorts everyone's thinking patterns. *Every* Christian has challenges to face in the power of the Holy Spirit; I am no different.

I am a Christian facing the challenge of transcending parental alcoholism. *When Jesus promised abundant life and inner peace to those who trust in him, he did not make an exception for me!* As I fellowship regularly with other believers who understand and encourage me, as I study God's Word to learn the truth about myself and about God, and as I walk in the power of the Holy Spirit seeking to make Jesus Lord of my life, I, too, will experience, "the peace of God which passeth all understanding" (Philippians 4:7 KJV).

APPENDIX 4

FORGIVENESS CONTRACT

My action plan for forgiving _____ (initials of the person I need to forgive).

In the space provided below, list the injustices for which you need to forgive this person. In the "Present Status" column, use the appropriate code numbers from the list that follows. Then list the ways you have responded to this person in the past, using an asterisk to indicate those responses for which you need to apologize; what you should do next; and the date by which you will do it.

Injustices I need to forgive   Present Status:

_____   _____

_____   _____

_____   _____

_____   _____

  0   I still have resentment and a desire to retaliate.

  1   I am out of fellowship with God because I have not forgiven.

  2   I have quit hurting the other person.

3   I am willing to want to apologize and forgive.

4   I want to apologize and forgive.

5   I am trying to determine if I should talk with the person.

6   I have apologized and am making restitution.

7   I have forgiven the person.

8   I am claiming the forgiving and the forgiveness.

9   I am praying that my memories will be healed.

10   I am working on keeping the issue closed.

11   I am learning assertive behavior to minimize future hurt.

P—Add a "P" in front of the numbers if you are praying about the situation the number represents.

T—Add a "T" in front of the number if you are talking with a reliable friend about it.

Ways I have responded in the past and those responses for which I need to apologize:

_____

_____

_____

What I should do next   Target Date:

_____   _____

_____   _____

_____   _____

Directions: "The action plan form on [this] page is designed to help us identify those we need to forgive. Make as many copies of it as you need so you will have one for each person you need to forgive. Remember . . . this is not a rigid process and that I am not suggesting a legalistic formula but rather, a way of systematically opening ourselves to God's direction on these matters and prompting ourselves to resolve them. Pray before working on these." (Richard Walters, *Forgive and Be Free* [Grand Rapids, Mich.: Zondervan, 1983], 124.)

NOTES

Introduction

1. Sandra Wilson, "A Comparison of Evangelical Christian Adult Children of Alcoholics and Nonalcoholics on Selected Personality and Religious Variables" (Dissertation Abstracts International, 1988), B49. University Microfilms No. 88–23876.

2. Ibid.

3. Joseph Veroff, Richard Kulka, and Elizabeth Douvan, *Mental Health in America: Patterns of Help-Seeking from 1957 to 1976* (New York: Basic Books, 1981). Thirty-nine percent of the people surveyed by these authors reported seeking counseling help from pastors. No other group, including professional counselors, was selected as frequently.

4. *Religion in America: The Gallup Report* (Princeton, N.J.: Princeton Religious Research Center, 1984).

Chapter 1. Understanding Alcoholism

1. *Working Paper: Projections of Alcohol Abusers, 1980, 1985, 1990* (Rockville, Md.: National Institute on Drug Abuse, 1985).

2. James R. Milam and Katherine Ketcham, *Under The Influence* (New York: Bantam Books, 1981), 8. These authors suggest since

alcoholism is so often the undiagnosed cause of listed "causes" of death (e.g., respiratory failure), it may actually be the number-one killer in the United States.

3. Stephen Van Cleave, Walter Byrd, and Kathy Revell, *Counseling for Substance Abuse and Addiction,* Vol. 12, Resources for Christian Counseling, Gary R. Collins, Ph.D., ed. (Waco, Tex.: Word, 1987), 42.

4. Robert Dupont, Jr., *Getting Tough on Gateway Drugs* (Washington, D.C.: American Psychiatric Press, 1984), 113.

5. Proverbs 23:32.

6. Vernon Johnson, *I'll Quit Tomorrow* (San Francisco: Harper & Row, 1980), 1–2.

7. Herbert Fingarette, *Heavy Drinking: The Myth of Alcoholism as a Disease* (Berkeley: University of California Press, 1988).

8. Jean Kinney and Gwen Leaton, *Understanding Alcohol* (New York: Plume, 1982), 38.

9. Ibid., 43.

10. Robert Dreger, "Does Anyone Really Believe That Alcoholism is a Disease?" *American Psychologist* 41 (1986):322.

11. Milam and Ketcham, *Under The Influence,* 189.

12. Ibid.

13. Herbert Gravitz and Julie Bowden, *Guide to Recovery: A Book For Adult Children of Alcoholics* (Holmes Beach, Fla.: Learning Publications, 1985), 8.

14. Wilson, "Evangelical Christian Adult Children of Alcoholics and Nonalcoholics," 10.

15. Kinney and Leaton, *Understanding Alcohol,* 55. These authors do a good job of summarizing etiological factors in alcoholism. See 51–69.

16. J. Kern, C. Hassett, P. Collipp, C. Bridges, M. Solomon, and R. Condren, "Children of Alcoholics: Locus of Control, Mental Age, and Zinc Level," *Journal of Psychiatric Treatment and Evaluation* 3 (1981):207–218.

17. Laurie Garrett, "Cells of Alcoholics, Non-drinkers Differ," *Cincinnati Enquirer,* 15 September 1988, A–13.

18. Donald W. Goodwin, *Alcoholism: The Facts* (New York: Oxford University Press, 1981), 72–76.

19. Robert Cloninger, "Genetic and Environmental Factors in the Development of Alcoholism," *Journal of Psychiatric Treatment and Evaluation* 9 (1983):5.

20. Goodwin, *Alcoholism: The Facts,* 72–76.

21. "Genetics and Alcohol," Fifth Special Report to the U.S.

Congress on Alcohol and Health, *Alcohol Health and Research World* 20 (1984):63–68.

22. Fingarette, *Heavy Drinking*, 52–53.

23. John Friel and Linda Friel, *Adult Children: The Secrets of Dysfunctional Families* (Pompano Beach, Fla.: Health Communications, 1988), 35–36.

24. Allan H. Bruckheim, "Alcoholism is Called Disease as Well as Behavioral Problem," *Cincinnati Enquirer,* 19 July 1988, D–2.

25. Claudia Black, Ph.D., *It Will Never Happen To Me!* (Denver: M.A.C., 1982), 3. The stereotypical "Skid Row bum" type of alcoholic comprises five percent or less of alcoholics in this country.

Chapter 2. The Alcoholic Family System

1. Jane Miller, "Alcohol Abuse in America: Problems and Solutions," *Alcoholism Magazine* (February 1983):8–9.

2. Friel and Friel, *Adult Children: The Secrets of Dysfunctional Families*, 47–49. For an excellent discussion of family systems, both functional and dysfunctional, see chapter 6. This is a valuable resource.

3. Two of many passages indicating this are Deuteronomy 6:6–7 and Ephesians 6:4.

4. Archibald Hart, *Counseling the Depressed*, Vol. 5, Resources for Christian Counseling, Gary R. Collins, Ph.D., ed. (Waco, Tex.: Word, 1987), 118.

5. By using Dachau (an infamous Nazi labor and death camp) to symbolize the utmost extreme of family dysfunction, I do not intend to minimize or trivialize in any way the suffering and horror of the Holocaust. I seek to convey the fact that there actually are some families in which children live in constant chaotic and life-threatening circumstances and where they may even be starved, tortured, and killed.

6. David Frye, "Griefwork and the Adult Children of Alcoholic Families," *Children of Alcoholics Review*, 10 and 11 (1986):8–12.

7. Proverbs 23:32.

8. Claudia Black, *It Will Never Happen To Me!* 15.

9. Charles Deutsch, *Broken Bottles Broken Dreams* (New York: Teachers College Press, 1982), 33–34.

10. Stephanie Brown, "Treatment of Adult Children of Alcoholics" (an Advanced Clinical Seminar presentation at professional workshop, Cherry Hill, N.J., June 1987).

11. Stephanie Brown, *Treating Adult Children of Alcoholics: A*

Developmental Perspective (New York: John Wiley & Sons, 1988), 106.

12. Ibid., 4.

13. Shirley Aldoory, "Research in Family Factors in Alcoholism," *Alcohol Health and Research World*, 3 (Summer 1979):4.

14. Claudia Black, *It Will Never Happen To Me!* 145.

15. Wilson, "Evangelical Christian Adult Children of Alcoholics and Nonalcoholics," 54.

16. Patrick Ward and Anton Krone, "Deadly Deals: Child Abuse in Chemically Dependent Families," *Focus on Family and Chemical Dependency* (November–December 1987):17.

17. Judith Seixas and Geraldine Youcha, *Children of Alcoholism: A Survivor's Manual* (New York: Harper and Row, 1985), 21.

18. Friel and Friel, *Adult Children: The Secrets of Dysfunctional Families*, 77–79.

19. Margaret Hindeman, "Child Abuse and Neglect: The Alcohol Connection," *Alcohol Health and Research World*, 3 (Winter 1977):2–7. Laura Russell, *Child Abuse and Alcoholism* (Rutherford, N.J.: Thomas W. Perrin, 1985). Mig Woodside, *Children of Alcoholics* (New York: Children of Alcoholics Foundation, 1982).

20. Russell, *Child Abuse and Alcoholism*, 12.

21. Ibid., 13.

22. Friel and Friel, *Adult Children: The Secrets of Dysfunctional Families*, 77.

23. Deutsch, *Broken Bottles Broken Dreams*, 43.

24. Woodside, *Children of Alcoholics*, 15.

25. Black, *It Will Never Happen To Me!* 136.

26. Woodside, *Children of Alcoholics*, 16.

27. Carol Williams, "Child Care Practices in Alcoholic Families," *Alcohol Health and Research World*, 4 (1987):74–77.

28. Friel and Friel, *Adult Children: The Secrets of Dysfunctional Families*, 78.

29. Black, *It Will Never Happen to Me!* 137.

30. Friel and Friel, *Adult Children: The Secrets of Dysfunctional Families*, 77.

31. Black, *It Will Never Happen to Me!* 135.

32. Grant Martin, *Counseling for Family Violence and Abuse*, Vol. 6, Resources for Christian Counseling, Gary R. Collins, Ph.D., ed. (Waco, Tex: Word, 1987).

33. Claudia Black, Stanley Bucky, and Susan Wilder-Padilla, "The Interpersonal and Emotional Consequences of Being an Adult Child

of an Alcoholic," *The International Journal of the Addictions*, 21 (1986):213–231.

34. Wilson, "Evangelical Christian Adult Children of Alcoholics and Nonalcoholics," 54.

35. Ward and Krone, "Deadly Deals: Child Abuse in Chemically Dependent Families," 17.

36. Jeffrey Brown, "Common Bonds of Family Tragedy: Alcoholism and Child Sexual Abuse," *Focus on Family and Chemical Dependency*, 1 (Jan.–Feb. 1988):18–19, 41–42, 46.

37. Brian Lynch, "Child Sexual Abuse in the Alcoholic Family," *Focus on Family and Chemical Dependency*, 6 (Nov.–Dec. 1986):26–27, 30.

38. Seixas and Youcha, *Children of Alcoholism*, 18.

39. Friel and Friel, *Adult Children: The Secrets of Dysfunctional Families*, 78–79.

40. Brown, *Treating Adult Children of Alcoholics*, 5.

41. Michael Liepman, William White, and Ted Nirenberg, "Children in Alcoholic Families," *Providing Care for Children of Alcoholics*, David Lewis and Carol Williams, eds. (Pompano Beach, Fla.: Health Communications, 1986), 39–64. These authors nicely summarize Steinglass's systemic conceptualization of the role of alcoholism in stabilizing the family, and they cite Smilkstein for the phrase "pathological equilibrium."

42. Booz-Allen and Hamilton, Inc., *An Assessment of the Needs of and Resources for Children of Alcoholic Parents* (Rockville, Md: National Institute on Alcohol Abuse and Alcoholism, 1974).

43. Margaret Cork, *The Forgotten Children* (Ontario: Addiction Research Foundation, 1969).

Chapter 3. Children in the Alcoholic Family

1. Jean Kinney and Gwen Leaton, *Understanding Alcohol* (New York: Plume, 1982), 39.

2. Jael Greenleaf, *Co-Alcoholic Para-Alcoholic: Who's Who and What's the Difference?* (Los Angeles: The 361 Foundation, 1981), 8.

3. Erik Erikson, *Childhood and Society* (New York: W.W. Norton, 1950).

4. Liepman, White, and Nirenberg, "Children in Alcoholic Families," 45.

5. Jerome Kagan, "Do Infants Think?" *Scientific American,* 226 (March 1972):74–82.

6. Black, *It Will Never Happen To Me!* 35.

7. Ibid.

8. Seixas and Youcha, *Children of Alcoholism,* 88.

9. Liepman, White, and Nirenberg, "Children in Alcoholic Families," 48.

10. Mark Worden, "Children of Alcoholics: Growing Up in Dysfunctional Families," *Focus on Family and Chemical Dependency,* 4 (May–June 1984):33, 38, 40.

11. Wilson, "Evangelical Christian Adult Children of Alcoholics and Nonalcoholics," 20.

12. Kirk Roberts and Edward Brent, "Physician Utilization and Illness Patterns in Families of Alcoholics," *Journal of Studies on Alcohol,* 43 (1982):119–128.

13. I. Nylander, "Children of Alcoholic Fathers," *Acta Paediatrica,* 49 (Jan. 1960):9–127.

14. Morris Chafetz, Howard Blane, and Marjorie Hill, "Children of Alcoholics," *Quarterly Journal of Studies on Alcohol,* 32 (1971):687–698.

15. Cork, *The Forgotten Children,* 61.

16. David Baraga, "Self-concept in Children of Alcoholics," 39 (Dissertations Abstracts International, 1978):368–B.

17. Brown, *Treating Adult Children of Alcoholics,* 107.

18. Psalm 127:3 KJV.

19. Brown, *Treating Adult Children of Alcoholics,* 39.

20. Cork, *The Forgotten Children,* 61.

21. Robert Ackerman, *Let Go and Grow: Recovery for Adult Children* (Pompano Beach, Fla.: Health Communications, 1987), 52.

22. Debra Moses, "A Child's Concept of Alcoholism," *Focus on Family and Chemical Dependency* (November/December 1986):29.

23. Ibid., emphasis added.

24. Wayne Kritsberg, *The Adult Children of Alcoholics Syndrome* (Pompano Beach, Fla.: Health Communications, 1986), 30–31.

25. Psalm 27:10.

26. Lawrence Crabb, Jr., *Effective Biblical Counseling* (Grand Rapids, Mich.: Zondervan, 1977), 129.

27. See Hebrews 12:15 for God's warning about the "root of bitterness."

28. Hart, *Counseling the Depressed,* 155–156.

29. *Children of Alcoholics: A Review of the Literature* (New York: Children of Alcoholics Foundation, 1985), 28.

30. William Bosma, "Alcoholism and Teenagers," *Maryland State Medical Journal*, 21 (1975):34–36.

31. Edward Caine, "Two Contemporary Tragedies: Adolescent Suicide/Adolescent Alcoholism," *Journal of the National Association of Private Psychiatric Hospitals*, 9 (1978):4–11.

32. Bosma, "Alcoholism and Teenagers," 34.

33. E. Fine, L. Yudin, J. Homes, and S. Heinemann, "Behavioral Disorders in Children with Parental Alcoholism," *Annals of the New York Academy of Sciences*, 273 (1976):507–517.

34. Bosma, "Alcoholism and Teenagers," 34.

35. George Barnes, "The Development of Adolescent Drinking Behavior: An Evaluative Review of the Impact of the Socialization Process Within the Family," *Adolescence*, 12 (1977):571–591.

36. Charles Deutsch, *Children of Alcoholics: Understanding and Helping* (Pompano Beach, Fla: Health Communications, 1983), 6.

37. B. Herjanic, M. Herjanic, E. Penick, C. Tomelleri, and R. Armbruster, "Children of Alcoholics," *Currents in Alcoholism, Vol. II*, F. Seixas, ed. (New York: Grune and Stratton, 1977), 445–455.

38. Deutsch, *Children of Alcoholics: Understanding and Helping*, 7.

39. Stephanie Brown and Timmen Cermak, "Group Therapy with the Adult Children of Alcoholics," Newsletter of the California Society for the Treatment of Alcoholism and Other Drug Dependencies (1980):7.

40. Robert Ackerman, *Children of Alcoholics*, 2d ed. (Homes Beach, Fla.: Learning Publications, 1983), 53. Ackerman cites Norman Garmezy as the originator of the term "invulnerables."

41. Emmy Werner, "Resilient Offspring of Alcoholics: A Longitudinal Study from Birth to Age 18," *Journal of Studies on Alcohol*, 1 (1986):34–40.

42. Baraga, "Self-concept in Children of Alcoholics."

43. Ackerman, Let Go and Grow: Recovery for Adult Children, 59. Ackerman cites a 1974 Polish study by Obuchowska.

44. Donald Miller and M. Jang, "Children of Alcoholics: A 20 Year Longitudinal Study," *Social Work Research and Abstracts*, 4 (1977):23–29.

45. Carol Williams, "Child Care Practices in Alcoholic Families," *Alcohol Health and Research World*, 4 (1987):74–77, 94.

46. Black, *It Will Never Happen To Me!*

47. Sharon Wegscheider-Cruse, Another Chance: Hope and Health for the Alcoholic Family (Palo Alto: Science & Behavior Books, 1981).

48. Joy Miller and Marianne Ripper, *Following the Yellow Brick Road* (Pompano Beach, Fla.: Health Communications, 1988), 52.

49. Ibid., 70.

50. Ibid., 59.

51. Ibid., 86.

52. Black, *It Will Never Happen To Me!* 24.

53. Miller and Ripper, *Following the Yellow Brick Road,* 106.

54. Black, Bucky, and Wilder-Padilla, "Consequences of Being an Adult Child of an Alcoholic," 226.

55. Black, *It Will Never Happen To Me!* 31.

Chapter 4. Characteristics of Adult Children of Alcoholics

1. Darlene Howard, *Cognitive Psychology* (New York: Macmillan, 1983), 419. Emphasis added.

2. Gravitz and Bowden, *Guide to Recovery,* 7.

3. Friel and Friel, *Adult Children: The Secrets of Dysfunctional Families,* 71. Emphasis in the original.

4. This overview was compiled from my research findings, from Friel and Friel, *Adult Children: The Secrets of Dysfunctional Families,* 25–26, and Kritsberg, *The Adult Children of Alcoholics Syndrome,* 35.

5. Janet Woititz, Ed.D., *Adult Children of Alcoholics* (Pompano Beach, Fla.: Health Communications, 1983), 4.

6. Thomas Perrin, *I Am an Adult Who Grew Up in an Alcoholic Family* (Rutherford, N.J.: Thomas W. Perrin, 1983).

7. Black, Bucky, and Wilder-Padilla, "Consequences of Being an Adult Child of an Alcoholic," 228–231.

8. Black, *It Will Never Happen To Me!* 105.

9. Kritsberg, *The Adult Children of Alcoholics Syndrome,* 36.

10. Seixas and Youcha, *Children of Alcoholism,* 59.

11. Ibid., 56.

12. Greenleaf, *Co-Alcoholic Para-Alcoholic: Who's Who and What's the Difference?* 10.

13. Seixas and Youcha, *Children of Alcoholism,* 59.

14. Daniel Goleman, "Those Who Repress Emotions Tend to Get Sick More Often," *Cincinnati Enquirer,* 17 March 1988, C–6.

15. John Powell, *Why Am I Afraid to Tell You Who I Am?* (Allen, Tex.: Argus Communications, 1969), 155.

16. American Health Magazine, "Childhood Stress Linked to Later Immunity," *The Cincinnati Enquirer,* 16 March 1988, E–5.

17. Barbara McFarland and Teresa Baker-Baumann, "The Food Fix in Some Alcoholic Homes," *Changes,* 2 (1987):16–18.

18. Timmen Cermak and Stephanie Brown, "Interactional Group Therapy with the Adult Children of Alcoholics," *International Journal of Group Therapy*, 3 (1982):375–89.

19. Wilson, "Evangelical Christian Adult Children of Alcoholics and Nonalcoholics," 57.

20. Toby Rice Drews, *Getting Them Sober*, Vol. II (South Plainfield, N.J., Bridge Publishing, 1983), 52.

21. Friel and Friel, *Adult Children: The Secrets of Dysfunctional Families*, 27.

22. Melody Beattie, *Codependent No More* (Center City, Minn.: Hazelden, 1987), 30.

23. Ibid., 31.

24. Ibid.

25. Friel and Friel, *Adult Children: The Secrets of Dysfunctional Families*, 27.

26. Ibid.

27. Melody Beattie, *Codependent No More*, 78–79.

28. Friel and Friel, *Adult Children: The Secrets of Dysfunctional Families*, 161.

29. Robert Ackerman, *Same House Different Homes: Why Adult Children of Alcoholics Are Not All the Same* (Pompano Beach, Fla.: Health Communications, 1987), 20.

30. This description of adult role behavior is based on my own clinical observations as well as those of Gravitz and Bowden (see *Guide to Recovery: A Book for Adult Children of Alcoholics*, 43–44) and Seixas and Youcha (see *Children of Alcoholism: A Survivor's Manual*, 48–49).

31. Michael Seabaugh, "The Vulnerable Self of the Adult Child of an Alcoholic: A Phenomenologically Derived Theory" (doctoral dissertation, University of Southern California, 1983).

32. Jefferson Breen, "Children of Alcoholics: The Subterranean Grieving Process," *Psychotherapy Patient*, 2 (1985):85–94.

33. Mark Worden, "Children of Alcoholics: Growing Up in Dysfunctional Families," *Focus on Family and Chemical Dependency*, 7 (1984):33, 38, 40.

34. Brown, *Treating Adult Children of Alcoholics*.

Chapter 5. Adult Children and the Alcoholic Family

1. Melody Beattie describes the Karpman Drama Triangle in chapter 8 (pages 77–88) of *Codependent No More*. She describes the

Karpman Drama Triangle and the accompanying roles, and states they are the observation of Stephen B. Karpman.

2. Cermak and Brown, "Interactional Group Therapy with the Adult Children of Alcoholics."

3. Barbara Wood, "Children of Alcoholics: Patterns of Dysfunction in Adult Life" (Paper presented at the Annual Convention of the American Psychological Association, Toronto, Ontario, August 1984).

4. Gary Smalley and John Trent, *The Gift of Honor* (Nashville: Thomas Nelson, 1987), 183.

5. Wilson, "Evangelical Christian Adult Children of Alcoholics and Nonalcoholics," 52.

6. Susan Beletis and Stephanie Brown, "A Developmental Framework for Understanding Adult Children of Alcoholics," *Journal of the Addictions and Health*, 4 (1981):187–203.

7. Thomas Perrin, *Psychotherapy with Adult Children of Alcoholics: A Structured Group Model* (Rutherford, N.J.: Thomas W. Perrin, 1984).

8. Francis Brown, S. R. Driver, and Charles Briggs, *A Hebrew and English Lexicon of the Old Testament* (Oxford: Clarendon Press, 1968), 457.

Chapter 6. Adult Children and Their Concepts of God

1. Andrew Meacham, "Child Abuse Comes Out of the Dark," *Changes*, 5 (Sept.–Oct. 1987):20–21, 28–29, 34–35.

2. Wilson, "Evangelical Christian Adult Children of Alcoholics and Nonalcoholics," 65.

3. Sara Hines Martin, *Healing for Adult Children of Alcoholics* (Nashville, Tenn: Broadman Press, 1988), 135.

4. David Seamands, *Healing of Memories* (Wheaton, Ill.: Victor Books, 1985), 97. Emphasis in the original.

5. Friel and Friel, *Adult Children: The Secrets of Dysfunctional Families*, 20.

6. David Seamands, *Healing of Memories*, 97. Emphasis in the original.

7. This is a portion of the note by Dr. Charles Ryrie on Proverbs 1:7 from *The Ryrie Study Bible: New American Standard Translation* (Chicago: Moody Press, 1978), 938.

8. Martha Janssen, *Silent Scream* (Philadelphia: Fortress Press, 1983), 107.

9. Wilson, "Evangelical Christian Adult Children of Alcoholics and Nonalcoholics," 65.

10. Ibid., 61.

11. Ibid., 66.

12. Gravitz and Bowden, *Guide to Recovery*, 15.

Chapter 7. Revealing the Secret: Learning to Share

1. Brown, *Treating Adult Children of Alcoholics*, 3.

2. John Jones, *The Children of Alcoholics Screening Test* (Chicago: Camelot Unlimited, 1983). The CAST and *The Children of Alcoholics Screening Test Manual* by John Jones may be ordered from Camelot Unlimited, 5 N. Wabash, Suite 1409, Chicago, IL 60602.

3. In my research, I used the CAST to discriminate evangelical Christian adult children of alcoholics (the experimental group) and nonalcoholics (the control group). The average score for adult children of alcoholics was 19.63, with a range of scores from 8 to 30 (of a possible 30). The average score for adult children of nonalcoholics was .32.

4. Friel and Friel, *Adult Children: The Secrets of Dysfunctional Families*, 171.

5. "Boys on Death Row: More Mad Than Bad?" *Harvard Medical School Mental Health Letter*, 3 (1988):6.

6. Jeremiah 17:9.

7. Gravitz and Bowden, *Guide to Recovery*, 39.

8. Ibid., 40.

9. Ibid., 37.

10. Sandra Wilson, "Getting Past Your Past: A Biblical Model of Mind Renewal Recovery for Christian Children of Alcoholics" (program presented at the Fullerton Evangelical Free Church, Fullerton, Calif., June 1987).

11. Wilder Penfield, *The Mystery of the Mind* (Princeton, N.J.: Princeton University Press, 1977), 148.

12. Charles Whitfield, *Healing The Child Within* (Pompano Beach, Fla.: Health Communications, 1987), 109.

Chapter 8. Renewing the Mind: Learning the Truth

1. Everett Harrison, "Romans," *The Expositor's Bible Commentary*, Vol. 10, Frank Gaebelin, ed. (Grand Rapids, Mich.: Zondervan, 1976), 128.

2. Brown, *Treating Adult Children of Alcoholics*, 4. Emphasis added.

3. Miller and Ripper, *Following the Yellow Brick Road*, 149.

4. See 2 Corinthians 10:5.

5. Brown, *Treating Adult Children of Alcoholics*, 107.

6. William Backus, *Telling the Truth to Troubled People* (Minneapolis: Bethany House, 1985).

7. I frequently recommend one or more of these: William Backus and Marie Chapian, *Telling Yourself the Truth* (Minneapolis: Bethany House, 1985); Jerry Schmidt, *Do You Hear What You're Thinking?* (Wheaton, Ill.: Victor Books, 1983); David Stoop, *Self Talk: Key to Personal Growth* (Old Tappan, N.J,: Revell, 1982); or Chris Thurman, *The Lies We Believe* (Nashville, Tenn.: Thomas Nelson, 1989).

8. Seixas and Youcha, *Children of Alcoholism*.

9. Ibid., 26.

10. Brown, *Treating Adult Children of Alcoholics*, 105.

11. Gravitz and Bowden, *Guide to Recovery*, 65.

12. Ibid.

13. My research indicated Christian adult children of alcoholics identified problems with distrust significantly more often than Christian adults from nonalcoholic homes.

14. See John 2:24–25.

15. See Jeremiah 17:9 KJV.

16. Gravitz and Bowden, *Guide to Recovery*, 57.

17. Brown, *Treating Adult Children of Alcoholics*, 105.

18. The Christian adult children of alcoholics in my study had sought counseling in the previous year significantly more often than the Christian adult children of nonalcoholics.

19. See Proverbs 11:14 and 24:6.

20. Gravitz and Bowden, *Guide to Recovery*, 56.

21. Black, "Adult Children of Alcoholics: Healing the Child Within" (seminar in Cincinnati, Ohio, December 1988).

22. Gravitz and Bowden, *Guide to Recovery*, 66.

23. W. E. Vine, *An Expository Dictionary of New Testament Words* (Old Tappan, N.J.: Fleming H. Revell, 1952).

24. See Romans 8:29.

25. William Backus and Marie Chapian, *Telling Yourself the Truth* (Minneapolis: Bethany House, 1985), 113.

26. Gravitz and Bowden, *Guide to Recovery*, 65.

27. Black, "Adult Children of Alcoholics: Healing the Child Within."

28. Although no one may ever satisfactorily reconcile the existence and effects of evil with the sovereignty of a loving God, Philip Yancey does perhaps the best job of any contemporary writer. See Yancey's *Where Is God When It Hurts?* (Grand Rapids, Mich.: Zondervan, 1977) and *Disappointment With God* (Grand Rapids, Mich.: Zondervan, 1988).

Chapter 9. Reclaiming the Emotions: Learning to Feel

1. Friel and Friel, *Adult Children: The Secrets of Dysfunctional Families*, 107.
2. Willard Gaylin, "Feelings," *Harvard Medical School Mental Health Letter*, 5 (1988):4–5.
3. See 2 Samuel 18:33–19:1.
4. Luke 10:21.
5. Matthew 23:37.
6. John 11:35.
7. Matthew 26:38.
8. Daniel Goleman, "Those Who Repress Emotions Tend to Get Sick More Often," *Cincinnati Enquirer,* 17 March 1988, C–6. Emphasis added.
9. Philip Yancey, *Where Is God When It Hurts?* (Grand Rapids, Mich.: Zondervan, 1977), 38.
10. Friel and Friel, *Adult Children: The Secrets of Dysfunctional Families*, 107.
11. Ibid.
12. Cermak and Brown, "Interactional Group Therapy With the Adult Children of Alcoholics."
13. Gravitz and Bowden, *Guide to Recovery.*
14. Ibid., 47. Emphasis in the original.
15. Black, "Adult Children of Alcoholics: Healing the Child Within."
16. Black, *It Will Never Happen To Me!* 109.
17. Ibid., 109–110.

Chapter 10. Counseling for an Accurate Identity

1. Self-esteem, i.e., one's evaluation of oneself, forms self-concept, identity, or self-image.
2. These are some of the books I recommend: David Carlson,

Counseling and Self-Esteem, Vol. 13, Resources for Christian Counseling, Gary Collins, Ph.D., ed. (Waco, Tex.: Word, 1987). Archibald Hart, *Feeling Free* (Old Tappan, N.J.: Fleming H. Revell, 1979). Chapter 7 of Hart's book is one of the best ever written on the subject. Josh McDowell, *His Image, My Image* (San Bernardino, Calif.: Here's Life Publishers, 1984). Robert S. McGee, *The Search for Significance* (Houston: Rapha Publishing, 1987). Bruce Narramore, *You're Someone Special* (Grand Rapids, Mich.: Zondervan, 1978). David Seamands, *Healing For Damaged Emotions* (Wheaton: Victor Books, 1981). Chapters 2 and 4–8 of Seamands's book are especially helpful. Maurice Wagner, *The Sensation of Being Somebody* (Grand Rapids, Mich.: Zondervan, 1975).

3. Gayle Rosellini and Mark Worden, *Taming Your Turbulent Past* (Pompano Beach, Fla.: Health Communications, 1987), 146.

4. Archibald Hart, *Feeling Free* (Old Tappan, N.J.: Fleming H. Revell, 1979), 126. Emphasis in the original.

5. Friel and Friel, *Adult Children: The Secrets of Dysfunctional Families,* 80.

6. Jay Adams, *The Biblical View of Self Esteem, Self-Love, Self-Image* (Eugene, Oreg.: Harvest House, 1986), 132.

7. Seixas and Youcha, *Children of Alcoholism,* 151.

8. Rosellini and Worden, *Taming Your Turbulent Past,* 112.

9. Ibid., 149.

10. Ibid., 151.

11. Ibid., 141.

12. Romans 3:23.

13. See Psalm 14:3 and Romans 3:10.

14. Seixas and Youcha, *Children of Alcoholism,* 160.

15. Rosellini and Worden, *Taming Your Turbulent Past,* 78.

16. Claudia Black, *Perfectionism* (monograph distributed at the "Adult Children of Alcoholics: Healing the Child Within" seminar held in Cincinnati, Ohio, December 1988).

17. Brown, *Treating Adult Children of Alcoholics: A Developmental Perspective,* 7. Emphasis added.

18. Ibid., 6.

19. I fully realize that I enter deep and turbulent waters when presenting my interpretation of a biblical view of humanity. Many knowledgeable, sincere evangelicals hold positions which differ from those presented here. I do not expect to resolve ancient theological debates.

20. See John 3:16 and Romans 5:8.

21. 1 John 3:1–2.

22. There are differing views about using counseling as an evangelistic opportunity. However, whether or not one chooses to present the gospel, it is misleading to omit the clear biblical teaching of total depravity when discussing a scriptural basis for personal identity.

23. David Seamands, *Healing Grace* (Wheaton, Ill.: Victor Books, 1988).

24. See Exodus 20:5.

25. This example is adapted from Robert McGee's summary of chapters 4–7 of his book, *The Search for Significance*, 95.

26. Friends in Recovery, *The Twelve Steps: A Spiritual Journey* (San Diego: Recovery Publications, 1988), 69.

27. Rosellini and Worden, *Taming Your Turbulent Past*, 118.

28. See Leviticus 19:18; Matthew 19:19; Mark 12:31; and Luke 10:27.

Chapter 11. Counseling for Respectful Relationships

1. Janet Woititz, *Struggle for Intimacy* (Pompano Beach, Fla.: Health Communications, 1985), 20.

2. Vine, *An Expository Dictionary of New Testament Words*, Vol. 3, 20.

3. Ibid., 21.

4. Beattie, *Codependent No More*, 198.

5. Ibid., 191.

6. Misbelief numbers four through nine are adapted from chapter 3 of Woititz's, *Struggle for Intimacy*, 23–58.

7. Genesis 2:24.

8. I first presented the basic concept of these defensive styles at a retreat for the women of Faith Evangelical Free Church in Milford, Ohio in May 1986.

9. Gravitz and Bowden, *Guide to Recovery*, 66.

10. Ibid.

11. Rosellini and Worden, *Taming Your Turbulent Past*, 164.

12. See Romans 14:4.

13. Gravitz and Bowden, *Guide to Recovery*, 72.

14. Vine, *An Expository Dictionary of New Testament Words*, 324.

15. Woititz, *Struggle for Intimacy*, 32.

16. Woititz, *Struggle for Intimacy*.

17. Sara Hines Martin, *Healing for Adult Children of Alcoholics* (Nashville, Tenn.: Broadman Press, 1988).

18. Hebrews 13:5b.

19. Beattie, *Codependent No More*, 200–201.
20. See Luke 18:17.
21. See Matthew 10:16.
22. Gravitz and Bowden, *Guide to Recovery*, 73.

Chapter 12. Counseling for Healthy Marital and Parenting Relationships

1. Rosellini and Worden, *Taming Your Turbulent Past*, 166.
2. Ackerman, *Let Go and Grow*, 160.
3. Ibid.
4. Smalley and Trent, *The Gift of Honor*, 133–134.
5. Friel and Friel, *Adult Children: The Secrets of Dysfunctional Families*, 60.
6. Lawrence Kutner, "Recognizing Sparks of Conflict: Disagreements Stem From Desire for Control and Freedom," *Cincinnati Enquirer*, 24 July 1988, E–5.
7. Seixas and Youcha, *Children of Alcoholism*, 94.
8. Quoted in Kutner, "Recognizing Sparks of Conflict."
9. 1 Peter 1:3.
10. Martin, *Counseling for Family Violence and Abuse*, 200.
11. Ibid., 201.
12. Ibid.
13. See Psalm 127:4–5.

Chapter 13. Counseling for New Family Roles

1. See 2 Corinthians 5:17.
2. Brown, *Treating Adult Children of Alcoholics: A Developmental Perspective*, 66.
3. Gravitz and Bowden, *Guide to Recovery*, 37.
4. Friel and Friel, *Adult Children: The Secrets of Dysfunctional Families*, 96.
5. Seixas and Youcha, *Children of Alcoholism*, 122.
6. Hebrews 10:24.
7. This discussion of specific limit-setting considerations borrows heavily from Seixas and Youcha, *Children of Alcoholism*, 115–116.
8. Seixas and Youcha, *Children of Alcoholism*, 113.
9. Ibid., 117–118.

10. The complete list of biblical instructions on honoring our parents is found in Smalley and Trent, *The Gift of Honor,* 42.

11. Friel and Friel, *Adult Children: The Secrets of Dysfunctional Families,* 97.

12. 2 Peter 3:9b.

Chapter 14. Counseling for Biblical God-Concepts

1. Herbert VanderLugt, "Unrealized Blessings," *Our Daily Bread* (Grand Rapids, Mich.: Radio Bible Class), 23 November 1988.

2. David Seamands, *Putting Away Childish Things* (Wheaton, Ill.: Victor Books, 1982), Preface.

3. Bauer, Arndt, and Gingrich, *A Greek-English Lexicon of the New Testament,* 2d ed. (Chicago: University of Chicago Press, 1979), 417.

4. See John 5:23, 14:6, and 15:23; and also 1 John 2:23.

5. Warren Myers and Ruth Myers, *Experiencing God's Attributes* (Colorado Springs: Navpress, 1978).

6. McGee, *The Search for Significance,* 82.

7. Philip Yancey, "Saturday Seven Days a Week," *Christianity Today,* 18 March 1988, 64.

8. I am indebted to my pastor, Dr. Raymond F. Dupont, Jr., for the concept of wandering, willing, and working worshipers.

Chapter 15. Counseling for Forgiveness

1. Wilson, "A Comparison of Evangelical Christian Adult Children of Alcoholics and Nonalcoholics."

2. Jeanette Lockerbie, *Forgive, Forget and Be Free* (San Bernardino, Calif.: Here's Life Publishers, 1981), 21.

3. Rosellini and Worden, *Taming Your Turbulent Past,* 32.

4. Miller and Ripper, *Following the Yellow Brick Road,* 6. Emphasis not in the original.

5. David Seamands, *Healing for Damaged Emotions* (Wheaton, Ill: Victor Books, 1981), 28.

6. Martin, *Counseling for Family Violence and Abuse,* 93.

7. Rosellini and Worden, *Taming Your Turbulent Past,* 179.

8. See Exodus 20:12, Deuteronomy 5:16, and Ephesians 6:2–3.

9. Hart, *Feeling Free,* 143.

10. That agreement with God's perspective on salvation is essential, since God's revealed view is always truth. For this reason, the Bible never speaks of God as being reconciled to people, but always of people being reconciled to God.

11. Charles Swindoll, *Improving Your Serve* (Waco, Tex.: Word, 1981), 67.

12. Christian adult children of alcoholics have found the following especially helpful: Lewis Smedes, *Forgive and Forget* (New York: Harper and Row, 1984); Richard Walters, *Forgive and Be Free* (Grand Rapids, Mich.: Zondervan, 1983), and Bruce Narramore and Bill Counts, *Freedom From Guilt* (Eugene, Oreg.: Harvest House, 1974).

13. Rosellini and Worden, *Taming Your Turbulent Past*, 179.

Chapter 16. Problems, Promise, and Privilege

1. Gary Collins, "Practical Counseling Update: Adult Children of Alcoholics," *Christian Counseling Newsletter*, 2 (1988):5.

2. Seamands, *Healing for Damaged Emotions*, 46.

3. In a 1989 interview-style article on Sharon Wegscheider-Cruse, one of the primary founders of the adult children of alcoholics movement, the writer acknowledged the growing influence of New Age thinking among adult children. He observed, "Now it seems that the 12-step concept is becoming incorporated in the broader New Age movement," and asked Wegscheider-Cruse, "What do you think of that trend?" In reply, she expressed her apprehension about the New Age "cult" and its effect on adult children of alcoholics, although the basis of her concern was entirely different from mine. This exchange between Wegscheider-Cruse and the writer appeared in *Changes* (May–June, 1989), the leading magazine for and about adult children of alcoholics; it illustrates the pervasive nature of New Age influence in the movement.

4. Kathleen W., *Healing a Broken Heart* (Deerfield Beach, Fla.: Health Communications, 1988), 15.

5. Gravitz and Bowden, *Guide to Recovery,* 104.

6. Ernie Larsen and Carol Larsen Hegarty, *Days of Healing, Days of Joy* (New York: Harper & Row, 1987).

INDEX

Sandra D. Wilson, Ph.D.

Sandra D. Wilson is a Christian psychotherapist specializing in counseling Christian adults raised in alcoholic and other dysfunctional families. A Phi Beta Kappa scholar, she holds a master's degree in clinical social work from the University of Louisville and a Ph.D. in counseling psychology from the Union Graduate School in Cincinnati. She also holds a B.A. in psychology from the University of Cincinnati where she was graduated summa cum laude.

Dr. Wilson is the counseling coordinator at Faith Evangelical Free Church in Cincinnati and a visiting professor of pastoral counseling and psychology at Trinity Evangelical Divinity School. She pioneered research in the evangelical Christian population of adult children of alcoholics and has presented her findings in professional journals and conferences. A nationally sought seminar and retreat speaker, Dr. Wilson and her husband, Garth, have been married thirty-one years and have two grown children, Becky and Dave.